Popular Music and Society

For Bernadette, James and Tim

Popular Music and Society

Brian Longhurst

Polity Press

Copyright © Brian Longhurst 1995

The right of Brian Longhurst to be identified as author of this work has been asserted in accordance with the Copyright, Designs and Patents Act 1988.

First published in 1995 by Polity Press
in association with Blackwell Publishers Ltd.

Editorial office:
Polity Press
65 Bridge Street
Cambridge CB2 1UR, UK

Marketing and production:
Blackwell Publishers Ltd.
108 Cowley Road
Oxford OX4 1JF, UK

Blackwell Publishers Inc.
238 Main Street
Cambridge, MA 02142, USA

ISBN 0 7456 1437 X
ISBN 0 7456 1464 7 (pbk)

A CIP catalogue record for this book is available from the British Library and the Library of Congress.

Typeset in 10½ on 12pt Plantin
by Graphicraft Typesetters Ltd., Hong Kong
Printed in Great Britain by Hartnolls Ltd., Bodmin, Cornwall

This book is printed on acid-free paper.

Contents

PART III   AUDIENCE

Figures

Tables

Boxes

Acknowledgements

I would like to thank Nick Abercrombie for inviting me to write this book, thereby giving me the opportunity to develop some thoughts on an area of culture which has always been very important to me. Thanks also to Nick Abercrombie and Celia Lury for their extensive and very helpful comments on two previous drafts. Their supportive criticism and encouragement improved the book greatly. Countless discussions with Nick over a long period of time have also influenced other areas of the book in all sorts of ways.

Most of the book was written during my first ever period of four months' academic study leave. I would like to thank those colleagues in the Sociology Department at the University of Salford who took on extra duties during this time and hope that I did not irritate them too much with my obvious glee at having some time to work on a project in a consistent and undisturbed way.

Some of the ideas in chapter 5 first saw light of day in collaborative work, to which Scott Lash contributed greatly. These ideas were also tried out in seminars in the Sociology Departments of the Universities of Lancaster, Edinburgh and Manchester and at the annual conference of the British Sociological Association. Thanks to everyone who participated and commented.

Some of the material in chapters 7 and 8 has benefited from comments passed by colleagues at a seminar in the Department of Sociology at the University of Salford. Discussions in the Lancaster/Salford Audiences group have also been of great help and I would like to thank all the participants for their input. Discussion of the work of Larry Grossberg proved particularly thought provoking. The publisher's readers' comments were also constructive.

Thanks additionally to Sue Smart who has always answered my hopelessly naive questions about word-processing in a helpful way and who sorted out some of the figures, when my limited skills were not up to the job. Ingrid Grimes copy-edited the book in a most efficient and interactive way. All at Polity Press have been a pleasure to work with from beginning to end, but Pam Thomas must be accorded special thanks.

At points this book argues that music is very important to members of society in emotional ways that cannot be put into words. That argument in part stems from my own feelings about music and personal life. Thanks therefore are due to my parents who always had music around and respected my own musical tastes, which cannot always have been easy. I would like to thank my father in particular, whose musical creativity I have not appreciated enough, for all the times he played 'The old music master' for me in the back room at Shakespeare Road when I was a child. Also going back to childhood, thanks to my cousin, Terry Boiston, who exposed me to Elvis Presley and Otis Redding, leaving me with continuing attachments.

As always, my biggest debts are to those who live with me, putting up with my current musical tastes. James Oxley-Longhurst continues to provoke a sense of wonder, educates me in Michael Jackson tapes, and impresses me by 'Walking the Dinosaur'. Tim Oxley-Longhurst was welcomed as the final alterations were being made to the manuscript. He cannot yet communicate his musical preferences, but I am sure he will. Bernadette Oxley puts on the music that I would not hear otherwise, listened to a significant part of my record collection one night in the early days and, most importantly, is always there.

The author and publishers wish to thank the following for permission to use copyright material:

American Sociological Review and Richard A. Peterson for Table 2.1 from David Berger and Richard A. Peterson, 'Cycles in Symbol Production: the case of popular music', *American Sociological Review* 40 (1975).

Blackwell Publishers for Figures 1.1 and 1.2 from David Held, *Introduction to Critical Theory* (1980).

Cambridge University Press for Box 19 from D. Laing, 'World Record Sales 1992', *Popular Music*, 12, 3 1993.

Jonathan Cape and Hill and Wang for Figure 6.2 'Myth Today' from *Mythologies* by Roland Barthes, translated by Annette Lavers. Translation © 1972 by Jonathan Cape Ltd. Reprinted by permission of Jonathan Cape and of Hill and Wang, a division of Farrar, Straus & Giroux, Inc.

Charly records for Box 11 from the sleeve notes for Jimmy Reed *Upside Your Head* (1980), by Cliff White, courtesy of Charly Records.

Constable Publishers Limited for Figures 2.6, 2.7, 2.8 and 2.9 from R. Wallis and K. Malm, *Big Musics from Small Peoples* (1984).

Cultural Trends for Tables 1.1, 2.2, 2.4, 2.5, 2.6, 2.7, 7.1, 7.2, 7.3, 7.4, 7.5 from *Cultural Trends* 7 (1990), 12 (1991) and 19 (1993).

Faber & Faber Ltd. for Box 5 from J. Savage, *England's Dreaming: Sex Pistols and punk rock* (1991) and Box 8 from J. J. Beadle, *Will Pop Eat Itself?: pop music in the soundbite era* (1993).

The Guardian for material in Boxes 1, 6 and 16 by Playthell Benjamin, Roger Cowe, Pat Fane, Caroline Sullivan. Copyright *The Guardian*.

HarperCollins Publishers Ltd and Hill and Wang for Box 17, an except from 'The Grain of the Voice' from *Image–Music–Text* by Roland Barthes, translated by Stephen Heath. Translation © 1977 by Stephen Heath. Reprinted by permission of HarperCollins and of Hill and Wang, a division of Farrar, Straus & Girous, Inc.

The Independent on Sunday for Box 2 by Jeremy Warner.

The International Federation of the Phonographic Industry for Figure 2.4 from *World Sales 1989* (1990); Table 2.3 from *World Sales 1993* (1994).

International Music Publications Limited for the lyrics quoted in Figure 6.6 from 'Material Girl' by Peter Brown and Robert Rans as recorded by Madonna.

Manchester University Press for Box 14 from D. Hatch and S. Millward, *From Blues to Rock: an analytical history of pop music* (1987).

The Observer for Box 21 by Steven Wells, copyright *The Observer*.

Open University for Figure 7.4 from R. Middleton and J. Muncie, 'Pop Culture, Pop Music and Post-war Youth: countercultures', Unit 20 of the Open University course on *Popular Culture*.

Open University Press for Figures 6.4 and 6.5 from R. Middleton, *Studying Popular Music* (1990); Table 6.1 from D. Laing, *One Chord Wonders: power and meaning in punk rock* (1985); Box 10 from D. Bradley, *Understanding Rock 'n' Roll: popular music in Britain 1955–1964* (1992).

Penguin Books Limited for Box 20 from David Robins and Philip Cohen, *Knuckle Sandwich: growing up in the working-class city* (1978) copyright © David Robins and Philip Cohen, 1978.

Pluto Press for Boxes 4 and 7 from S. Steward and S. Garratt, *Signed, Sealed and Delivered: true life stories of women in pop* (1984) and Box 12 from J. Burchill and T. Parsons, *'The Boy looked at Johnny': the obituary of rock and roll* (1978).

Routledge Publishers for Figure 2.3 from Paul Bagguley, 'Post-Fordism and Enterprise Culture: flexibility, autonomy and changes in economic organization' in R. Keat and N. Abercrombie (eds), *Enterprise Culture* (1991); Figure 5.7 from E. Ann Kaplan, *Rocking around the Clock: music television, postmodernism, and consumer culture* (1987); Figure 6.6 from Barbara Bradby, 'Like a Virgin-Mother?: materialism and maternalism in the songs of Madonna' from, *Cultural Studies*, 6 (1992); Figures 6.8, 6.9, 6.10 and Box 18 from A. Goodwin, *Dancing in the Distraction Factory: music, television and popular culture* (1993); Figure 7.3 from J. Clarke, S. Hall, T. Jefferson and B. Roberts, 'Subcultures, Cultures and Class: a theoretical overview' in S. Hall and T. Jefferson (eds), *Resistance through Rituals: youth subcultures in post-war Britain* (1976); Box 22 from H. Jenkins, *Textual Poachers: television fans and participatory culture* (1992).

S.T. Publishing for Box 3 from George Marshall, *The Two Tone Story* (1990).

Serpent's Tail Limited for Box 15 from D. Toop, *Rap Attack 2: African rap to global hip hop* (1991).

Souvenir Press for Box 9 from C. Gillett, *The Sound of the City: the rise of rock and roll* (1983).

University of Massachusetts Press for Figure 3.3 reprinted from *On Becoming a Rock Musician* by H. Stith Bennett (Amherst: University of Massachusetts Press, 1980), copyright © by The University of Massachusetts Press.

Virago Press and Random House, Inc. for Box 13 from M. Angelou, *Singin' and Swingin' and Gettin' Merry like Christmas*, copyright © by Maya Angelou 1976, published by Random House 1976 and Virago Press 1985.

Every effort has been made to trace all the copyright holders but if any have been inadvertently overlooked the publishers will be pleased to make the necessary arrangement at the first opportunity.

Introduction

This book is written for undergraduate students. It aims to provide an introduction to the area of popular music and society that will be useful to those taking courses in the areas of the sociology of culture, cultural studies, communication studies and media studies. It will also be of interest to those more general readers wanting an overview of contemporary developments in the sociological study of popular music. My aim has partly been to locate the analysis of popular music in the context of more general debates about culture, its analysis and effects.

The book includes accounts of the main theories in the area of popular music, as well as reviewing the most important substantive studies which have appeared in this field. It also includes a significant amount of empirical data where relevant. In addition to words on the page, the book uses three main devices to convey information and illustrate the accounts and theories.

Figures which often summarize whole arguments or the most salient parts of them are used in a number of places. These summaries are represented in diagrams or lists of points. I have created some of the figures and others are drawn from other sources, which are given with the figures. My view is that a clear diagram is often a useful way of conveying the sense of an argument and can help in the understanding of the overall structure or main themes. It is a device which is under-used in sociology.

There are also a number of tables in the book. In the main these contain quantitative data and are distinguished from figures on that basis. The data given most often refer to the United Kingdom, though figures are also provided for world record sales and so on.

Salient points to be drawn from the tables are discussed in the text of the book. However, the data may also be of use in student project work and essays, where other issues may be important.

The third device is the box. Boxes have been used to set off material which goes beyond the main flow of the text, but which illustrates key points. The boxes also use some of the less sociological writing on popular music, which can be very informative and provoke thought on the nature of contemporary music. I hope these boxes might encourage the reader to seek out this literature, which contains some of the most pleasurable writing on pop music. There is also a fair amount of quotation from important sources which is used in a direct way in the main text of the book.

The book is written in the belief that the pleasures of pop music and its analysis can be combined. It is a common experience for anyone teaching a course on the media to be approached at some point by a student who says that their enjoyment of television or film has been ruined by the analysis carried out on them. Those of us who teach such courses can often recall similar feelings when we were first introduced to the study of media. My (perhaps inadequate) response is to suggest that the pleasures of analysis can lead to new enjoyment of the media texts themselves. In my view, this is a part of the 'sociological imagination' and something to be welcomed. I hope that the arguments and studies reviewed in this book contribute to such analytic satisfaction. Certainly, working through the material did not detract from my enjoyment of pop music and often stimulated me to explore new areas in a different frame of mind or dig out old, and almost forgotten, records and tapes. I hope some of this comes through in the text.

In the book, I use 'popular music' as an overall term. There is much debate about the meanings of terms like pop and rock, and this is an issue which is examined on several occasions within the text. At this early stage, however, I ask the reader to go along with me in adopting a relatively broad and open categorization of popular music.

Finally, I should say that more detail on the contents of each chapter can be found at the end of chapter 1, where the logic of the arrangement of the chapters should be apparent from the discussions and criticism of general theories contained therein.

1

Arguments and Framework

The aims of this chapter are: to introduce the most important, sociologically informed, general accounts of the nature and place of popular music in society; and to criticize these accounts in moving toward a framework to be used in the subsequent presentation of the material in this book. Three bodies of literature are considered: first, the work of Adorno on the culture industry and popular music; second, the Weberian examination of rationalization; and third, contemporary approaches which seek to move away from some of the themes central to these earlier accounts. Most space is devoted to the first two approaches as they will not be treated at length elsewhere, though issues they raise are examined in a number of other places. Aspects of the third body of literature are considered in rather more detail in chapters 7 and 8.

Adorno and popular music

The British sociologist and pop writer Simon Frith draws attention to the key importance of the work on music of Theodor Adorno in the following way:

Adorno's is the most systematic and most searing analysis of mass culture and the most challenging for anyone claiming even a scrap of value for the products that come churning out of the music industry. His argument . . . is that modern capital is burdened by the problem of overproduction. Markets can only be stimulated by *creating*

needs . . . needs which are the result of capital rather than human
logic and therefore, inevitably, false. The culture industry is the central agency in contemporary capitalism for the production and satisfaction of false needs. (1983:44–5)

This book takes up Frith's argument that Adorno's analysis is a
challenge to those who seek to recognize some value in pop music.
However, my suggestion is that the generality of Adorno's work
represents a challenge of a rather different kind to those who want
to engage in the systematic and specific analysis of the place of pop
music in society. I shall explain why Adorno's arguments represent
such a challenge to analysis in a short while. However, before this
is possible it is necessary to examine his position in more detail.

Adorno (1903–69) was a member of the Frankfurt School of
theorists and writers, founded at the University of Frankfurt in 1923,
who developed critical theory as an attempt to further social change
from within a broadly Marxist understanding of the structure of
society. Along with other figures such as Max Horkheimer (1895–
1971), Herbert Marcuse (1898–1979) and, most recently, Jurgen
Habermas (b. 1929), Adorno criticized capitalism's control over
social life and the subsequent inequalities this causes. In his work
with Horkheimer, Adorno maintained that the culture industry was
central to capitalist domination (Adorno and Horkheimer 1977).

In contemporary capitalist societies the culture industry produces
forms of culture which are commodities: that is, culture which is
produced to be bought and sold on a market. It possesses exchange
value and the companies that produce culture do so to make a profit
from it. According to the Frankfurt School writers, such commodification had become increasingly widespread, penetrating all aspects
of cultural production and social life. This led to a standardization
of the products of the culture industries, which in turn induced a
passivity in those who consume the culture industry products. Held
(1980:94) explains that:

> The main characteristics of the culture industry reflect the difficult
> problem it faces. It must at once both sustain interest and ensure that
> the attention it attracts is insufficient to bring its produce into disre-
> pute. Thus, commercial entertainment aims at an attentive but pas-
> sive, relaxed and uncritical reception, which it induces through the
> production of 'patterned and pre-digested' cultural entities.

For Adorno popular music is a part of the culture industry. An
important claim that Adorno makes about popular music is that it

is standardized. In his view, the whole of the popular music product is standardized including types of songs, songs themselves and parts of songs. Thus, if Adorno was writing about popular music today, instead of in the 1930s, 1940s and 1950s, he might argue, first, that popular music is divided into a number of standardized types: heavy metal, country, folk, blues, soul and so on, which are immediately recognizable to the audience. Second, he might maintain that the music and songs within these types are themselves standardized into a small number of different structures. Therefore, a musicological analysis would show that one heavy metal track is very much like another in its essential structure and form (Walser 1993). There are a small number of components to such tracks and on Adorno's account these are interchangeable. As Adorno says, 'The beginning of the chorus is replaceable by the beginning of innumerable other choruses' (1990:303).

In Adorno's account the parts of a piece of popular music are interchangeable. Gendron (1986) explains such 'part interchangeability' through the example of a mass-produced car. Thus 'virtually any mechanical part from any 1956 Cadillac Eldorado (e.g. a carburettor) can be substituted for any other 1956 Eldorado without disturbing the functional unity of the overall mechanism' (p. 20) or, to take another example suggested by Gendron, the speakers from one stereo system can be substituted into another and the system will normally still work. Part interchangeability is very important to rationalized industrial systems and variation exists often to ensure that only parts made by one manufacturer can be used in its own product to keep the market demand for such parts buoyant. Hence, it is possible to substitute a particular part from one Ford Fiesta for that in another Fiesta though not to place that part into a Renault Clio. However, certain parts, such as the tyres, may be more likely to be interchangeable.

Adorno calls the type of variation that exists between such standardized products, 'pseudo-individualization'. Such variations do not alter the basic structure of the product as they represent only surface changes. For example, the addition of racing stripes to a Ford Fiesta may affect its appearance to the taste of its owner, but they will not alter its performance. Adorno suggests that the variations in popular music are of this type. The details of the popular song may be changed but the essential structure or form remains the same.

Goodwin gives an example of how these ideas of part interchangeability and pseudo-individualization might be applied to the contemporary music scene. He says that:

pop songs often utilize the same or very similar drum patterns, chord progressions, song structures, and lyrics while being distinguished by marketing techniques (the construction of 'personalities' involved in selling, say, New Kids on the Block, the make-up once worn by the rock band Kiss), performance quirks (Michael Jackson's 'hiccup', Madonna's 'controversial' videos) or rhetorical gestures (Pete Townsend's 'windmill' swing at his guitar, Chuck Berry's 'duckwalk'). (1992:76)

Adorno's analysis of popular music is built upon a comparison of popular music with 'serious' music. He argues that it is possible to distinguish standardized popular music from 'serious' music, where the detail of a section of music only takes on meaning in relation to the piece as a whole and standardization does not exist in the way that it does in popular music. Adorno's argument about 'serious' music rests on the valuation of a intimate relation between the specific parts and the overall nature of the whole of a piece of music, which give the piece its own particular distinctiveness and individuality. Great works of music, like those of Beethoven, are distinctive and original. The parts of the piece come together to form a whole, which is not simply the sum of the parts. It is an artistic creation which uses the parts to create an overall meaning. The substitution into the piece of a different part would seriously affect the meaning of the whole piece.

According to Jay (1973:182), the distinction drawn by Adorno between these types of music relates to issues of the market and the context in which music is produced and consumed. It is not that Adorno was a conservative who simply liked classical music because it was better in an unexplained way. As Jay argues: 'The real dichotomy, Adorno contended was not between 'light' and serious 'music' – he was never a defender of traditional cultural standards for their own sake – but rather between music that was market-oriented and music that was not.' The main features of popular and serious music as distinguished by Adorno are summarized in figure 1.1.

The Frankfurt School argued that the principles of mass production applied to the production of culture as well as the production of goods like motor cars. In this view popular music would be produced in an industrial way. However, Adorno's analysis ran into a specific problem at this point, as much pop music is not written on a production line but rather in what he called a handicraft fashion. Thus, the writing of a piece of standardized popular music

'Serious' music	'Popular' music
Every part/detail depends 'for its musical sense on the concrete totality and never on a mere enforcement of a musical scheme'	Musical compositions follow familiar patterns/frameworks: they are stylized
	Little originality is introduced
Themes and details are highly interwoven with the whole	Structure of the whole does not depend upon details – whole is not altered by individual detail
Themes are carefully developed	Melodic structure is highly rigid and is frequently repeated
Details cannot be changed without altering the whole – details almost contain/anticipate the whole	Harmonic structure embodies a set scheme ('The most primitive harmonic facts are emphasized')
	Complications have no effect on structure of work – they do not develop themes
Consistency is maintained between formal structure and content (themes)	Stress is on combination of individual 'effects' – on sound, colour, tone, beat, rhythm
If standard schemes are employed (e.g. for dance) they still maintain a key role in the whole	Improvisations become 'normalized' (the boys can only 'swing it' in a narrow framework)
	Details are substitutable (they 'serve their function as cogs in machines')
Emphasizes norms of high technical competence	Affirms conventional norms of what constitutes intelligibility in music while appearing novel and original

Figure 1.1 The structure of production and consumption of 'serious' and 'popular' music
Source: Held (1980:101)

might be carried out by a lone individual sitting at home with a pen
and paper, who would not be constrained by the discipline of producing standardized parts for a production line. For Adorno, this
showed the remnants of a earlier form of production, which was
not subject to capitalist work patterns. Despite this, he maintained
that the popular music industry was industrialized in other very
important ways. Most notably it was promoted and distributed in
accord with industrialized principles, which also characterized its
manufacture.

According to Adorno, the listener to industrialized popular music
is caught up in a standardized and routinized set of responses. Adorno
argues that he or she is distracted and inattentive. In this sense, pop
music is a part of the everyday background of contemporary social
life. For example, we do not listen to it in the way that musical
experts think that we should listen to a Beethoven symphony: that
is, by sitting down and giving it all our attention, and seeing how
the parts relate to the whole in creating the kind of meaning that
Beethoven intended to communicate.

In Adorno's view, the pleasure derived from popular music is
superficial and false. Thus the listener may be what Adorno calls
'rhythmically obedient'. He or she is a 'slave to the rhythm', following the standardized beat of the song and becoming overpowered or
conditioned by it. For Adorno, individuals who enjoy these pleasures are corrupted by immersion and are open to the domination of
the industrialized, capitalist system. Another type of pleasure, which
Adorno calls 'emotional' is also dangerous. Feelings of emotion
brought on by the popular song are false or immature, rather than
deep or penetrating. There is no comparison between such feelings
and the sorts of emotion which can be generated and expressed by
the best forms of serious music. The distinctions that Adorno draws
between the audience responses to serious and popular music are
summarized in figure 1.2.

Adorno's argument implies that the production, textual form and
audience reception of popular music are all standardized, revealing
a similar essential structure. Industrial production in capitalist societies gives rise to a standardized product, which is used in superficial ways by the audience, who desire or express a wish for such
industrial products because of their familiarity. Such a system reinforces the domination of society by those who control the industrial
apparatus; the capitalist or bourgeois class, as the vast majority of
the population are passive and falsely happy owing to their manipulation by the culture industry, which feeds them products which

'Serious' music	'Popular' music
To understand a piece of serious music one must experience the whole of it	The whole has little influence on reception and reaction to parts – stronger reactions to part than whole
The whole has strong impact on reaction to details	The music is standardized into easily recognizable types, whole are pre-accepted/known prior to reception
Themes and details can only be comprehended in the context of the whole	Little effort is required to follow music – audience already has models under which musical experiences can be subsumed
The sense of the music cannot be grasped by recognition alone, i.e. by identifying music with another 'identical' piece	Little emphasis on the whole as musical event – what matters is style, rhythm (the movement of the foot on the floor)
Effort and concentration are required to follow music	Leads back to familiar experiences (themes and details can be understood out of context because listener can automatically supply framework)
Its aesthetic disrupts the continuum of everyday life and encourages recollection	A sense of the music is grasped by recognition – leading to acceptance
	Pleasure, fun gained through listening are 'transferred' to the musical object, which becomes invested with qualities that stem from mechanism of identification
	The most successful, best music is identified with the most often repeated
	Music has 'soporific effect' on social consciousness
	It reinforces a sense of continuity in everyday living – while its reified structure enforces forgetfulness
	Renders 'unnecessary the process of thinking'

Figure 1.2 Differences between 'serious' and 'popular' music in responses encouraged/demands made upon listener
Source: Held (1980:103)

INDUSTRIAL PRODUCTION

(including promotion and distribution, though actual song production often
takes a craft form)

POPULAR MUSIC

(is standardized and contrasted with serious music)

THE LISTENER

(is distracted and inattentive; obedient and emotional)

Figure 1.3 Adorno's account of popular music

they think that they want. The different aspects of Adorno's thesis
are summarized in figure 1.3.

It has already been suggested that Adorno's approach attempts to
characterize the nature of popular music, its production and consumption. Adorno wanted to develop a critique of this along the
lines of a critical theory derived from Marx. As such, the theory
covers a lot of ground and seeks to mount a critical attack on much
contemporary music and culture, which would show how it was
implicated in the oppression of the working class in capitalist society. Some of the problems with this account are examined in the
next section.

Adorno and pop: some criticisms

In considering the criticisms that can be made of Adorno's thesis,
it is important to recognize that these formulations seem to have
some applicability to contemporary music. Thus, there does seem to
be a great deal of standardization of pop music around different
forms and the commodity status of the product seems increasingly
prevalent. However, a number of points can and have been made
against the sort of approach outlined by Adorno. The more

specific of these are considered first followed by some more general considerations.

Gendron suggests that Adorno confuses what he calls functional and textual artefacts. An example of a functional artefact is a washing machine and of a textual artefact a compact disc. Gendron points to a key difference between text and functional artefact, when he says that: 'A text (whether written or oral) is a universal, whereas a functional artifact is a particular. However, to be marketed and possessed, every universal text must be embodied in some functional artifact (paper, vinyl discs)' (1986:27). Thus, when a person buys a compact disc he or she is actually buying a combination of functional and textual artefacts. The universal artefact, according to Gendron (p. 27), is the recording that appears on the disc, which is a product of the recording process, mixing and so on (dimensions of the recording process are considered at greater length in chapter 3). However, before it can be sold, this universal artefact needs to be 'embodied' in a functional artefact. The extent to which both of these dimensions are industrialized should be investigated but it cannot be assumed that they are equally industrialized and rationalized, in the same sorts of ways. Thus, the universal artefacts which are the product of the music industry may be produced under industrialized conditions whereas the actual recordings may not be, as was pointed out above, and recognized by Adorno when he talked of the handicraft nature of much song writing. However, there are problems with this conceptualization of handicraft, as it does not in itself actually examine the nature of song production or the nature and extent of technology which is used in the process. This suggests that sociological analysis of the production of music needs to pay attention to two different levels: the more macro-level structure of the pop music industry and the more micro-level of the social production of pop music itself, which takes place in the context of this organization of the music industry, but which is not simply determined by it.

Furthermore, Gendron argues that the part interchangeability of the functional artefact is largely a consequence of its being produced on an assembly line. 'In this system of production, every whole (e.g. the automobile) is assembled out of qualitatively different parts, each of which is taken at random from qualitatively indistinguishable batches' (1986:26). However, in Gendron's view, the increased use of technology in the production of music actually *expands* the degree of variation possible. For example, this may be seen in the marketing of music in a number of different formats, which leads to greater availability of different forms. Further, the importance of the relatively cheap cassette tape also increases the variety of available music, which can also be copied by those who have bought the original tape.

Middleton (1990:38) makes a related point when he suggests that Adorno pays insufficient attention to the 'specificity of cultural goods', which he explains by quoting from Frith that 'music can never be *just* a product (an exchange value), even in its rawest commodity form; the artistic value of records has an unavoidable complicating effect on their production'.

In addition to not recognizing the specificity and variations in the nature of cultural production, Adorno does not pay enough attention to the struggles which take place between different cultural producers (Middleton 1990) and to the competitive market relations which prevail in the different sectors of the music industry. Thus, in speaking of the culture industry there is a tendency to neglect variations between different sections of that industry and the precise patterns of relations between different companies.

Another of the key problems of Adorno's approach is that he does not allow for enough diversity in the structure and form of popular music texts (Middleton 1990). Adorno wrote a good proportion of his work on popular music in the late 1930s and early 1940s. At this point it may have seemed that the products of the popular music section of the culture industry were standardized. However, it is more difficult to sustain this thesis in the light of the current variation in pop music styles, though we may still wish to take seriously as matters for empirical investigation the extent to which this is true, rather than superficial variation. There is a problem here, however, in that it is not always easy to decide what is fundamental, and what is superficial, textual variation. This distinction might conceivably work for the very standardized songs produced from Tin Pan Alley in the 1930s, but it is not so easily applicable to some more recent forms, or to free-form jazz. The further elucidation and consideration of this point depends upon analysis of the structure of musical texts themselves and the tools that can be used in this exercise (see chapter 6).

In a similar way Adorno's account of the reception of pop music is very unspecific. He makes a number of generalizations which are not backed up by evidence of a substantive kind. Before his suggestions could be accepted, it would be necessary to consider the different ways in which people actually relate to popular music. Thus, it might be difficult to argue that people respond to Take That and Frank Zappa in similar ways. What is more, he does not consider in enough detail the different sorts of pleasure that are a part of the consumption of popular music. Some forms of music may be valued because they are exceptionally good to dance to, others may invite contemplation, and so on. These pleasures are not all as superficial as Adorno seems to think.

These more specific criticisms can be related to the general nature and basis of Adorno's account, in terms of four areas.

1   Immanent method

Middleton (1990) suggests that many of the problems of Adorno's work stem from his initial focus on a particular type of musical work itself. In his view, Adorno generalizes from within the Western tradition of 'serious' music, and compares other forms against this. These are then seen to be of less value. A more proper procedure would be to proceed in a non-judgemental way, rather than implicitly or explicitly comparing different forms of music against the ideal of aspects of the Western classical tradition. This involves the suspension of critical judgement about value. A similar point is made by Gendron (1986).

2   Historical and social location

Adorno's approach is too constrained by his own historical and social location, of being a highly educated, musically literate German intellectual of the mid-twentieth century. Owing to his lack of reflection on the effects this may have, his approach has many difficulties in coping with social and historical change in music making, as he continued to value a particular and very specific form of music. However, as Gendron (1986) points out and as has been noted several times above, there are senses in which Adorno's theory does seem to explain features of contemporary pop music, such as the kind of superficial variation identified by Goodwin (1992); and the extent to which Adorno's theory illuminates aspects of contemporary pop needs consideration.

3   Innovation

In a way related to these other general points, Adorno pays insufficient attention to the dynamic and changing nature of music.

Popular music has developed considerably since Adorno put forward his ideas, and consideration needs to be given to the issue of whether musical innovation and the development of new technologies actually alters aspects of musical production in quite significant ways.

4 Analysis

As Adorno's account is so general it constrains detailed analysis of the specific nature of musical production, textual variation and consumption. My suggestion is that, as well as problematizing pleasure, Adorno militates against sociological exploration and analysis. Before the relevance of such a theory can be determined, there needs to be investigation of the changing nature of the music industry, the ways in which music is actually produced in different places and times, the specific political effects of music in different contexts, the extent of textual variation between forms of pop music, and the different ways in which music is consumed and produces pleasure. We are now much more able to consider these issues as there has been much research carried out since Adorno's time, some of which is reported upon in this book. However, as a general theory, we have to ask if Adorno's account allows the kind of detailed analysis which is necessary for the proper evaluation of pop music in society.

Having made these points against Adorno, I want to consider the relevance of the work of Max Weber on rationalization to the contemporary study of music.

Weber, rationalization and McDonaldization

A different and potentially illuminating approach to the place of music and culture in society can be found in the work of the German sociologist Max Weber (1864–1920) and in subsequent Weberian writers. Weber's sociology is based around a typology of different types of social action: rational action towards a goal, rational action towards a value, affective action, and traditional action. One of the central themes of his work is that Western societies are becoming increasingly rationalized, as forms of rational action become more central. An example of this form of action and social organization is a bureaucracy. Weber's ideal type of this form of organization consisted of elements such as a clear hierarchy of positions,

■ efficiency
■ calculability
■ predictability
■ control

Figure 1.4   Dimensions of McDonaldization
Source: Ritzer (1993)

a division of labour, written documentation, promotion and recruitment on merit, government by rules, and impersonal relations between bureaucracy members and clients. Bureaucracies were
becoming increasingly common, and in important ways society was
bureaucratized and rationalized. This was not necessarily a bad thing
in Weber's mind, though his work did also have a pessimistic tone and
he talked of becoming imprisoned in the 'iron cage' of bureaucracy.

Moreover, this would seem to be even more likely, and depressing
perhaps, if many other areas of social life were being organized
along the lines identified by Weber. A contemporary argument that
this is clearly the case has been made by the American sociologist
George Ritzer (1993). Ritzer suggests that the dominant form of
organization of social life is not bureaucracy as identified by Weber,
but the similar type of rationalization exemplified by the McDonald's
fast food restaurant. Ritzer argues that a large number of other
social organizations are being organized along lines similar to the
fast food restaurant. He calls this 'the McDonaldization of society'.
Thus sport, education, and medical care, to take just three of the
examples examined by Ritzer, increasingly exhibit features similar to
McDonald's. The main dimensions of this sort of organization are;
efficiency, calculability, predictability and control (see figure 1.4).
The organizations are organized to deliver the goods in an efficient
way, eliminating wasteful operations in the working practices of staff
and not keeping the customer waiting for long periods. Every aspect
of the production and delivery of the good is measured and calculated. Hence, the burgers and rolls in McDonald's restaurants are
of a precise size and are cooked for an exactly measured period of
time. The products and surroundings in McDonaldized organizations are standardized and predicable. The idea is that a hamburger
will look and taste the same in New York, London, Paris or Mos-
cow. Finally, the processes in organizations like McDonald's are
controlled with clear lines of management.

Ritzer suggests, rather like Weber, that despite the rationalization processes involved in McDonaldization, such organizations can be irrational and inefficient. For example, we may have to queue for a relatively long time for a hamburger and may find the lack of variation in the quality boring and unexciting. Further, other types of organization develop, which attempt to produce experiences which are not routinized and predictable in the McDonaldized fashion.

An important aspect of Ritzer's argument is his suggestion that our leisure time has become rationalized. Hence, not only are the production of goods and the places where we consume them rationalized, but our time and wider leisure activities also. The places where we might have escaped from office or state bureaucracies in earlier times have themselves become organized along the rationalized, McDonaldized model.

It has been argued that these processes of rationalization are applicable to pop music. Weber (1958) identifies the particular nature of the rational structure of Western music and his argument suggests that:

> The value of musical rationalization is the transformation of the process of musical production into a calculable affair operating with known means, effective instruments, and understandable rules. Constantly running counter to this is the drive for expressive flexibility. (Martindale and Riedel 1958:li)

As Goodwin (1992:76) explains:

> It is suggested that just as capitalist societies need increasingly to rationalize production to bring *order* to the creation of commodities, so Western music also creates a network of rules for music making. Thus a universal notational system and precise measurement of tonal and rhythmic differences comes to define what music *is*.

In an argument which is examined in more detail in chapter 3, Goodwin (1992) finds evidence that the development of new forms of technology and their application to music involves the rationalization of the nature and production of musical texts along Weberian lines. He identifies three dimensions to this: 'harmonic rationalization, temporal rationalization, and timbral conformity'.

Goodwin (p. 83) explains that:

> Harmonic rationalization occurs partly, for instance, through the elimination of microtonality that is involved in many modern synthesizers.

This has implications for the globalization of music because many non-Western musics depend on microtones that are difficult to achieve on Western synthesizers.

Thus, there is a limiting of the range of tones which we might expect to hear in music. Temporal rationalization occurs through technology like the drum machine, which can produce a precise number of beats per second, thus structuring the overall nature of a piece of music. Timbral conformity occurs through the ways in which the sounds from synthesizers are often pre-set at the factory which means that 'the new machines produce the same sounds whoever plays them, whenever and wherever they are played' (Goodwin 1992:84).

On a Weberian interpretation, production in the music industry might increasingly be organized along rational lines. Thus, different aspects of a piece of music may be constructed in different places and brought together for completion if they have been recorded at the same rate of beats per minute. This increases the importance of the beat which structures the whole piece of music. Moreover, tracks can be constructed from a limited range of sounds in a rapid fashion, by people skilled with computers rather than musical instruments. A further discussion of the use of new technologies in this process can be found in chapter 3.

In addition, the delivery of the musical product is increasingly taking place in large leisure supermarkets. In a shop such as HMV or Virgin in the centre of Manchester the music is lined up in tidy boxes and packets, self selected by the customer and taken to a till to be paid for. There are relatively few staff in evidence and they mainly interact with customers to take their money. By contrast, record shops more frequently used to be places where the potential purchaser could ask advice from the expert sales person who would allow the customer to listen to several records of his or her own choice before deciding on a purchase, or not as the case was. Such modes of interaction would now only be expected in the increasingly marginalized specialist shops. Table 1.1 offers evidence of the increasing importance of the McDonaldized specialist chains and the decline of the larger independent specialists in the retailing of recorded music in Britain. The potential purchasers of the music might work in organizations structured along McDonaldized lines. Thus, in Douglas Coupland's novel *Generation X* (1992), the young characters have had a series of McJobs in the past and at the beginning of the movie version of *Wayne's World*, Wayne describes his

Table 1.1 Retailers of recorded music: numbers of UK outlets

Numbers(a)

	1984	1985	1986	1987	1988	1989	1990	1991	1992
Specialist chains	167	..	238	326	361	338	365	427	432
Multiples	1,857	..	1,798	1,810	1,774	1,857	1,899	1,904	1,857
Independent specialists									
Large (b)	375	..	333	401	437	330	175	152	126
Medium (c)	673	..	752	778	792	641	339	366	347
Small (d)	1,159	..	929	846	763	821	857	666	648
Others (e)	800	..	800	800	800	800	800	800	800
Total	3,007	..	2,814	2,825	2,792	2,592	2,171	1,984	1,921
Total	5,031	..	4,850	4,961	4,927	4,787	4,435	4,315	4,210

(a) Numbers are not calculated at the same time in each year.
(b) Sales of 1,000 or more units per week.
(c) Sales of 500–1,000 units per week.
(d) Sales of 100–500 units per week.
(e) An estimate of all other independent specialists selling fewer than 100 units per week.

Source: Cultural Trends 19 (1993:52); from Gallup

career in terms of lots of jobs which entail wearing a name-badge and a hairnet. In themselves the consumers of music might be affected by these same processes of rationalization.

Rationalization and McDonaldization: some criticisms

As will be examined in more detail in chapter 3, it is not clear that rationalization is the only process at work in the production of contemporary popular music. Thus, some writers have argued that there will always be dimensions which are not rationalized and the musical production will escape from this kind of straitjacket. Frith (1992:74) captures several aspects of this notion when he maintains that:

> The industrialization of music hasn't stopped people from using it to express private joys or public griefs; it has given us new means to do so, new ways of having an impact, new ideas of what music can be. Street music is certainly an industrial noise now, but it's a human noise too so it is perhaps fitting to conclude that the most exciting and political music of the early 1990s should be the hip-hop sounds of young urban black bands like Public Enemy, groups that are heavily dependent on both the latest technology and street credibility.

Goodwin suggests that rap and hip-hop music, while using technologies that might imply rationalization, have broken with conventionalized forms. He argues that 'what is really striking about the recent development of popular music is its progressive shift away from conventional tonality and structural conformity'. Furthermore, 'extremely avant-garde sounding recordings that thoroughly challenge the conventions of tonality and song structure have routinely charted' (1992:92–3).

In addition, the consumers of this sort of music might try to escape from the structures of rationalization in which they are forced to work. The characters in *Generation X* seek escape from their McJobs, and Wayne and Garth in *Wayne's World* develop their own forms of creativity in running their own cable access television programme and in their appropriation of heavy metal music.

As with the account offered by Adorno, the arguments about rationalization seem over-general, again implying the need for a more specific and empirically based understanding and theorization of the precise nature of musical production, products and consumption. While general theories can provoke thought and may capture significant aspects of contemporary practice, they need to be evaluated in the context of the application of the theory to a range of different cases. This may often lead to a reformulation of the theory with more specific reference. The argument here is not about theory *per se*, but concerns the attempt to stretch a theory to cover all cases in different contexts.

Audience power and creativity

The two general accounts considered in this chapter so far have stressed themes of commodification, standardization and rationalization. In different ways they are both pessimistic accounts of contemporary culture and popular music. Both of the theories continue to have influence upon interpretations and understandings of popular music. However, in recent years a number of writers have sought to understand the limits to the influence of mass culture and rationalization. This has often entailed a move away from consideration of what culture does to its audience towards an evaluation of the ways in which audiences use the products of the culture industries in their own lives. The contours of these developments have now been traced by a number of different authors (for example, McGuigan 1992), who show the way in which the sort of critique of the culture industries put forward by Adorno and Horkheimer was superseded by the theory of hegemony associated with the work of the Italian Marxist writer Antonio Gramsci (1891–1937). Hegemony is explained by Abercrombie (1990:201) in the following terms:

> In such a view, popular culture cannot be seen as a simple imposition of dominant ideology on subordinate classes. While cultural relations have to be understood in terms of the antagonistic relationships between the bourgeoisie and the working classes, bourgeois culture is not *simply* dominant. One cannot speak of domination here but rather the struggle for hegemony – that is, moral, cultural and political leadership. For Gramsci, the bourgeoisie can achieve hegemony only to the extent that it can accommodate subordinate class values. The establishment of hegemony is thus a case of *negotiation* between dominant and subordinate values.

Such an approach entails the attempt to understand how members of society negotiate with the products of the culture industries. These developments are reviewed at greater length in chapters 7 and 8 of this book. However, one of the key suggestions of recent versions of this sort of approach is that audiences have a great deal of power in negotiating with the texts of media products. Thus, for example, Fiske has argued:

> against the common belief that the capitalist cultural industries produce only an apparent variety of products whose variety is finally illusory for they all promote the same capitalist ideology. Their skill in sugar coating the pill is so great that the people are not aware of the ideological practice in which they are engaging as they consume and enjoy the cultural commodity. I do not believe that 'the people' are 'cultural dopes'; they are not a passive, helpless mass incapable of discrimination and thus at the economic, cultural, and political mercy of the barons of the industry. (1987:309)

This leads Fiske into consideration of the ways in which media texts are used in different ways in audience members lives. For example, he writes of Madonna in the following way:

> The meanings of the Madonna look, as of the Madonna videos, cannot be precisely specified. But that is precisely the point, the pleasure that they give is not the pleasure of *what* they say, but of their assertion of the right and the power of a severely subordinated subculture to make their own statements, their own meanings. Madonna's invitation to her girl fans to play with the conventions of patriarchy shows them that they are not necessarily subject to those conventions but can exercise some control over their relationship to patriarchy and thus over the sense of their identity. (p. 233)

Fiske's more recent work has received a somewhat hostile reception, one criticism being that it leads to a simple celebration of popular culture, and suggests that opposition to domination can be found in all its forms. It may be that, in attempting to focus attention on the different ways in which products of the culture industries can be used, Fiske (and others like him) have played down the dimensions of the culture industry identified by Adorno. However, this does not mean that the implications of this work should be ignored, and the ideas of activity and creativity on the part of the audience need to considered in empirical terms alongside those of commodification, standardization and rationalization.

A framework for analysis

The implication of the discussion in this chapter so far is that there is a need to pay detailed attention to the different dimensions of production, the nature of the product, and its consumption. To structure such consideration in this book, I have organized the discussion in accord with a production, text and audience scheme. In its essentials this scheme is very simple. It argues that any cultural object such as a book, play, film, television programme, or record should be thought of as a text. These texts do not come into existence spontaneously, but result from production processes which involve various different institutions. In some cases such production may be relatively simple. Thus when I write a lecture for delivery to my students, I may sit down with a pen and paper and write a text which is then delivered orally to them. In other cases, production is exceedingly complex. Thus, a record will be the outcome of a complex set of procedures involving different people and social processes, including musicians, recording engineers, record producers, playing instruments, interaction in a recording studio, mixing tapes, the manufacture of records in a factory, and so on. Such cultural objects are not only produced, they are also consumed, or read, by an audience or audiences and it is necessary to study the processes that occur here. These can be represented diagrammatically, as in figure 1.5.

This scheme leads to at least five sets of issues or questions which need to be examined in sociological analysis. First, there are a set of concerns raised by the consideration of what is meant by production and producers. Here, it is important to examine the way in which producers like musicians or novelists are located within a range of contextualizing social institutions. Thus, the musician may be contracted to a multinational corporation with interests in many different fields, or, at the other end of the scale, he or she could write music for their own interest and never have it published or performed. It can be suggested that most cultural production takes place within an economic context where the profit motive is paramount and this will have effects, however mediated, on the text.

Second, it is important to consider precisely *how* production takes place. It is important to examine not just *who* produces, and the wider economic and institutional contexts for such production, but the actual nature of the processes of production themselves. Therefore, it will be necessary to consider whether people collaborate in

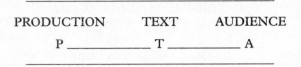

Figure 1.5 Production, text and audience scheme

the production of the text. Also, whether one organization, or group, has the power to prevent another group or individual from developing ideas: for example, is one institution like the State attempting to prevent another like a rock group from recording certain songs? Furthermore, it is important to consider whether there are conflicts within a company or group involved in cultural production.

Third, there are a range of issues raised by the description of the cultural object as a text. One consequence of this depiction is that a text such as pop record is thought to have a structure, which can be examined through analysis. In chapter 6 of this book a number of different concepts which are used in the analysis of texts are identified. It is also important to recognize that, at least partly because of the way in which they are structured, there can be different interpretations of texts and the meanings they contain.

Fourth, there are issues deriving from the idea of an audience and what is meant by this term. Thus, the particular make-up of the audience for any particular text should be investigated and we may want to consider the way in which a text or set of texts is used by different social groups. For example, do contemporary heavy metal fans listen to Led Zeppelin differently from rock fans from the late 1960s? Also, it is important to consider the ways in which texts produce certain identifications for us when we watch, read or listen to them. Thus, when some people listen to guitar-based music, they pretend to be playing the electric guitar themselves, thus in some way identifying with the guitar player. This is similar to identifying with the hero of a narrative, and it is no accident that players like Eric Clapton and Jimi Hendrix were known as guitar heroes.

Fifth, it is important to consider *how* it is that a text is consumed. This may involve examination of whether a record is listened to on a Walkman, a small stereo, or a system costing thousands of pounds, as these may alter the ways in which the text is understood and the forms of pleasure which are derived from it. Does an individual listen to a text alone in his or her bedroom, or dance to it at an all-night rave? The detail of social context can have a great effect on meaning and form of appropriation of a text. These different aspects

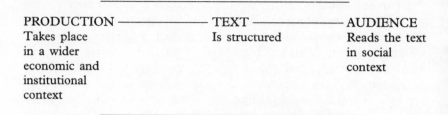

Figure 1.6 Developed production, text and audience scheme

can be mapped on to the basic production, text and audience scheme as shown in figure 1.6.

Popular music can be examined in the context of such a production, text and audience scheme. In what follows this framework is adopted to structure the presentation of material. In chapter 2, the wider institutional and economic context of popular music production is considered: this includes a discussion of the patterns of ownership in the pop music industry, an examination of the nature of the markets for the products of that industry, details of the income derived from rights in the industry and consideration of the ways in which 'globalization' of the music industry is occurring.

In chapter 3, on the social production of music, more 'micro' and detailed aspects of musical production are considered. This includes examination of the subcultures of musicians, the social backgrounds of pop musicians and the detail of more 'amateur' musical production in local contexts. The chapter includes discussion of the changing division of labour in the popular music production process and the effects of technological change on these processes.

In chapters 4, 5 and 6 attention moves from the production of texts to the nature of texts themselves. Chapter 4 considers a range of material and issues deriving from the history of popular music, its political orientation and connections with sexuality. Included in this chapter is a discussion of pop and postmodernism.

Chapter 5 develops the discussion of these matters through an analysis of black music. This includes examination of the problems of attributing music to different racial groups and includes three case-studies of blues and soul, ska and reggae, and rap and hip-hop. Again, these discussions involve consideration of some of the different dimensions of the debate around postmodernism in contemporary culture.

Chapter 6 focuses on the structure of texts and how they convey meanings. It begins with a discussion of the limits of musicology in the study of popular music, before considering different aspects of musical meaning. This involves the introduction of some key terms from structuralism and semiotics. The chapter continues with an examination of the debate on the relative importance of words in the creation and communication of musical meaning, before analysing the recent debates on music video.

Chapters 7 and 8 consider different dimensions of the audience for popular music. Chapter 7 looks at some of the most important recent accounts of text/audience relations, then goes on to consider some data on the trends in consumption of different musical texts by different parts of the audience. This is followed by a description of some of the main contours of the examination of music as it is used and developed by different subcultural groups.

Chapter 8 considers the literature on fans, and summarizes the most important accounts which have been produced on the attachment of fans to individual groups and artists, and some of the recent theorizations of fan activity in general. This is followed by examination of the debates on the increasing difficulty of defining the relations between production and consumption in the sphere of popular music, returning in conclusion to some of the issues raised by the studies of local music-making described in chapter 3.

The production, text and audience scheme thus structures the presentation of the material to be examined in this book. There are a number of different sociological dimensions to the analysis which run through the application of this scheme. Thus, attention is paid at different points to dimensions of class, gender, race, age and place. Any sociological analysis worth its salt has to do this. The utilization of these dimensions as threads running through the book does mean that there is no chapter entitled 'Women and Pop', for example, or no chapter on young people and music, and so on. However, examinations of all these dimensions will be found.

There are also a number of specific concepts and issues examined in this book, which are important in contemporary cultural studies and the sociology of culture. These have to do with, for example, the value that is placed on particular pieces of music and the struggle which takes place between different social groups around music. The salience of these issues is identified as they are introduced in particular contexts, rather than overburdening the discussion at this introductory stage.

Summary

This chapter has considered:

- Adorno's account of popular music and criticisms that can be made of it;
- Weber's account of rationalization and its development into the thesis of McDonaldization by Ritzer;
- some criticisms of the rationalization idea;
- recent work which has moved beyond Gramsci's account of hegemony to emphasize audience power and creativity;
- the production, text and audience framework for the analysis of culture and the issues it raises;
- the structure of the rest of the book.

PART I

PRODUCTION

2

The Pop Music Industry

This chapter covers four main areas. First, it characterizes the economic structure of the contemporary popular music industry, examining patterns of market domination, relations between the structure and wider social and economic change, and employment patterns. Second, it outlines the data on the material production of the industry, summarizing the information on what the music industry produces and where it is sold. Third, the chapter considers the income derived from the ownership of rights in the music industry. Several authors (for example, Frith 1987) have pointed to the centrality of such rights to the contemporary music industry. The nature of copyright is explained and the different rights in the music industry distinguished. Data on the income from rights and membership of the collecting societies is included. The idea that the industry is moving away from the exploitation of rights to the use of trademarks is considered, before the chapter concludes with an examination of some of the issues raised by the contemporary globalization of the music industry. Consideration is given here to the ideas of cultural imperialism and transculturation.

The structure of the pop music industry

As was explained in chapter 1, all pop music is produced within a social context, and a great deal of it is produced from within an industry attempting to generate profits. This being the case, how is the pop music industry currently structured?

Company	Larger company	Base country
EMI	Thorn-EMI	Britain
Polygram	Philips	Netherlands
Sony	Sony	Japan
Warner	Time-Warner	United States
BMG	Bertelsmann	Germany
MCA	Matshushita	Japan

Figure 2.1 Dominant companies in the music industry
Source: derived from Negus (1992)

The popular music industry is dominated by six companies: EMI Music, Polygram, Sony Music Entertainment, Warner Music International, BMG Music Group and MCA, who produce over 70 per cent of recorded pop music (Negus 1992:1). As is shown by figure 2.1, these companies are parts of other larger companies. The picture which emerges clearly from this brief characterization is of the dominance of the music industry by six firms which are parts of larger, or parent, companies with a wide range of commercial interests. The music industry is therefore concentrated and dominated by conglomerates.

Concentration refers to the fact that the ownership of an area of production is concentrated in the hands of a small number of companies. Concentration can be discussed across an economy as a whole or in terms of specific sectors. It is often expressed by what economists call the *concentration ratio*, 'which measures the degree of concentration within a particular sector by taking the proportion of the market controlled by the top five firms in the sector' (Murdock and Golding 1977:23). On the figures given by Negus (1992), the concentration ratio for the music industry would be over 70 per cent.

The music industry has been concentrated for a good part of the twentieth century (Negus 1992). However, it is important to recognize that concentration ratios vary historically. For example, in their discussion of 'cycles in symbol production' in the American pop music industry, Peterson and Berger (1990), demonstrate significant variation in the four and eight firm concentration ratios between 1948 and 1973, as is shown in table 2.1. The American industry was most concentrated in the early 1950s, with the four firm concentration ratio varying between 71 per cent and 89 per

Table 2.1 Number of firms and market shares in the weekly Top 10
of the popular music single record market, by year

Year	Labels	Firms	Firms with only one hit	Concentration ratio 4-FIRM	8-FIRM
1948	11	11	5	81	95
1949	9	8	3	89	100
1950	11	10	3	76	97
1951	10	8	2	82	100
1952	12	11	5	77	95
1953	12	11	3	71	94
1954	13	12	4	73	93
1955	16	14	7	74	91
1956	22	20	10	66	76
1957	28	23	8	40	65
1958	35	31	19	36	60
1959	46	42	29	34	58
1960	45	39	20	28	52
1961	48	39	16	27	48
1962	52	41	21	25	46
1963	52	36	15	26	55
1964	53	37	17	34	51
1965	50	35	16	37	61
1966	49	31	13	38	61
1967	51	35	15	40	60
1968	46	30	17	42	61
1969	48	31	14	42	64
1970	41	23	5	51	71
1971	46	21	7	45	67
1972	49	20	5	48	68
1973	42	19	4	57	81

Source: Peterson and Berger (1990:142)

cent. It was least concentrated in the early 1960s, before becoming
more so in the early 1970s. Some further discussion of the factors
behind these changes can be found in the examination of the development of rock and roll in chapter 4.

The parent companies of the 'big six' music producers which

Conglomerate	Examples of other interests
Thorn-EMI	lighting, domestic appliances, retail outlets, security systems, computer software, electronic technology
Philips	lighting, electronic and electrical goods
Sony	domestic and industrial audio and visual products, semiconductors, telecommunications goods, Columbia Pictures
Time-Warner	film, cable, television and publishing
Bertelsmann	newspapers, magazines, books, record clubs, cable television
Matshushita	electronic goods

Figure 2.2   Other interests of dominant companies in the music industry
Source: derived from Negus (1992)

dominate the pop music industry are also active in other sectors of the economy. As is shown by figure 2.2, they are conglomerates having a wide range of interests, which focus in the media field. Murdock and Golding (1977), in an influential examination of the structure of contemporary media industries, suggest two reasons for this process of diversification across different spheres on the part of the conglomerates which produce a range of different products. First, they argue that such strategies facilitate the maintenance of overall profits even when individual sectors suffer from a lack of potential for expansion due to falling demand; and second, that the process provides the opportunity for one sector to 'cushion' another where profitability has declined due to other factors. A recent discussion of the ways in which different areas can be combined is contained in the examination of Thorn EMI in box 1, where it is suggested that Thorn EMI is a rather unstable combination of two main areas: music and technology.

A related strategy is that of 'vertical integration' where 'oligopolistic concentration of the record industry was maintained by control of the total production flow from raw materials to wholesale sales' (Peterson and Berger 1990:143). For example, an artist may record in a studio owned by a company which manufactures a disc from the recording at one of its plants, which is then reviewed in a magazine owned by that company (which may also include a review of the film

Box 1 Branson sale can't hide flip side at Thorn EMI

VIRGIN has been good news for Thorn EMI. Richard Branson's sale of his record business to finance the airline has left Thorn EMI with a larger music business and its biggest boost to half-year profits, which were badly in need of a lift.

The group used to be a technology business with a bit of music on the side. Now it is increasingly a music business where technology is an irritation which won't go away. True, there is a big rental business (mainly Radio Rentals in this country) but it seems almost inevitable that rental operations will eventually be sold, floated off or otherwise disposed of.

The logic of separating music and rental is overwhelming, just as the logic of putting together Thorn and EMI in the first place defeated many observers. Since the latter happened, there is no guarantee the former will not, but chairman Sir Colin Southgate has indicated in the past that separation is the direction in which the group is moving.

He was not available yesterday, but Smith New Court analyst Bruce Jones pointed out that he had suggested some time ago that rental might be floated off. The trouble is, there seems to be a conflict between the need to

float and the opportunity. "He said six to nine months ago that rental would be floated only when one side of the business was holding the other back," Mr Jones said. "The problem is, now that is happening, it isn't possible."

In a statement, Sir Colin was sanguine about difficult trading conditions. "Despite these circumstances, our strong financial position enables us to make significant investments in our core music and rental businesses to ensure they continue to meet our stated objectives," he said.

The rental operation turned in an 18 per cent increase in profits in the first half of the year, although currency swings had something to do with the size of that rise. But behind the figures lies the uncertainty of possible legal changes in the US, the threat of which has perhaps been heightened by the bad publicity attracted by Rent-a-Center.

The chain, which claims almost a third of the US market, was accused earlier this year of improper practices in persuading clients to enter contracts they could not afford, and in extracting payments from them. Thorn EMI has vigorously refuted the allegations and earlier this month appointed former senator Warren Rudman, who is now associated with the group's lawyers, to conduct an inquiry.

Legal changes are probably a bigger threat, but still reason-

ably remote. One possibility is a bill which would reclassify rental activities as credit business, thus bringing it within very tight regulation. Most importantly, the high interest charges included in rental payments would be severely constrained.

Thorn EMI insists there is little chance of such a change happening, but the threat and the scandal have cast a cloud over the group's apparent success in narrowing its activities to two

main spheres, after a long struggle to escape from the conglomeracy of the 1980s.

Time after time, the group was forced to announce that sales of defence or lighting interests had been called off — notably when talks with GEC broke down in August. The chart shows that it is the remaining peripheral businesses which have held back profits this time. HMV's loss is a little misleading, since this is primarily a second-half business. Nevertheless, last

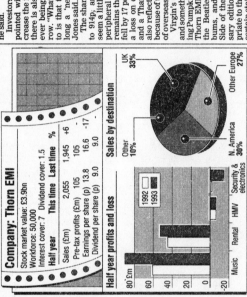

Company: Thorn EMI

- Stock market value: £3.9bn
- Workforce: 50,000
- Interest cover: 7   Dividend cover: 1.5

Half year	This time	Last time	%
Sales (£m)	2,055	1,945	+6
Pre-tax profits (£m)	105	105	-17
Earnings per share (p)	13.8	16.6	-17
Dividend per share (p)	9.0	9.0	

Half year profits and loss

(bar chart, £m, 1992 / 1993: Music, Rental, HMV, Security & electronics)

Sales by destination

(pie chart: UK 33%, Other Europe 27%, N. America 30%, Other 10%)

year's final result of £2.6 million profits on sales of £323 million is hardly inspiring, and certainly unsatisfactory.

Security and electronics, encompassing the defence businesses, is even more unpleasant. A loss of almost £15 million is blamed on contract deferral and cost overruns but, as Smith New Court's Mr Jones commented, investors just want to see the back of these businesses. "People are bored with the continuing problems," he said.

Investors were also disappointed with the failure to increase the interim dividend, but there is also a sense of jam forever being promised for tomorrow. "What it really comes down to is that this has been for too long a 'next year' stock," Mr Jones said.

The share price fell from 949p to 914p, and while this might seem a little rash on the basis of peripheral problems, the fact remains that earnings per share fell by 17 per cent. This includes a loss on disposals of Lighting and a Thames TV stake, but it also reflects a higher tax charge because of the higher proportion of overseas profits.

Virgin's Janet Jackson, UB40 and something called the Smashing Pumpkins have done well for Thorn EMI so far this year, but the Beatles Red and Blue albums, and Pink Floyd's Dark Side of the Moon 20th anniversary edition seem more appropriate to the group's current uncertain state.

Source: *The Guardian*, 24 November 1993

made by the artist for a film company owned by the same conglomerate) and sold to the public in a shop owned by the company.

The concentrated nature of the pop music industry has led to complaints that the dominant companies can use their power against the interests of consumers. An example of this arose in Britain during 1992 and 1993 over the pricing of Compact Discs. The House of Commons Committee that investigated this matter suggested that prices of CDs were too high in Britain, especially by comparison with the United States. Leaving aside the merits of the arguments from the different protagonists, which were subsequently decided in favour of the record companies, it is clear that there was resentment against the concentrated nature of the market and its dominance by conglomerate concerns, as is shown by the article reproduced in box 2.

Within this overall picture of a market dominated by a small number of very large companies, attention has often been drawn to the innovative role of small 'independent' record companies. Thus, Peterson and Berger (1990) argue that a period of concentration in the music industry is followed by a burst of creativity when the previously unmet demand on the part of the public for different sounds is unleashed and fed by smaller innovative companies. They suggest that this happened during 1955–9 after the advent of rock 'n' roll in 1955. A similar case can been made for the effects of punk in Britain during 1977 and subsequently, though it is important to recognize that demand itself may be influenced by shifts in consumer preferences, which are related to changes in consumer culture.

This has led some journalistic writing to focus on the creative stance and effects of small, independent record companies such as Atlantic (Gillett 1988) and Stax (Guralnick 1991) which are perceived to have produced particularly distinctive and interesting music. It is suggested that the smallness and intimacy of such companies facilitated the production of particularly innovative sounds which broke free from the standardized products of the dominant record companies. Furthermore, it is argued that such companies were better able to represent the aspirations and feelings of their artists and audiences than the large corporations.

Negus (1992) offers a critique of such approaches. He maintains that a dichotomous distinction between the large, conservative conglomerates and the small, innovative independents is misleading as the recording industry is actually 'a web of major and minor companies' (Negus 1992:17). Thus, larger companies will, for example:

Box 2   Monopoly inquiry into UK music industry

BRITAIN's £1bn-a-year music industry is to be referred to the Monopolies and Mergers Commission in a decision likely to cause a political furore and deep divisions among government ministers.

Sir Bryan Carsberg, Director-General of Fair Trading, has privately told industry leaders that he believes 'a complex monopoly' exists in the supply of compact discs and that competition has not been working effectively. Artists such as Mark Knopfler of Dire Straits have also complained about the price of CDs.

An announcement is due to be made on Thursday, shortly after the Commons National Heritage Committee publishes a damning report on the price of CDs.

Sir Bryan's decision flies in the face of his predecessor, Sir Gordon Borrie, who said last year that there were no grounds for an MMC inquiry. Ministers at the Department of Trade and Industry are believed to oppose interference with one of Britain's most successful industries and biggest export earners, but are powerless under the Fair Trading Act to contest Sir Bryan's decision.

The MMC will be given nine months for the investigation. It is to be asked to concentrate on the application of copyright laws to the music industry, which MPs on the national heritage committee believe keep CD prices artificially high and prevent an inflow of cheaper imports.

Maurice Oberstein, executive vice-president of PolyGram, said any meddling with the copyright laws would be 'a hugely dangerous enterprise' that would almost certainly backfire and destroy a thriving industry. It would also have profound implications for other successful British industries such as pharmaceuticals and publishing. 'I can tell you right now that it would have hardly any impact on the price of CDs, but would be highly destructive of smaller independent record producers and retailers. 'Why are they picking on us? Copyright exists in all kinds of industries and it applies all over the world. We are not allowed to export our product to the US. If we could, the price of CDs would be lower.'

He also claimed that 'almost all of us lose money on our UK trading. We make money out of our overseas royalties, which is a huge benefit to the UK economy, but it is a total red herring to say we are profiteering at the British consumer's expense.'

Mr Oberstein, whose comments were echoed by Rupert Perry, UK chief executive of EMI Records, said he found it 'simply incredible' that Sir Bryan had 'caved into the rantings' of the Commons select committee.

'I could have told you what that committee was going to write before they even sat down to think about it. They wouldn't listen to our arguments. They wouldn't look at the figures.'

The British market in CDs is dominated by just four players: PolyGram, Thorn EMI, Warner Records and Bertelsmann Group. Though Sir Bryan accepts that no evidence exists of a cartel, he is concerned that copyright laws and binding contracts between artists and music companies have the effect of creating a 'complex monopoly'.

They also, he believes, severely restrict imports of cheaper CDs from the US. According to the industry, there is no significant difference between the wholesale price of CDs in Britain, which averages about £5 per disc, and its US counterpart.

Much of the blame for high CD prices, the industry claims, lies with retailers. It says prices are lower in the US largely because of the economies of scale that US producers enjoy.

Source: *Independent on Sunday*, 9 May 1993. Author Jeremy Warner

fund smaller ones to develop particular artists; set up 'independent looking' companies of their own; and adopt small group working practices which resemble those in smaller companies.

It is illuminating in this respect to consider the example of 2 Tone records. The first record on 2 Tone, *Gangsters* by the Specials, was recorded 'independently' and then manufactured and distributed by Rough Trade, an 'independent' record company. Radio airplay and live appearances by the Specials led to record industry attention and an interesting deal with Chrysalis Records, which is discussed in box 3.

Negus (1992) draws attention to the webs and networks which operate in the music industry:

> These organizational webs, of units within a company and connections to smaller companies, enable entertainment corporations to gain access to material and artists, and to operate a coordinating, monitoring and surveillance operation rather than just centralized control. The corporation can still shape the nature of these webs through the use and distribution of investment. But it is a tight–loose approach, rather than a rigidly hierarchical form of organization; tight enough to ensure a degree of predictability and stability in dealing with collaborators, but loose enough to manoeuvre, redirect or even reverse company activity. (Negus 1992:19)

This characterizes the interconnections between the small and the dominant companies in the music industry in a fashion which reflects the influence of writers who maintain that Fordist methods of mass production, organization and promotion (so called after the model of Ford's development of the mass production of cars) are increasingly being replaced by post-Fordist ones in contemporary capitalist societies. The differences between these regimes are summarized in figure 2.3.

Box 3   The birth of 2 Tone Records

THIS further stamp of approval from John Peel only added to the circus of record company suits that turned up at every gig, along with the likes of new wave fave Elvis Costello, who was an early convert to the 2 Tone sound. A & M, Arista, Island, CBS, Virgin, Warner Bros. They were all sniffing around, offering larger and larger amounts of money to get the hottest property on the market at the time. Christ! Mick Jagger was turning up in person to represent Rolling Stone Records! The band couldn't believe it was all happening to them, but rather than get carried away with it all, they knew exactly what they wanted out of any deal. A distribution deal for their 2 Tone label, giving them the freedom to record what they wanted and to sign other groups of their choice.

At the end of the day, it was Chrysalis who finally got the Special A.K.A. to put pen to paper by agreeing to their demands . . . The stumbling block with other labels had been 2 Tone. Everyone wanted the Specials, but nobody wanted the label. At Chrysalis too, there were some arguments over creating a separate label identity, but in the end it was agreed to do just that because the band were too good to lose.

The 2 Tone idea might have put the others off, but the extra money involved turned out to be peanuts. 2 Tone was allowed to record ten singles a year by any band and Chrysalis were obliged to release at least six of them. The budget for each single was only £1,000, and so it was just like giving the Specials another ten grand advance with the added bonus of the chance to discover new talent and more chart success. For that, the Specials signed a five album deal, with options up to eight LPs. With most bands doing well if they are still in business after the 'difficult second album', Chrysalis were certainly taking no chances about losing their new signings half way along the road to Beatledom.

2 Tone was never a separate entity from Chrysalis, although those directly in control decided what was released on it. In effect it was just a trading name for Chrysalis. There were no fancy 2 Tone contracts and bands on 2 Tone were actually signed to Chrysalis. For this, Chrysalis paid 2 Tone a 2 per cent royalty on top of that offered to the bands. 2 Tone might have been a revolutionary challenge to what had gone before, but when all was said and done Chrysalis still held all of the aces.

Source: Marshall (1990:17)

Fordism	Post-Fordism
Mass consumption	Fragmented niche markets
Technology dedicated to the production of one product	General flexible machinery
Mass, assembly-line production	Short-run batch production
Semi-skilled workers	Multiskilled workers
Taylorist management strategy	'Human relations' management strategy
General or industrial unions	No unions or 'company unionism'/no-strike deals
Centralized national bargaining	Decentralized local or plant-level bargaining
Geographically dispersed branch plants	Geographically concentrated new industrial districts flexible specialist communities

Figure 2.3   Ideal types of Fordism and post-Fordism
Source: Bagguley (1991:155)

According to Bagguley (1991:154), the 'central element of a Fordist economic structure is mass production articulated to mass consumption'. Thus, the characterization of the culture industry produced by Adorno which was considered at length in chapter 1, could be said to depict a Fordist structure. Standardized products would be produced on production lines, under the control of a hierarchical management, to be consumed by a public with very little choice over what was available to them. In a post-Fordist system, there would be far more flexibility in production, with work groups often organized into teams with a variety of tasks, a move toward the production of a greater range of products addressed to different markets, with the aim of giving consumers a greater choice. For the post-Fordist industry: 'the emphasis is on breaking down rigid job classifications both horizontally between functions and vertically within the hierarchy of authority, implying "multiskilling" on the one hand, and participation on the other' (Bagguley 1991:157). Hence, it can be argued that working practices in a small company might not be that different from those in a small team in a much bigger one which has moved away from Fordism and bureaucracy. Negus (1992:14–16) argues that this process has occurred in the music industry, resulting 'in a proliferation of project groups and team-based working practices' and contributing 'to a blurring of previous hierarchical distinctions' (p. 15).

However, there are a number of criticisms which can be made of this idea of post-Fordism. Bagguley (1991) suggests that it concentrates mainly on manufacturing industry to the neglect of services, tends to ignore divisions of race and gender, and to over-estimate the extent of the spread of post-Fordist practices, which may be confined to a relatively small number of industries in specific locations in the world.

A connected development in the culture industries has been: '[a] shift in authority from those people directly concerned with production to those who are essentially concerned with other aspects of the company. Marketing and finance departments grow in importance by comparison to those concerned with production' (Abercrombie 1991:177). The different dimensions of what this actually means for the working practices in a record company and the promotion of artists are examined in more detail in chapter 3. However, it has been argued that rises in employment in the marketing and administration areas of the music industry have sometimes offset falls which have taken place in employment in manufacturing. An example of this occurred in 1988 in the United Kingdom when there were:

> a number of pressing plant closures and although the continued buoyancy of the retail market continued to increase employment in marketing and administration, the size of the fall in manufacturing employment reduced total estimated employment in the recording sector by around 150 to just over 9,000. (*Cultural Trends* 1990:39)

Continuing this theme of employment in the industry, inspection of the data contained in table 2.2 reveals a fall in the number of businesses involved in the manufacture of records and tapes in the United Kingdom from 260 in 1985 to 189 in 1989. However, total employment has gone up from 4,000 in 1984 to 5,900 in 1989, with a decrease to 5,400 in 1988. There has been a concentration in the number of businesses involved in the manufacture of records and tapes, allied with an overall increase in employment over this period.

In this chapter so far, attention has concentrated on the most

Table 2.2 Manufacture of gramophone records and pre-recorded tapes
United Kingdom

	Number of businesses	Gross output (£ millions)	Gross value added (£ millions)	Total employment
1984	234	195.2	75.5	4,000
1985	260	254.7	114.3	4,700
1986	236	303.2	143.1	5,500
1987	228	365.1	165.0	5,800
1988	221	400.5	159.0	5,400
1989	189	425.8	144.2	5,900

Source: *Cultural Trends* 12 (1991:24); from *Business Monitor PA345*, HMSO

Table 2.3 Top ten territories by share of world market

1993	Sales (USD) (millions)	%Share
USA	9,833.1	32.3
Japan	5,082.4	16.7
Germany	2,690.7	8.8
UK	1,976.0	6.5
France	1,848.6	6.1
Canada	896.8	2.9
Netherlands	618.8	2.0
Mexico	572.8	1.9
Australia	545.6	1.8
Spain	493.7	1.6

Source: International Federation of the Phonographic Industry (1994)

important general aspects of the music industry. The next section considers some different dimensions of what that industry actually produces.

Products of the music industry

The main functional artetacts (Gendron 1986 – see chapter 1) produced by the music industry are records and tapes. As is shown by table 2.3, the most important markets for these products are in the United States, Japan and Europe.

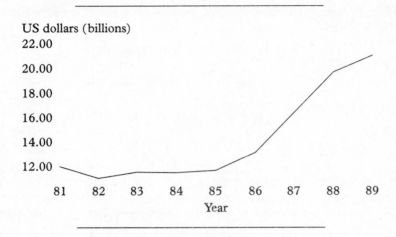

US dollars (billions)

Figure 2.4 World sales of sound recordings 1981–9
Source: International Federation of the Phonographic Industry (1990)

The recent history of sales for the record industry world wide has been divided into three phases (Hung and Morencos 1990:64). The first phase, from 1969 to 1978, involved expansion with the value of retail sales increasing from 'USD 2 billion in 1969 to USD 10.2 billion in 1978' (p. 64). The second phase, a recession from 1979 to 1984, corresponds to the general world recession and the increased effects of home taping made easier by the market penetration of cassettes. The third, recovery, phase developed from 1985, and the value of sales of sound recordings increased from 1985 as shown by figure 2.4.

The expectation is that this expansion will continue. The value of world music sales in 1992 was USD 28,893 million, compared with USD 26,361 million in 1991. CDs are becoming increasingly important in these sales figures. For example, their worldwide sales value increased from USD 975 million in 1991 to USD 1,163 million in 1992. However, cassettes generate the most money representing a value of USD 1,240 million in 1991 and USD 1,602 million in 1992 (International Federation of the Phonographic Industry 1992).

Three important themes can be noted from the review carried out in this section. First, the market for records and tapes is concentrated in the USA, Japan and Europe, though the value of the markets in other areas of the world can be expected to grow rapidly. Second, there have been fluctuations in the value of the market. Third, the relative importance of CDs is increasing, but the cassette still generates the largest share of income from sales. However, it is very important that other means of the generation of income are examined, as these can be seen to be increasingly salient, and the chapter now turns to this area.

Income from rights

The manufacture and sale of tapes and discs are obviously important sources of income for the popular music industry. However, income derived from rights is also very significant and 'a considerable part of the turn-over of the music industry is now being derived from "the exchange of immaterial items" based on the rights to produce a musical work or its performance' (Fabbri 1991, pp. 109–14, as quoted by Negus 1992:12). Thus, Frith contends that:

> For the music industry the age of manufacture is now over. Companies (and company profits) are no longer organized around making *things* but depend on the creation of *rights*. In the industry's own jargon, each piece of music represents 'a basket of rights'; the company task is to exploit as many of these rights as possible, not just those realized when it is sold in recorded form to the public, but also those realized when it is broadcast on radio or television, used on a film, commercial or video soundtrack, and so on. (1987:57)

In the context of the music industry, copyright centres on intellectual property right, which is:

> the right given to the creators of original literary, dramatic, musical and artistic works, and [which] also extends to the creators of original sound recordings, films, broadcasts, cable programmes and the typographic arrangement of published editions. (*Cultural Trends* 1993:56)

In addition, 'The concept of copyright embodies the further principle that although the creator of the work may want to retain the copyright, he may allow others to use his material providing they pay him for it' (p. 56).

As is shown by figure 2.5, three types of right can be identified, which are collected on different bases. Frith (1987) shows that these rights are subject to international variations. Thus:

Right	Basis for collection
Performing	'for use of the musical material . . . collected on behalf of writers and publishers when music is performed or broadcast'
Public performance	'paid for the privilege of broadcasting or playing the actual recording (rather than the song) in public'
Mechanical	'paid to the copyright holder every time a particular song or piece of music is recorded'

Figure 2.5 Rights in the music industry
Source: Negus (1992:13)

France and the USA, for example, have never acknowledged a performing right in records as such (and it was not until the 1976 Act
that jukebox operators in the USA had to get a license from ASCAP/
BMI for their use of songs as songs. (p. 58)

A problem for the individual copyright owner is the collection of the
income which should stem from the ownership of such rights.
Therefore, income from these rights is collected on behalf of copyright owners by collecting societies.

The three types of right identified in figure 2.5 can further be
grouped into performing and mechanical. The Performing Right
Society, which was founded in 1914, is the principal collecting agency
for performing rights in Britain. Its membership, split between writers, publishers and copyright owners and successors, is detailed in
table 2.4, showing a very gradual increase over the period 1984–92,
made up in the main from an increase in the number of writer
members.

The income collected by the Performing Right Society has increased steadily over the past nine years. Data on this are displayed
in table 2.5. As can be seen, there are four main sources of this
income: public performance royalties, radio and television royalties,
overseas royalties, and investment. Radio and television are very
important royalty payers, and the royalties from this source are
greater than the other public performance royalties added together.
'However the gap between the two sources is narrowing: in 1984
public performance royalties amounted to 24 per cent and 38 per

Table 2.4 Performing Right Society membership (a)

	1984	1985	1986	1987	1988	1989	1990	1991	1992
Writers	14,959	16,171	17,046	17,729	18,135	19,084	19,731	20,584	22,057
Publishers	2,389	2,436	2,361	2,318	2,302	2,330	2,312	2,344	2,394
Copyright owners and successors	1,171	1,185	1,195	1,220	1,231	1,232	1,215	1,232	1,244
Total	18,519	19,792	20,602	21,267	21,668	22,646	23,258	24,160	25,695

(a) As at 1 July of each year. Each category of membership is further divided between 'full', 'associate' and 'provisional' members.

Source: *Cultural Trends* 19 (1993:56); from Performing Right Society

Table 2.5 Performing Right Society: summary income and expenditure accounts

£ thousands

	1984	1985	1986	1987	1988	1989	1990	1991	1992
Income									
Public performance royalties	16,261	18,031	21,115	24,511	30,581	34,248	38,428	41,235	43,600
Radio and television royalties	25,909	27,862	33,099	35,947	40,293	42,036	44,339	45,863	48,031
Overseas royalties:									
Republic of Ireland(a)	na	na	na	na	na	1,861	2,539	3,472	4,456
Commonwealth	978	409	629	585	541	745	619	644	904
Foreign affiliated societies	21,371	24,220	26,450	29,752	28,834	32,420	37,372	39,044	43,081
Investment	3,173	3,965	3,990	4,499	3,891	5,706	7,741	6,629	4,949
Total	67,692	74,387	85,283	95,294	104,410	117,016	131,038	136,887	145,021
Expenditure and income distribution(b)									
Administration and licensing costs (net)(c)	12,379	13,893	15,303	17,033	19,236	20,588	23,754	26,348	27,794(d)
Distributed income:									
Writer members	26,687	29,618	34,081	37,641	41,242	45,051	49,139	50,648	53,658
Publisher members	17,791	19,132	21,727	24,300	26,625	31,009	34,725	35,591	36,255
Foreign affiliated societies	10,027	10,685	12,716	14,580	15,770	18,589	22,167	23,955	23,204
Donations, awards and copyright promotion	222	301	333	382	530	576	523	454	477
Transfers to/(from) reserves	–	500	200	–	–	250	200	50	(1,350)

(a) In 1988, Irish Music Rights Organisation (IMRO) was established to assume responsibility for the Society's increasing work in the Republic of Ireland. Prior to 1988, public performance, radio and television royalties in the Republic had been an integral part of domestic collection and distribution. Consequently 1989 figures are not fully comparable with those for earlier years.

(b) With the exception of income distributed to foreign affiliated societies, published figures on distributed income are presented only as rounded percentages. Consequently total expenditure does not precisely equal total income.

(c) Net of recoveries, but before tax.

(d) Excluding £4 million capitalized write-off on Performing Right On-Line Membership Services (PROMS) project.

Source: *Cultural Trends* 19 (1993:57); from Performing Rights Society Yearbooks

cent of total income respectively, while in 1992 the corresponding figures were 30 per cent and 33 per cent' (*Cultural Trends* 1993:58).

Phonographic Performance Limited (PPL), which was founded in 1935, collects royalties for record companies and artists in the United Kingdom. Data on the source and amount of revenue collected by this society are given in table 2.6. The biggest source of revenue is currently public performance, followed by the BBC and Commercial Radio. As can be seen, the importance of public performance has increased steadily over the period shown.

Mechanical Copyright income is collected in Britain by the Mechanical Copyright Protection Society (MCPS), which was founded in 1924. 'The MCPS represents some thousands of composers and publishers of music in the UK, and agreements with reciprocal companies overseas effectively give it representation of over one million composers and music publishers around the world' (*Cultural Trends* 1993:60). The amounts collected over the period 1983–92 are detailed in table 2.7, showing a rapid increase over this period.

Frith (1987) has further argued that the contemporary music industry has moved beyond this world, where exploitation of rights is central, to a different structure, when he says that:

> In this multi-media setting the relationship of intellectual and industrial property is once more confused, and it increasingly seems that pop stars are better thought of as designer goods rather than as creative artists. The importance of image for sales – whether specific images like A-Ha or corporate images applied (as with Duran Duran) to every aspect of 'company' product (records, posters, tee shirts, videos, etc., etc.) – puts musicians under the protection of trade mark and registered design rather than that of copyright. (p. 72)

As Lury (1993:85) explains:

> A trademark provides a legal shield around the name, slogan, shape, or character image and, in conjunction with product licensing, makes it possible for the original proprietor to transfer this sign to second and third parties for a limited period of time in exchange for royalties.

It has been suggested that such developments are taking place across a number of different media. Indeed, it may be that they enable performers to move between different media more easily through the transfer of their image, and thus to break down the divisions which exist between media. What has been termed 'branding': 'the forging of links of image and perception between a range

Table 2.6 Phonographic Performance Limited: sources of revenue (a)

£ thousands

	1983/4	1984/5	1985/6	1986/7	1987/8	1988/9	1989/90	1990/1	1991/2	1992/3(b)
Public performance	1,879	2,057	2,584	3,149	4,104	5,975	8,999	10,417	12,262	12,673
Satellite and cable	–	–	–	–	–	–	–	–	–	110
Telephone services	216	361	327	427	456	170	94	75	73	70
BBC	4,417	5,000	5,702	6,716	6,950	7,212	8,182	8,169	8,848	9,539
Commercial television	253	335	285	336	362	425	399	563	469	500
Commercial radio	3,239	3,120	3,086	2,439	3,719	6,883	5,914	4,965	4,761	5,330
Broadcast dubbing	–	–	–	–	–	–	–	–	–	700
Commercial dubbing										
– BPI	–	–	–	–	–	–	–	705	813	920
Other (c)	497	603	651	895	1,068	1,697	2,589	2,815	1,475	1,050
Total	10,500	11,475	12,636	13,963	16,659	22,363	26,178	27,710	28,701	30,892

(a) Gross revenues.
(b) Estimated.
(c) Interest.

Source: *Cultural Trends* 19 (1993:59); from Phonographic Performance Limited

Table 2.7 Mechanical-Copyright Protection Society: receipt and payment of royalties

£ thousands

	1983/4	1984/5	1985/6	1986/7	1987/8	1988/9	1989/90	1991(a)	1992
Royalties received	13,383	14,694	16,558	19,748	22,245	26,288	34,462	113,092	87,130
Royalties distributed	12,055	14,047	15,346	17,471	20,401	23,603	28,609	106,090	84,323
Of which:									
Royalties arising from overseas	1,700	1,900	2,000	2,100	2,500	2,700	2,300	4,884	4,198

(a) The MCPS changed its year-end to end-December in 1991 to bring it into line with the other major collecting societies. The figures for 1991 therefore cover the *18 month period* to 31 December.

Source: *Cultural Trends* 19 (1993:61); from *Annual Reports*, Mechanical Copyright Protection Society

of products' (Lury 1993:87), facilitates the development of images that are transferable between different media. Such transferability of images means that the music industry has become increasingly connected to other media industries. As is discussed elsewhere in this book (especially in chapters 3 and 6), one of the implications of these developments is the increasingly prominent view that the music industry should not be examined primarily in terms of *manufacturing* but in the context of the promotion of images and signs. Thus, it may be equally seen as a service industry, where the product is an experience. In important respects, advertising and promotional practices (Wernick 1991; Lury 1993) are central to contemporary culture. They are not simply added on to a previously produced product. Promotion of goods across different sectors is increasingly important. Michael Jackson is not simply a recording artist, but an image which connects a number of different areas of culture. Of course, problems arise for the images and the companies whose profitability is connected to it when the personal life of the real person affects the image.

If the image definition of such products or brands is clear enough, they can be sold all over the world, without alterations for different cultures and markets, rather like Coca-Cola, for example. This is both a manufactured product and an image or symbol of American life. Concerns about the effects of the prominence of such symbols has led to debate about the globalization of culture generally, and of music more specifically.

Globalization and the transmission of music

It was explained earlier in this chapter that the main markets for pop music products are in the United States, Europe and Japan. The United States and Britain have in turn dominated the production of popular music for sale in the world market (Negus 1992). It seems likely that world markets will be increasingly opened up to the products of these music industries. Though often relatively small in terms of size, the markets in many of the countries outside the established main markets are among some of the fastest growing in the world. These include countries in Latin America (e.g. Bolivia and Chile), Eastern Europe (e.g. Poland and Hungary), Africa (e.g. Nigeria), the Middle East (e.g. Israel) and Asia (e.g. Taiwan). It seems obvious that the nature of domestic music production may be

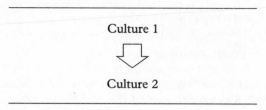

Figure 2.6   Cultural exchange

Source: Wallis and Malm (1990:173). First published in Wallis and Malm, *Big Music from Small Peoples*, Constable, 1984

Culture 1

Culture 2

Figure 2.7   Cultural dominance

Source: Wallis and Malm (1990:174). First published in Wallis and Malm, *Big Music from Small Peoples*, Constable, 1984

affected by the attempts of the big music companies to sell in these markets.

In such a context, Wallis and Malm (1990:173–8) have argued that patterns of cultural transmission can be classified into four types: 'cultural exchange', 'cultural dominance', 'cultural imperialism' and 'transculturation'. In cultural exchange (see figure 2.6): 'two or more cultures or subcultures interact and exchange features under fairly loose forms and more or less equal terms' (Wallis and Malm 1990:173). An example of this process would be the (illegal) taping of a record which is exchanged on a reciprocal basis with a friend. In more global terms, it could entail the ways in which reggae adopted elements from black American soul groups which have then been fed back to black American forms in subsequent years.

In cultural dominance (see figure 2.7), by contrast, one form of culture is imposed by a powerful group on a weaker one. For example, in school we may be forced to listen to particular forms of music to the exclusion of others because the approved forms were perceived to be proper music. Such a process occurred on a wider scale in Africa where: 'missionaries working in Kenya and Tanzania supported by a colonial administration exerted pressure on local culture. Schools were established at mission stations where native

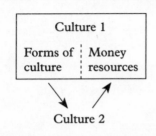

Figure 2.8   Cultural imperialism

Source: Wallis and Malm (1990:175). First published in Wallis and Malm, *Big Music from Small Peoples*, Constable, 1984

pupils were taught a mixture of European and Christian values and music' (Wallis and Malm 1990:175).

In cultural imperialism (see figure 2.8), 'cultural dominance is augmented by the transfer of money and/or resources from dominated to dominating culture group' (Wallis and Malm 1990:175). Wallis and Malm suggest that 'examples of the money transferred are profits made by subsidiaries of record companies belonging to the dominating culture, or copyright money. The resources can be gifted musicians, pieces of music, or unique traditional musical instruments which are removed to museums in a dominating culture area' (p. 175). It has been argued that the dominance of the United States in the transmission of music represents a form of cultural imperialism. This was a great concern in Britain in the 1950s when commentators such as Richard Hoggart (1958) were appalled by the prospect of the Americanization of British popular culture by rock 'n' roll and other American cultural forms (Hebdige 1988).

Garofalo (1992a) has pointed to three main problems with this thesis of cultural imperialism. He argues, first, that it tends to underestimate the amount of resistance to domination that can occur in even subjugated cultures. Second, he maintains that it tends to 'conflate economic power and cultural effects' (p. 4). It is important to recognize, in this argument that cultural dominance does not simply follow economic dominance. Third, he contends that the cultural imperialism thesis often rests on the premise that unspoilt cultures of the dominated are corrupted by the imposed cultures from the West. In criticism of this aspect of the cultural imperialism thesis, Collins (1992) argues that the forms of 'Western' music which are influential in South Africa are actually developments of

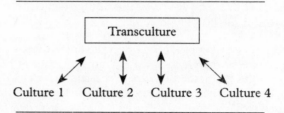

Figure 2.9 Transculture

Source: Wallis and Malm (1990:177). First published in Wallis and Malm, *Big Music from Small Peoples*, Constable, 1984

forms which were earlier exported from Africa in the days of slavery. These forms are being reclaimed in interaction with music developed along a different route in Africa itself. Collins (1992:194) argues that:

> 20th century African popular performers have found three ways of circumventing the problem of 'cultural imperialism' and producing a viable contemporary art form in touch with the common person. These are through the progressive Africanization or de-acculturation of genres which were initially modeled on foreign ones, by the creative use of the black dance-music 'feedback' from the New World, and by continuing the old African tradition of protest music.

Garofalo's (1992a) view is that reality is more complicated than the thesis of cultural imperialism allows and that the complexities may be better understood through the concept of transculturation. According to Wallis and Malm (1990:176), transculturation 'is the result of the worldwide establishment of the transnational corporations in the field of culture, the corresponding spread of technology, and the development of worldwide marketing networks for what can be termed transnationalized culture, or *transculture*' (see figure 2.9). The emergence of 'world beat' could be seen as an example of this process. Another term sometimes used for this sort of culture is global culture. The music of Madonna or Michael Jackson might be said to be transcultural or a form of global culture. As Garofalo (1992a:6) argues:

> Can it be that the 25 million or so people outside the United States who bought Michael Jackson's *Thriller* were all simply the unwitting dupes of imperialist power? Or, is it conceivable that Jackson produced an album which resonated with the cultural sensibilities of a broad international audience?

The effects of this process may be leading towards the creation of what Appadurai (1990) has called mediascapes:

> 'Mediascapes', whether produced by private or state interests, tend to be image-centered, narrative-based accounts of strips of reality, and what they offer to those who experience and transform them is a series of elements (such as characters, plots and textual forms) out of which scripts can be formed of imagined lives, their own as well as those of others living in other places. (p. 299)

Thus, it may be that globally we are witnessing the creation and expansion of mediascapes made up of a variety of elements which are used in alternative ways in different places by particular groups of people. Furthermore, such mediascapes would not be the product of one group or controlling organization, but involve complex negotiations and struggles around the placing together of different elements. The mediascape is like a landscape in that it can be seen in different ways from alternative perspectives and is relatively open to different uses. The idea suggests that configurations of media are very complex, and that while they are affected by the operation of power, they are not simply subject to the whims of powerful corporations or governments. A landscape may be affected by the decisions of the powerful – a motorway may be built through it for instance – but such decisions may be fought, or parts of the landscape may come under the control of smaller owners and so on.

In this sort of approach the attempt is made to move away from more simplistic accounts resting on notions of the overpowering strength of a few capitalist corporations who can do more or less as they want. It suggests that more attention should be paid to the production (and consumption) of music in specific local contexts, as part of a consideration of the interaction of the global and the local. However, it is important to recognise the leading role of large corporations and to study their aims and the potential effects they can have in a detailed fashion.

Summary

This chapter has considered:

- the current patterns of ownership and control in the pop music industry, pointing to the concentration of the industry by conglomerates;

- the status of 'independent' record companies and the ideas of Fordism and post-Fordism;
- the nature of the markets for the products of the pop music industry;
- the importance of copyright, distinguishing different types of right, the value of the income they generate and the membership of the collecting societies in the United Kingdom;
- the possible replacement of copyright by trademark;
- some characterizations of processes of cultural exchange and transmission, including a discussion of the thesis of cultural imperialism and the possibility of a trend towards transculturation or globalization.

3

The Social Production
of Music

This chapter examines a number of different aspects of the production
of music. The components of such production are set out clearly in
box 4. Some of the aspects of the industry referred to in box 4 have
already been examined in chapter 2, especially lesson 4 on publishing. This chapter focuses on the more 'micro' aspects of the production of music. It begins with a discussion of the most important
sociological studies of musicians. Without musicians there would be
no music and consequently no music industry at all. However, it has
been argued that, owing to technological advance, the musician is
being replaced by machines. This chapter considers this argument,
especially in the final section on the issue of the effects of technological change.

The review of the sociological studies of musicians begins with a
consideration of those accounts which focus on groups of musicians, particularly the pioneering work of Becker. This introduces a
number of themes concerning the relationship between making music
and being artistic. These are considered in more detail through the
work of Frith and Horne (1987) before the section concludes with
a review of some of the most important studies of music-making in
particular local environments.

The next section looks at the most important aspects of what goes
on in record companies and the recording process itself. A particular
focus here is on the changing role of the producer and the nature
of social processes in the studio. The third main section in the
chapter picks up the issue of the role of technological change in
some detail. It first considers the more general relations between
technology and society before applying these themes to contemporary pop music.

Box 4   The music industry in ten easy lessons

1 The band   A group of hopefuls, longing for a hit record, for fame, fortune, and *Top of the Pops*.

2 The manager   The manager's role is to mother the band, to organize their day-to-day life, to negotiate work and contracts. A manager's primary function is to take care of business and finances. 'Super-managers' such as Simon Napier-Bell (Marc Bolan, Wham!), who help create their acts and often manage a whole stable of artists, still exist, as do management agencies; but more often they are simply friends who become involved. More and more women are entering this area.

3 The A & R department   Unless they want to produce their record completely independently, a band's first aim is to get a record contract. Every company has an A & R (Artists and Repertoire) department. A & R workers – most of whom are men – go out to gigs and listen to tapes that are sent in. If they like a band or artist, they will usually commission a demo-tape to be made fairly quickly in a small studio; if that turns out well, the act will be signed to the label. The A & R department is sometimes known as 'Um & Ah', due to its indecisiveness.

4 Publishing   Every time a song is played on the radio or TV, or is performed by someone else, royalties are due to the writers. Their collection is dependent on the song having been published, and most record companies now have their own publishing companies. A group writing their own material may choose to set up their own company or to sign to someone else. Publishing companies spend their time looking for potential hit song writers. Like A & R, they are responsible for signing new names, and they also collect royalties from cover versions and plays of work published by them.

5 The studio   The control-room is run by two, sometimes three, people. The *producer's* job is to direct the overall sound. Some, like Phil Spector, impose their ideas on artists who are there simply to make the basic noise he wants. Most, however, work with the artists, offering criticisms and suggestions until both sides are reasonably happy. The *engineer* makes the machinery do what the producer wants, getting the required effect out of the equipment. Increasingly, producers and engineers are working together as a permanent team, moving together from studio to studio to do different sessions, although all studios still have a resident engineer, and sometimes even a house producer. The *tape op*, or second engineer, is essentially a luxury employed by larger studios to help the engineer, set up equipment, make tea, etc. Producers, engineers and tape ops are nearly always men, as are the technicians and studio managers; studio bookings are invariably handled by women.

6 *Production, packing and sales*
From the studio, the tapes are taken and made into masters, the mould from which records are pressed in the factory. A sleeve is designed and printed, the records are put inside them, and they are then packed and sent out to the shops. Dealers can phone in with orders, but chainstores such as Our Price and W. H. Smiths will negotiate huge bulk-orders of records they think will be popular. Records are also sold by reps, who go round shops trying to persuade managers to buy their product. Though the travelling reps are usually men, most of the work involved in getting a record from cutting to shop is done by women. The larger the company, the more likely it is that all the work will have been carried out by their own staff: smaller companies will employ outside agencies or pay multinationals such as EMI to press, pack, distribute or market their records.

7 *Promotion*   When the record is released, the priority is to get it played on the radio. This is the job of the promotions department, whose 'pluggers' try to persuade radio-show producers and DJS to give their songs airplay (by taking them out to dinner, for instance). This department also ensures that record shops have advertising posters and display their records, and that the shops are provided with tour programmes and other promotional material. The artist and/ or their publishing company may also decide to employ independent pluggers to push certain records.

8 *Press*   Meanwhile, the press department is working hard to get our budding stars splashed all over the media. They liaise with the media, commission photo-sessions for publicity shots, try to get records and gigs reviewed, send out press releases to tell everyone what artists are doing, dream up gimmicks, 'leak' gossip, and approach editors with ideas for stories. Most of this work is done by women and within the record company, although some people prefer to hire their own publicists/agencies.

9 *Touring*   In general, the bigger the show, the bigger the entourage. Any tour will usually have roadies to move and set up equipment, lighting crews, sound crews, and an engineer to mix the sound live. This area, again, is almost exclusively male.

10 *DJs and journalists*   These play an essential part in getting a record across to potential customers!

Source: Steward and Garratt (1984:60–1). From *Signed, Sealed and Delivered,* Pluto Press

Musicians: culture, social origins and performance

Jazz musicians

One of the earliest and most important discussions of the culture of a group of musicians was written by the American sociologist Howard Becker (1963). Despite having worked as a jazz musician himself, Becker was primarily interested in jazz musicians as a 'deviant group' in connection with his revision of the sociology of deviance in accord with the thesis of labelling. Basing his account on the participant observation of jazz musicians in Chicago, Champaign-Urbana (Illinois) and Kansas City (Missouri) mainly in 1948–9, Becker focused on the following points:

> (1) the conceptions that musicians have of themselves and of the non-musicians for whom they work and the conflict they feel to be inherent in this relation; (2) the basic consensus underlying the reactions of both commercial and jazz musicians to this conflict; and (3) the feelings of isolation musicians have from the larger society and the way they segregate themselves from audience and community.
> (p. 83)

He argued that these musicians explicitly differentiated themselves from the rest of society, calling non-musicians 'squares'. The musician, as an artist, was expected to deviate from conventional ways of behaving. The 'square' was ignorant of the ways of musicians but was also feared as 'the ultimate source of commercial pressure' (p. 90). Thus, the musician wished to follow his/her artistic sensibility and expression but was in danger of being forced along the lines of commercialism by the dictates of the tastes of the 'square'. The musician reacted to the pressure generated by this situation in one of two main ways: either by remaining within the jazz community and attempting to stay true to his/her artistic beliefs or by compromising and going commercial. Both reactions were based on dislike of the 'square', which could lead, according to Becker, to the attempt on the part of the musicians to separate themselves physically from the audience.

Becker also discusses the nature of the career of these sorts of musicians, extending his analysis to suggest that: 'The antagonistic relationship between musicians and outsiders shapes the culture of the musician and likewise produces the major contingencies and crisis points in his career' (p. 102). He shows how the career of the jazz musician was based on an informal network of connections who helped the musician to secure employment. However, those who controlled the most important cliques had adopted the commercial orientation. This further exacerbated the pressure of commercialism and the market on the jazz musician, who sometimes responded by adopting 'the orientation of the craftsman' (p. 112), where the musician was not interested in the music actually being played but focused on performing in a proficient or correct manner. In summary with regard to the musician's career, Becker maintains that:

> the emphasis of musicians on freedom from the interference inevitable in their work creates a new dimension of professional prestige which conflicts with the previously discussed job prestige in such a way that one cannot rank high in both. The greatest rewards are in the hands of those who have sacrificed their artistic independence, and who demand a similar sacrifice from those they recruit for these higher positions. This creates a dilemma for the individual musician, and his response determines the future course of his career. Refusing to submit means that all hope of achieving jobs of high prestige and income must be abandoned, while giving in to commercial pressures opens the way to success for them. (pp. 113–14)

Becker argues that the family acts as a constraint or 'problem' for the male jazz musician, whose desire for freedom often clashes with the views of parents for the younger musician, and of wives for older players. The jazz musicians therefore expressed, and attempted to live out, a particular type of masculinity, based around notions of freedom of artistic expression and liberation from family ties. The centrality of this to male musicians is brought home by the analysis of women musicians by Bayton (1990) who shows that women musicians had to cope with the demands of children and family life in a way that male partners did not. Thus, babysitting arrangements would be the woman's responsibility and children and babies would often have to be brought to band practices, something which was never the case for male musicians.

Becker's work is important because it identifies some key aspects of the culture of this group of musicians, including the difference between art and commerce, and the dislike of the audience who do not understand 'art'. However, it may not be possible to generalize from this group, who were studied at a particular time and place. It is important therefore to broaden this analysis by coming more up to date and by examining other forms of music.

Christian (1987) and White (1987) also examined the nature of jazz through participant observation of jazz bands. White studied a professional band's engagement at a jazz club in Zurich and Christian researched various semi-professional bands in the English Midlands. White echoes many of Becker's points in his discussion noting, for example, how some jazz musicians suggested that he should learn to read music as: 'you can do the shows and the cabaret thing – there's a lot of bread in all that game' (White 1987:199). Furthermore, he argues that the lack of stability in the lives of the male jazz musicians interfered with the possibility of a stable family life (p. 212).

The musicians studied by Christian had avoided the pressure towards commercialization by not becoming, or attempting to become, full-time jazz musicians. They earned small amounts of money, which were normally sufficient only to cover their costs and expenses (and in some cases not even these). The groups were subject to the market but mainly in the form of ensuring that they have a place to play. Christian explains that there is:

> [a] precarious and fluctuating balance between, on the one hand, efforts to maintain musical integrity as expressed in the values and conventions held by most jazz musicians – that their music is not primarily a commercial commodity but a creative artistic activity – and, on the other hand, the need to operate within a market situation in order to find opportunities to play . . . compromises have to be made, sometimes in terms of what they play but more often in terms of the level of payment they can expect . . . most semi-pro jazzmen would rather not play at all than completely sell out to popular taste. (Christian 1987:238–9)

The two main themes revealed first by Becker have been reinforced through this brief review of contemporary jazz musician culture: first, the way in which musicians distinguish commerce from art; and, second, the desire for the musician to be perceived as an artist, rather than subservient to commercial goals. These themes also run through much contemporary rock and pop music, where they have been confronted in alternative ways by musicians in different social circumstances, as is shown in the next part of this section.

Art and pop

The most comprehensive tracing of the interconnections between art and pop music can be found in the work of Frith and Horne

(1987). Developing some aspects of the work of Becker, they are interested in 'how, in art schools, a particular tension between creativity and commerce is confronted and how pop music works as a solution' (Frith and Horne 1987:3). Frith and Horne identify the structure and changing nature of the place of art schools in the English education system, and show how attempts to make the art schools more vocational and responsive to the needs of industry have run up against the widely held conception of what it means to be an artist (p. 30). The 'romantic' notion of the artist as a 'bohemian' entails ideas about individual creativity, freedom of artistic expression, the conflict between true art and the market and so on.

From the late 1940s and early 1950s, when they connected to, and bred a mode of appreciation of, black american jazz, the art schools went on to attract and produce a significant number of the most important and influential rock musicians of subsequent decades. Frith and Horne identify three main waves of musicians: the rock bohemians, who 'simply picked up the bohemian *attitude* and carried it with them into progressive rock' (Frith and Horne, 1987:100), the pop art bands 'who applied art *theories* to pop music making' (p. 100) and the pop situationists, who were central to the development of punk rock in the late 1970s. Some of the musicians and colleges involved are detailed in figure 3.1. The art colleges provided spaces for these bands and musicians to rehearse and practice, and often their first audiences from other students at the college. The later musicians and bands, as well as some of their managers, wanted to put some contemporary ideas about the relation between art and society, and the political role of art through pop music into practice. The art education of Malcolm McLaren, the future manager of the Sex Pistols, which is set out in box 5, is illustrative of some of the main themes outlined by Frith and Horne.

The earlier rock bohemians espoused notions of artistic freedom and individualism, which developed into their own attempts to produce pieces of rock art, often 'complex' in form. It was possible at this moment to sell lots of records (as albums) and still not to be seen to be 'selling out' to the marketplace, thus 'solving' the dilemma of the jazz musicians identified by Becker, by integrating art and commerce. The later situationists were more aware of the intertwining of pop, commerce and art. They were not so concerned to remain authentic artists, and therefore to be above commerce, as to subvert both terms, suggesting that art and commerce were inextricably linked and that art could not be defined outside of commercial relationships, which were not necessarily to be criticized. The

College	Musician
Liverpool	John Lennon, Deaf School, Orchestral Manoeuvres in the Dark
Newcastle	Eric Burdon
Sidcup	Phil May, Dick Taylor, Keith Richards
Ealing	Ron Wood, Pete Townsend, Thunderclap Newman, Freddy Mercury
Kingston	Eric Clapton, Keith Relf, Sandy Denny, John Renbourne, Tom McGuiness
Camberwell	Syd Barrett
Wimbledon	Jeff Beck
Hornsey	Ray Davies, Roger Glover, Adam Ant, Viv Albertine, Mike Barson, G. Lewis, Rob Gotobed, Lester Square, Steve Walsh
Croydon	Mike Vernon
Sutton	Jimmy Page
Harrow	Charlie Watts, Marco Pirroni
Hammersmith	Cat Stevens
Newcastle University	Bryan Ferry
Ipswich/Winchester	Brian Eno
Royal College	John Foxx and Ultravox
St Martin's	Glen Matlock, Lora Logic
Central	Lene Lovitch, Les Chappell, Joe Strummer
Epsom	Richard Butler
Northampton	Kevin Haskins and Bauhaus
Coventry	Hazel O'Connor, Jerry Dammers, the Specials, Selecter, 2 Tone movement
Leeds	Marc Almond and Soft Cell, Green Gartside, the Mekons
Manchester	Linder, the Ludus
Edinburgh	Joe Callis, the Rezillos
Sheffield	Richard Kirk

Figure 3.1   Art schools and pop musicians in Britain
Source: adapted from Frith and Horne (1987)

Box 5   The art-school career of Malcolm McLaren

IN autumn 1963 [age 17] Malcolm started evening classes in life-drawing at St Martin's School of Art on Charing Cross Road but his mother objected to the nudes on display, so, still under the thumb of his family he transferred to 3-D design and graphics. To be accepted by the new system of art education, Malcolm needed two extra O levels, and enrolled in an Edward school for a booster course. He passed, but was in the wrong educational area for St Martin's: instead, he was accepted by Harrow Art School to begin a Dip.AD in autumn 1964 . . . which, in his account of McLaren's early life, Fred Vermorel describes as 'the centre for miles around for Bohemian frenzy, mixing the local gay community with beatniks, drug pedlars, sexual delinquents and Mods' . . . By degrees Malcolm began to see himself as an avant-gardist, searching for a key with which to unlock his deep anger and resentment. Between 1965 and 1968, he passed through a number of art schools and polytechnics

(Reigate, Walthamstow, Chelsea, Chiswick) under a series of names falsified for the purpose of getting grants. Throughout this period he took up and discarded ideas from ideas then in currency . . . Common to these was the idea of art being indivisible from everyday life, indivisible particularly from commerce and the environment . . . Malcolm had entered Croydon [Art School] in the autumn of 1967: the course provided him with more freedom than hitherto and, as importantly, a community of peers . . . all were involved in a sit-in that developed in Croydon a week after the famous Hornsey Art School action. On 5 June [1968], the art students barricaded themselves in the annexe at South Norwood and issued a series of impossible demands . . . After the Croydon sit-in, Malcolm Edwards entered Goldsmiths' in autumn 1968 to study film and photography . . .

Source: Savage (1991:18, 23–4, 26, 28–9, 37). *England's Dreaming*, Faber and Faber

art industry could be exploited from within, there was no need to attempt to create a 'pure' space outside of it.

In his book *Lipstick Traces*, Greil Marcus (1993) points to the interconnections between the Dadaist art movement of the Cabaret Voltaire in Zurich in 1916, the Lettrists in France in the 1940s and 1950s, the Situationists in Paris in the 1950s and 1960s and punk rock in Britain in the 1970s. Such interconnections between art and pop music are also traced by Savage (1991) and for American punk by Heylin (1993). They came to the fore in the 1970s and have remained there ever since, reconstituting some of the dilemmas about

Stage

1	acquiring an instrument
2	finding someone to play with and a place to play
3	increasing skills and forming groups
4	getting songs
5	working-up or 'getting down'
6	structuring the set
7	finding a gig
8	getting to the gig
9	playing the room

Figure 3.2   Stages in the local rock career
Source: adapted from Bennett (1980)

being an artist and earning a living expressed by earlier generations of musicians.

The studies considered in this section so far have focused on more professional musicians in the main. However, music is also made, in the local context, by those who do not, in the immediate future anyway, expect to make a living from it. It is important therefore to consider the social processes at work in this realm. Furthermore, it is important to remember that the musicians discussed by Becker and Frith and Horne, will have started their careers by playing in local groups.

Local music-making

One of the most comprehensive and important studies of the nature of local music-making can be found in *On Becoming a Rock Musician* by H. Stith Bennett (1980). Bennett's study is based mainly on fieldwork done between 1970 and 1972 in the state of Colorado in the United States. He divides his analysis into four main parts: 'group dynamics', 'rock ecology' 'mastering the technological component' and 'performance: aesthetics and the technological imperative'. Following the approach developed by Becker, Bennett traces the process through which a person becomes a local rock musician and plays to an audience. He identifies a number of stages in such a career, which are summarized in figure 3.2.

The budding rock musician has first to acquire an instrument. Most often the first source of an instrument is the musician's parents.

However, theft has also been used as a way of developing an individual's or a band's resources. There are well-documented cases of this in rock journalism. For example, Savage (1991) describes how Steve Jones of the Sex Pistols stole equipment in the early days of the band, and Rogan (1993) alludes to the illegal activities of Johnny Marr of the Smiths in the pursuit of a new guitar and amplifier. According to Bennett, the problems involved in the acquisition of instruments and equipment represent economic barriers to becoming a rock musician.

After the instrument has been acquired, the beginner often attempts to learn to play on his or her own. This might involve attempting to play along with some favourite records. However, most beginners realize that they can learn only so much in this way and begin to seek other musicians to play with. This can happen in different ways but often involves contacts with friends or friends of friends, who might form the nucleus of the beginner's first group. Groups form and re-form very quickly and can often be very loose in membership. Further, groups can often re-form out of pools of musicians who have been in a variety of groups. Bennett suggests that this is also often based on networks of friends and acquaintances. However, bulletin boards in colleges, for example, were also significant. In other contexts, advertisements in music papers have brought band members together. After people have come together to form a budding group, it is important for them to find somewhere to practice. Given the space needed and the noise produced by using electric instrumentation, this can often be quite difficult. Garages and basements were the sorts of places often used by the bands studied by Bennett. These factors constitute a social barrier for the budding rock musician.

As has already been noted, Bennett points to a rapid turnover in the membership of groups. He suggests that the relationship between the skill of the individual relative to the rest of the group is very important in this process, which is summarized in figure 3.3. Bennett gives a graphic example of a 'musical status degradation ceremony':

We had picked Mike up in Denver where he was sorta hanging out after his group in Texas broke up. For a while there everything was cool and we were playing steady, but we were progressing too . . . you know what I mean? . . . playing new songs and doing originals and getting our sets really together. Then you'd start hearing these mistakes in the bass, it was really ragged . . . just sorta falling apart. The

Individual skills	Group skills decrease	same	increase
decrease	3	4	5
same	9	2	6
increase	8	7	1

Situations 1, 2, and 3 are stable group configurations:
1 = a 'good' group: the beginning of steady gigs
2 = a transitional stage: the end of steady gigs
3 = a disintegrative stage: 'natural death'

Situations 4, 5, and 6 are unstable group configurations which result in 'firing and hiring' – the individual is displaced by the group: an individual status degradation ceremony, or a group status enhancement ceremony.

Situations 7, 8, and 9 are unstable group configurations which result in 'quitting and looking' – the group is displaced by the individual: an individual status enhancement ceremony, or a group status degradation ceremony.

Figure 3.3 The levelling process of attributed musical skills in rock groups
Source: reprinted from *On becoming a Rock Musician*, by H. Stith Bennett (Amherst: University of Massachusetts Press, 1980:31), copyright © 1980 by The University of Massachusetts Press

thing is Mike was getting hung up on speed. First he was just popping and finally he was shooting up every morning. And he just looked like shit warmed over. Finally we just had to get rid of him, he was bringing the whole group down. (Piano player, quoted by Bennett 1980:33)

In the main, the sorts of groups studied by Bennett were 'copy' groups who relied on non-original material. This meant that group practice and rehearsals mainly involved the 'getting' of songs from a record. The groups did not use sheet music or musical notation in this process but developed their material by a process of trial and error from the recorded form. There are important issues here concerning the way in which a recorded form, which might involve extensive multi-tracking and over-dubbing, is transformed into

something that can be played live by a small group of four or
five musicians. Bennett argues that the local musician listens to the
recordings with a 'recording consciousness' (1980:126), which enables the musician to hear the different components of the recordings and the technical aspects of its construction, and to translate
them into practical ways of playing in the local group.

Furthermore, Bennett suggests that:

> after a song is *gotten* it must be transformed into a performable entity.
> After a song may be known in its individual parts it cannot be said
> that the *group* knows the song until the process of *working-up* (which
> is not so ironically also known as *getting-down*) has been concluded.
> (1980:145)

This involves repetitive practice. The next stage in the process is the
organization of the worked-up songs into a set or sets, which often
entails thinking through the pacing of the performance and trying to
produce an overall effect out of the discrete elements which have
been learned as separate songs.

The groups have to find gigs and get to the gig. As this normally
involves transporting themselves and the equipment, access to a van
is very important and a musician with a van might be accommo-
dated within a group in preference to a more accomplished player
without one. Bennett divides gigs into four main categories: social
(including sponsored ones with free admission, breakeven and fundraising types) which 'refers to situations which are concerned with
pure sociation events, gatherings, which are primarily ends in themselves' (Bennett 1980:85); ceremonial (for example, weddings); bar;
and concert. Concert gigs are relatively rare and are normally played
by the local group as a support for the more well-known group. The
bar gig is very important to the local group (which, given the male
nature of most bars, will affect the potential for participation of
women). As Bennett says in general about the bar:

> The economic mainstay of local groups is the local bar. A bar gig is
> a more complex economic event for the group than either the social
> or ceremonial one-nighter – it could mean 'Friday and Saturday nights'
> or 'six nights a week' depending upon the clientele the bar services,
> but it always means a performance reality which is purchased as
> entertainment in the same way as mixed drinks and bar chatter. Bar
> owners and managers consider the group an economic investment
> which draws customers to the site; from their viewpoint they are
> paying the group for the number of bodies it pulls through the door.
> (p. 91)

The group has to adapt and set up its equipment to play the room, which can affect the nature of the performance and the musical event in different ways. The physical make-up and acoustics of rooms can have effects. There are also important differences between playing inside and outside.

Bennett's book is important in illustrating many different aspects of the local musician's life and career and, like Becker, for illuminating some of the dilemmas in the local musician's life: finding someone to play with, deciding what to play, agreeing on the time to practice and so on. However, it is subject to some limitations: first, it is now rather dated; second, it discusses rock music of a particular type and period; third, it is located in one place in the main; and fourth, the musicians considered are mainly men and Bennett plays little attention to the issue of gender. It is important, therefore, to examine some other, more recent, accounts of local music-making to extend the scope of the approach pioneered by Bennett.

A more recent study of the making of rock music in a local context can be found in *Rock Culture in Liverpool* by Sara Cohen (1991). Cohen spent a year between October 1985 and October 1986 carrying out unstructured interviews and participant observation on 'bands without record contracts that therefore functioned on the margins of the industry' (p. 5). The sorts of bands she studied tended to have been together between two and three years, and to consist of four or five white men aged between 20 and 30. The pattern of instrumentation in the groups tended to be similar, being guitar and drum based. Cohen focuses on two of these bands in particular: the Jactars and Crikey it's the Cromptons!

Cohen makes a number of important points about the bands and different aspects of local music-making, some of which echo, in a rather different context, the themes developed by Becker and Bennett. First, she shows how the groups are based in particular social settings and how important their participation in one studio was, as they tended to interact with other bands based at Vulcan Studios in Liverpool. Second, she examines the issues around the gaining of instruments for the band, particularly the difficulties of securing the necessary finance.

Third, she discusses the way in which the bands developed their own songs. The bands studied by Cohen were primarily interested in writing their own material. They would play the occasional cover version, but an important aspect of their self-perception as musicians was their originality. This contrasts with the copy groups examined by Bennett. Cohen points to 'four main themes implicit in the music-making of the Jactars': an 'emphasis upon natural talent', a 'simple and clean sound', 'originality', and 'musical incompetence as style' which were shared by Crikey it's the Cromptons! (p. 169). There were differences between the bands in the ways in which they developed their material but they had similar notions of creativity and originality. In part, this stemmed from a post-punk ethos of creativity, to be developed outside of what the bands themselves saw as the established sounds of a mass culture.

Fourth, despite this anti-commercialism, the bands were interested in getting record deals. Cohen describes in some detail the reactions of record companies to the material sent to them by the bands, and the bands' attempts to get record companies to listen to their music. Thus, the bands were seeking success even if this was defined in terms which did not include doing anything to sell records. Likewise, over 50 per cent of the wider sample of local bands studied by Cohen had some kind of management (p. 59). However, despite this, legal and financial affairs remained difficult and were often implicated in the breakup of bands.

In addition to the factors noted so far (and there are other aspects which make Cohen's book useful in the developing literature on local music-making) it is the fifth factor which is the most important: the bands' masculinity and attitudes towards women. Cohen notes how the relations between different bands tended to be like gang rivalry (p. 35). Furthermore, the band was a social unit, being in a band was a 'way of life' (p. 38) for the male members, and the only woman member of one of the bands was systematically marginalized. These practices and attitudes were reinforced by the performances of the bands. Women were seen in terms of visual image (p. 81) not as musicians, and were hence involved as 'mostly backing singers and non-instrumentalists' (p. 206). In Cohen's account, at gigs 'the community and solidarity the bands strove for was predominantly masculine. While women generally liked to dance, their male counterparts were reluctant to do so' (p. 101). Women were seen as a problem for the bands and were 'actively excluded'. This reinforces the theme identified by Becker where wives and families were seen to be a problem for the jazz musician, and the gendered nature of music-making identified by Bayton (1990, 1992, 1993).

The most comprehensive study of local music-making to date was undertaken by the anthropologist Ruth Finnegan (1989) between 1980 and 1984 in Milton Keynes. In her book, *The Hidden Musicians*,

Finnegan describes seven musical worlds which she found in this English new town: classical, brass band, folk, musical theatre, jazz, country and western, and rock and pop. She draws a series of contrasts between the worlds (which can often overlap, as members can belong to more than one) in terms of how the playing of music is learned, how it is performed and how it is written. She identifies a number of different social institutions which support music and the patterns of organization of the musical worlds and, in general, points to the importance of music to everyday life in Milton Keynes in providing pathways for urban living. In this respect, Finnegan's detailed empirical study suggests that music is a core activity in the structuring of contemporary social life: an argument which has been made in far more theoretical terms by writers like John Shepherd (for example, 1991).

Finnegan shows the large number and variety of bands that were active in the pop and rock world at this time. She divides them into three main categories. First, there were 'the young, relatively inexperienced and recently formed bands' (Finnegan 1989:110), often formed by people still at school. Second, there were the groups 'who had left school and were beginning to perform in local clubs or youth clubs for a small fee' (p. 111). Third, there were those bands who:

> had established a secure position in pub and club circuits, outside as well as within Milton Keynes, played in upwards of 50 or 100 performances a year, and, while still towards the amateur rather than the professional end of the scale, brought in substantial fees. (p. 114)

Despite the existence of these different types of band, some overall patterns were identified. First, the groups were predominantly made up of men; second, the groups aimed at giving live performances; and third, the groups wanted to be paid, though remuneration varied greatly.

Finnegan uses her detailed research to confront some of the main themes arising from the literature on pop music. First, she argues that pop music cannot be simply seen as the music of youth, as the category of youth is cross-cut by many other social divisions and youth is actually a fairly wide category, encompassing people of a variety of ages. Thus:

> Youth predominated, for even mixed audiences also included young people, but family audiences were nothing unusual and it would be

misleading to conclude – despite the widespread image – that rock bands played exclusively to either teenagers or young people under 25. (pp. 123–4)

Second, she examines the view that pop music is produced by those who are uneducated or unemployed and again finds that this assumption is unwarranted. She suggests that the picture on education was mixed and that 'of band members who gave details nearly two-thirds were in jobs' (p. 124). This figure in particular might not hold for other times and places, as at this point Milton Keynes could be said to be relatively prosperous.

Third, Finnegan examines the idea that pop music expresses a form of rebellion. This is a theme which is treated at greater length in chapter 4, though Finnegan suggests that evidence from her study makes it difficult to generalize about this and the idea of protest was not 'generally borne out by this study' (p. 127).

Finnegan argues that there were a number of common themes running through the rock and pop music world. First, the musicians in this world tended to possess less knowledge about other players in it, compared with members of other musical worlds. However, certain individuals would be well known. Second, there were shared ideas about playing and learning. Echoing the account of Bennett (1980), the pop musicians were self-taught and joined bands in the early stages of learning an instrument. Moreover, there was a common pattern to the instrumentation in the bands, where 'the standard combination was guitars (rhythm and lead), bass guitar, and drums, together with vocals' (Finnegan 1989:129).

The most important common feature of the pop musicians' world, according to Finnegan (p. 129), was 'their interest in expressing their own views and personality through music-making'. Finnegan claims that this is a 'stress on individuality and artistic creation which accords ill with the mass theorists' delineation of popular music' (p. 129). However, for the mass theorists like Adorno, this may be a 'false' individuality and creativity, and they would not necessarily accept the participants' own view of their creativity.

According to Finnegan, such creativity was often expressed in the musicians' desire to compose their own music, where: 'playing in a band provided a medium where players could express their own personal aesthetic vision and through their music achieve a sense of controlling their own values, destiny and self-identity' (p. 130). This brings the discussion back to the themes raised by Becker in his account of jazz musicians, as the notion of self expression repeats

---

directors

president or managing director

artist and repertoire   marketing   public relations
publicity and press   radio and television promotion   sales
business affairs/finance and legal   manufacture and distribution
administration and secretarial

Figure 3.4 The division of labour in a record company
Source: derived from Negus (1992:38)

the idea of the artist, above commerce, at the core of the jazz musicians' beliefs. However, it should be remembered that these ideas of artistic achievement and autonomy may be more wished for than actually achieved. Moreover, it may be easier for the local musician to remain relatively separated from the music industry as he or she may not have to deal with it to any great extent. Such avoidance becomes more difficult as the artist seeks to earn a living from his or her activities, exacerbating musicians' concerns about remaining authentic as artists, rather than 'selling out'. This theme will be returned to in this book, but, before it can be considered, attention needs to be given to some of the processes at work in the institutions which these musicians confront, and which some of them will become part of, and in many ways as the discussion continues it should become clearer that the opposition between creativity and industry is oversimplified.

The pop process

Negus (1992:38) suggests that all record companies share a division of labour of the type shown in figure 3.4. This section examines these different places in the division of labour, how they interconnect, and the different contributions they make to the overall musical product.

The Artist and Repertoire (A & R) division or staff have primary responsibility for the signing and development of artists at the record company. However, in accord with the general points made by Abercrombie (1991) which were outlined in chapter 2, Negus

(1992:50) suggests that other divisions and groups of staff, especially marketing divisions, have increased their influence over these dimensions in recent years. Despite this, A & R remains very important and, according to Negus, has continued to work along principles set during the 1960s, when the 'rock tradition' developed. He (1992:53) suggests that six criteria are used in the assessment of potential artists:

'1   the live, stage performance;
2   the originality and quality of the songs or material;
3   the recorded performance and voice;
4   their appearance and image;
5   their level of personal commitment, enthusiasm and motivation;
6   the achievements of the act so far.'

The reference points for the predominantly male A & R staff, who may previously have worked as 'music writers, disc jockeys, musicians' promoters and sales' (Negus 1992:56), or have come into the industry from the 'college rock tradition' (p. 57), are the stars of the Anglo-American rock tradition. There is a certain antipathy to the video and more image-based pop bands which fall outside this tradition. This may be because an album band may have a longer life and can be expected to reap more consistent rewards for the company over a longer period of time. Moreover, in accord with this 'rock' tradition, importance is placed on the quality of live performance. This relates to the idea that rock is a public or 'street' form. Within rock and pop music, as in other areas of social life, the street has been seen as an area of male dominance and camaraderie. This is illustrated by a comment from a rare female worker in A & R quoted by Negus (p. 59):

I'll tell you why I think there are not many women in it. Because, number one, it's a very chauvinistic industry, it really is. Number two, the A & R lifestyle does not suit the majority of women at all. The fact of going out every night to clubs, being up all night in sleazy, dodgy clubs or whatever.

Once it has been decided that an act should be signed, they have to be developed and marketed from within the company. The interaction here between the A & R and marketing departments is central (Negus 1992:63). The image of the group or artist is developed, with attention being paid to current trends. There may be an attempt to 'brand' the artist, in line with the general developments outlined in chapter 2. Thus, one executive interviewed by Negus:

> spoke of attempting to 'brand' artists. By this he meant that the unique quality of an act would become instantly recognizable and condensed into a specific image which could become a trademark. This director referred to the presentation of U2, who were not signed to the company he worked for, but whose marketing he spoke of with great admiration. (p. 71)

It is important to understand that this process of 'branding' does not simply occur with the more recognizably 'pop' acts, such as Kylie Minogue or Take That, but is applicable to rock acts like U2 or Bruce Springsteen, who are often thought to possess more 'authenticity'. These distinctions between pop and rock and their accrued meanings are be discussed more fully in chapter 4, and the ways in which artists are branded as stars in chapter 6. The A & R and marketing departments both have their roles in the development of the product to be sold in the rock/pop marketplace.

Negus (1992) examines the different aspects of these departments of the record company. For the most part, he emphasizes the collaborative nature of the interaction between these different activities (p. 134); however, he also points to significant conflict in this domain. He maintains that A & R staff have become increasingly resentful of the intrusion of the promotional staff at earlier stages in the recruitment processes. The importance of marketing and promotion means that these activities are important in the shaping of a sound and image. Hence, in Negus's view:

> Many companies, responding to an increasing emphasis on marketing in the wider global economy, have attempted to make the informal dialogue between marketing and artist and repertoire more explicit by providing marketing with a formal veto on the artists who are signed. (p. 148)

The development of pop videos as promotional devices and their importance during the 1980s attest to the increasing importance of marketing and promotion and to their role within the creative process. Increasingly, promotional and marketing strategies are formulated at an earlier stage of the creation of a musical product, where a number of processes and tasks such as producing, engineering and mixing have been examined.

The producer tends to have overall control of the recording process, and he/she may be seen as filling the same sort of role as a director in film production. The A & R department will often try to match the artist with a producer who may have been successful with particular types of act and music previously. In the past, the producer may have been contracted to a particular company and worked with a large number of that company's acts. However, by the early 1960s producers were becoming akin to artists in their own right and some were known for their own sounds. A well-known case of this is Phil Spector, whose 'wall of sound' is still instantly recognizable and seen as Spector's invention, based on his orchestration of musicians and skills in the recording studio. A similar, but less well-known, example from the early 1960s in Britain can be found in the work of Joe Meek, whose sound, which can be found on records like *Telstar* and *Robot* by the Tornadoes, still has devotees. Today some producers are as well known as artists.

A similar movement towards greater importance can be traced for some record engineers. The distinction between the producer and engineer is put neatly by Negus (1992:84) when he explains that: 'while the producer works as director of proceedings, the engineer is involved in technically finding the combination of settings to create the sounds required'. Some engineers have become quite well known, though they would normally be ranked below the record producer in importance. However, it should be recognized that the process by which some more established acts have become involved in the production of their own music, facilitates the development of the role of the engineer, who would assist the group in putting into practice their own ideas: a role filled by some producers in the past. Furthermore, this points to some fluidity in the tasks performed by different components of the recording process over time.

The process of development of the occupation of 'recording engineer' or 'sound mixer' has been traced by Kealy (1990). He suggests that there are three modes of collaboration in pop music production: 'craft-union', 'entrepreneurial' and 'art'. He characterizes these modes in terms of a number of different dimensions as shown in figure 3.5. The content of these dimensions in the different modes is shown in figure 3.6. Kealy traces the development from the craft to the art modes of production. In the craft mode, which was dominant in the immediate post-war period, the recording engineer was expected mainly to use the acoustic properties of the studio to attempt to reproduce as far as possible a 'realistic' reproduction of a concert hall sound. The occupation was organized

- technology of recording
- recording aesthetic
- social organization of studio collaboration
- job responsibilities of the mixer
- occupational ideology of sound mixing

Figure 3.5 Dimensions of the modes of pop music production
Source: derived from Kealy (1990)

	Technology of recording	Recording aesthetic	Social organization	Job responsibilities	Occupational ideology
Craft	acoustic properties	realism	professional/ unionized	formal/ impersonal	'in the grooves'
Enterpreneurial	tape	hit sound	fluid	open	selling
Art	multi-track	art	collaboration	rapport	expression

Figure 3.6 Craft, entrepreneurial and art modes of collaboration in popular music production
Source: constructed from Kealy (1990)

around trades unions and relationships in the studio were formal and demarcated, with little overlap between tasks. Kealy suggests that:

> The basic standard used to judge a sound mixer's work was whether the sound was 'in the grooves'. The good mixer-craftsman would make sure that unwanted sounds were not recorded or were at least minimized, that the desired sounds were recorded without distortion, and that the sounds were in balance. The recording technology itself, and thus the sound mixer's work, was to be unobtrusive so as not to destroy the listener's illusion that he was sitting in Philharmonic Hall rather than in his living room. The *art of recording* was not to compete for the public's aesthetic attention to *the art that was being recorded.*
> (p. 211)

The entrepreneurial mode of sound recording developed during the 1950s. The introduction of tape for recording facilitated the introduction of a new aesthetic and social relations. Smaller studios developed which wanted to create sounds that would be hit records;

they were not concerned with the reproduction of concert performance. The social organization of the studio loosened and the responsibilities of the mixer/engineer opened up, with the previous modes
of craft unionism and professionalism breaking down. The studios
became concerned to sell their sounds, often on the labels that were
based in the small studio itself, such as Sun, based in Memphis,
who first recorded Elvis Presley in the mid-1950s, and Stax, also
located in Memphis, which recorded a large number of soul singers
and groups in the 1960s. There was a new entrepreneurial spirit
often based around the owner of the label, who was often directly
involved in record production. Examples include Sam Phillips at
Sun and Ahmet Ertegun at Atlantic.

The art mode of sound recording developed in the 1960s. Technology had further developed, with the introduction of multi-track
recording. The concern of many pop artists, and associated mixers
and engineers, was now to produce an artistic statement, which
might be an experiment in sound. The engineer or mixer moved
into a more collaborative relationship with the artist working in the
studio, and there was a desire to establish a rapport between the
engineer and the artist which would enable them to express themselves in the resulting music.

While these modes of organization can be seen as developing in
a chronological fashion, it is important that they also be treated as
ideal types. It can further be suggested that one does not necessarily
replace the other. For example, it may that bigger studios still operate
in accord with the craft mode, while smaller studios are predominantly in the entrepreneurial mode.

A related, but different, view to that of Kealy is expressed by
Struthers, who distinguishes between 'three rival aesthetics of recorded music' (1987:255): 'realism', 'perfectionism' and 'performance'. He suggests that realism was the earliest aesthetic, based in
the idea that: 'recordings should strive towards a faithful reproduction of the original performance' (p. 242). Such realism became
increasingly untenable as: 'using multi-track magnetic tape recording, the final recording is assembled and 'reconstructed' from a
number of fragments, and so there is no 'original' of which that
published recording can be a reproduction' (p. 244). This leads to
the perfectionism of which Struthers writes. The final aesthetic,
performance, places emphasis on the performance of the musician,
and his or her expressive qualities, which are captured in the
recording.

The ways in which these different roles might be changing in relation to the introduction of new technology is considered in the next section. However, before this, I want briefly to consider some other dimensions to the pop production process. The places in the division of labour in a record company were summarized in figure 3.4 above. I have already examined the role of A & R and mentioned the importance of the marketing department and its close relationship and potential conflict with A & R. Negus (1992) points to the importance of a number of the other dimensions of the process, examining the intimate relationship between publicity and the music press, despite the critical reactions of artists like Pat Kane of Hue and Cry as illustrated by box 6.

Like many other areas of society, pop and rock music can be seen as an aspect of a 'promotional culture' (Wernick 1991), where principles first formulated in the advertising of goods such as soap powder are increasingly applied to spheres like politics and university life. Pop and rock are heavily promoted forms and it can be argued that many of their meanings derive from their image in a marketplace. Music is promoted and analysed in the press, the music press and in music magazines. Further, music is promoted through the music video or 'promo'. There is a developing literature on video, which will be considered at length in chapter 6. Another important mode of advertising of musical wares is radio. A general examination of music and radio is beyond the scope of this book, being a topic in its own right. Such a general account can be found in the work of Barnard (1989). An extended consideration of the role of pirate radio in the 1960s is given by Chapman (1992) and an introductory account of radio in general can be found in Crisell (1986). More recent examinations of radio have pointed to the fragmentation of contemporary radio into a number of different specialist stations (Barnes 1990). It seems likely that radio will remain important in generating record sales even if the stations become increasingly specialized.

Record companies employ secretarial and administrative staff, often in familiar gendered roles involving the support of male staff. The products of the musical process also need to be made and distributed, and many of the more routine jobs in manufacture are performed by women, as illuminatingly discussed in the passage reproduced in box 7.

Having examined the nature of the production process and the division of labour in the music industry, I now wish to consider the relationship between music and technology. Particularly to see how this can be seen as re-patterning some of the relationships so far described.

Box 6   Rock criticism in the music press

'The bulk of pop writing at any time is embroidered press office material; the majority of pop writers end up subbing advertorial for after-shave.' Rock musician **Pat Kane** takes rock critics to task.

ROCK criticism? An oxymoron. The only truly critical acts in popular music are musical ones: I don't like the noises I hear around me, so I'm going to make or choose better/different ones. If rock 'n' roll is 'democracy in action – anyone can do it' (Lester Bangs), then why read others' opinions when you can make your own sounds, or choose your own soundscape? Your ears never tell you lies: rock critics *always* do.

And rock critics? For the most part, poxy morons. The bulk of pop writing at any time is embroidered press-office material; the majority of pop writers eventually settle for their own dusty little corner of a Condé Nast office, subbing advertorial for aftershave. The most interesting writers are the ones who endure, year after year, on magazines like NME or Melody Maker: forever foaming wildly at the next bunch of sallow-cheeked musical youth to come round the bend. They are particularly despicable. But at least they have their reasons.

Consider the basic lot of the long-term professional pop scrivener. It (I use the preposition wisely) is usually highly educated, yet utterly impoverished – a dangerous, distorting mixture. Despite years of training in the humanities, it finds itself reduced to a form of aesthete's beggary. The need to blag trips to Antwerp with Anthrax, or stuff down the crepes at some corporate mega-babe launch, reduces that precious critical distance to almost nil.

The reviews that result from this feudal employment are either slavishly reverential – which at least ensures that PR departments will keep the home-phone ringing. Or they're venomous and excessive – fuelled by self-loathing at continual compromise, and a kind of reckless bedsit nihilism.

I'll concede that these pressure-cooker conditions (young men and women writhing in the steam of their own insecurities and inadequacies) can make for some precocious writing. But it's a long trawl: and I usually just skim the pages looking for abusive references to a certain West-of-Scotland pop-soul duo by the name of . . .

Alright, I have an axe to grind: well, perhaps a machete to swing indiscriminately. My loathing of all rock critics – other than the self-evident pantheon (Marcus, Savage, Marsh, Bangs) – partly comes from having been at the end of some of their pathological attacks over the last eight years of my own career.

The golden rule that we broke at the start of our career and suffered for ever since was this: never give a more intelligent justification of your own music than the critic is able to. By doing so, you remove their whole raison d'être. Play the noble savage, hide your erudition under a comely fuzziness of mind, and the five-star ratings will be yours for as long as you want them. But push your own critical intellect too far and you will see the whites of their eyes.

A cursory flick through my cuttings renders up many such jewels of pundits-in-pique. 'May the bargain-bin save us from Sociological Pop Stars . . . Smart-Alec paranoid Scots, with gap sites where their shoulders should be . . . Tortuous lyrics, overripe melodies and everything framed in quotation marks. Don't they ever get tired of themselves?'

All this merely adjectival abuse – right down to the level of 'I've seen more soul in a billiard ball' and (I kid you not) 'Fuck off and die' – runs like water off a rocker's Gaultier. One can feel a certain empathy with the scattier rock critics; at least their writing displays a passionate, bilious commitment. Much more worrying is the advent of the Quality Music Establishment – represented pre-eminently by Q magazine but backed up by beanfeasts like the Mercury Music Awards (the 'Booker' of the pop world).

If the inky critic acts like a drunken gatekeeper between audience and artist – whose erratic behaviour at least allows the rocker all the random luck of schizophrenic reviewing – then the Quality Police are fully armed border guards. Only artists with corporate passports can get past them into the glare of public approval these days.

In an age of supposed relativism of taste and judgment, the presumption of Quality Rock-Crit is breathtaking: Q magazine proclaims its albums guide to be 'the best in the world,' Professor Simon Frith, chair of the Mercury judging panel, has predicted that one day 'the endorsements of rock critics will have as much influence as the blurbs on book covers.'

What's behind this elevation of critical reasoning, of talk-about-pop music, is a major marketing crisis for the music business. Teenage singles buyers no longer lead musical taste, no longer create lasting stars: their rap and rave purchases have almost no connection to mainstream tastes in the album charts – the area that makes the corporations money. Over-25s mostly stick with established artists in their CD buying. So how do you get a 30-year-old married couple to risk their recession surplus on new releases?

Through elitist pop discourse, of course: the deliberate manipulation of status and credibility. If you're buying any new albums, intones the deep ideology of Q and the Mercury Awards, buy the ones that the experts say really matter. Rock academics and broadsheet scribblers, solicitors after the financial health of globe-straddling multinationals: same as it ever was. Only worse.

And the saddest thing about this current critical situation? That musicians and record companies are now looking for, or looking to be, 'Q-type' or 'Mercury's' artists: pointlessly chasing after criteria of excellence which these new, pumped-up commissars of rock can't even be consistent about themselves.

When pen-pushers start interfering with sound-makers – when the power of their response even shapes for a single second what musicians do musically – then the whole situation is completely upside down. They know the way, said Kenneth Tynan, but they can't drive the car, Music critics, get back under the Rock. And stay there.

Source: *The Guardian*, 6 September 1993

Box 7 The other side of women in rock

THIS is the invisible, decidedly unglamorous side of the industry, the places where many of the 'women in rock' work. Most of the major labels – and, indirectly, the independents – probably employ as many women as men, perhaps even more: 'tea ladies', secretaries, receptionists, canteen staff, cleaners, and almost anyone servicing the needs of people within the industry will be female. Women also do all of the menial work that cannot yet be done more cheaply by machines: they assemble the basic parts of instruments, solder the wires and chips of electrical equipment and, in the pressing and packing plants, it is women who check the quality of discs, put them in their sleeves and pack shop orders into boxes ready for distribution. They are anonymous factory-workers at the bottom of the company hierarchy, and almost every record is handled by them at some point. Which gives them, if they choose to use it, an enormous amount of power ... EMI's plant at Middlesex is, in fact, reputed to be one of the better factories: it is unionized, working conditions are fair, and the company was happy to let me visit. The manager ... is a large, middle-aged, genial man who calls his staff 'girls' (some of them are grandmothers), and thinks his secretary is wonderful. He forgot to mention her name: he calls her 'Darling'. He meant well.

Source: Steward and Garratt (1984:63–4). From *Signed, Sealed and Delivered*, Pluto Press

Pop music and technology

In considering the way in which technology interacts with pop music, there are two important matters which require immediate attention: first, the definition of technology; and second, the general nature of the interaction which is being suggested. I shall examine these issues before reviewing some of the particular roles of technology in the production of popular music.

MacKenzie and Wajcman (1985) suggest that there are three definitions of technology. First, technology may be defined as 'sets of physical objects', irons, buses, cars, CD players, tape recorders and so on. Second, technology may refer to human activities as well as simple physical objects. These physical objects only become technology when they are used in human activity: 'a computer without programs and programmers is simply a useless collection of bits of metal, plastic and silicon' (p. 3). Third, there is the definition of technology as not only objects and activity but as knowledge as well.

In this approach, technology is not really technology without 'know-how'. When a lecturer uses an overhead projector, he or she has to know how to switch it on, how to place the overhead slide on the right way up and how to focus the machine on the screen, otherwise the overhead projector is simply an ugly box. These are relatively simple forms of knowledge and activity (though it is interesting to see how difficult many lecturers find them!), and many forms of technology require more detailed and expert knowledge, and more complicated operations for them to function properly.

It is often assumed that technology is very important in affecting the nature and development of society. In its strongest versions this thesis is called 'technological determinism'. In an important discussion and critique of this thesis, the cultural theorist and critic Raymond Williams suggests that:

> The basic assumption of technological determinism is that a new technology – a printing press or a communications satellite – 'emerges' from technical study and experiment. It then changes the society or the sector in which it has 'emerged'. 'We' adapt to it because it is the new modern way. (1983:129)

MacKenzie and Wajcman (1985:4) suggest in a similar vein that technological determinism: 'is the theory that technology is indeed an independent factor, and that changes in technology cause social changes. In its strongest version, the theory claims that change in technology is the most important cause of change in society.' These writers argue that the thesis of technological determinism rests on two important premises: first, a prior separation of technology from society, where technology is at some point seen to be outside society; and second, that 'technical change causes social change' in a direct and unmediated sort of way.

There are two major problems with simple technological determinism. First, 'the characteristics of a society play a major part in deciding which technologies are adopted' (MacKenzie and Wajcman 1985:6). If this is accepted it is hard to see technology as an independent factor. One point here is that technologies may be invented but not then developed, or fail, for social reasons. Some technologies lose out for reasons which are not necessarily simply technological. Thus the cartridge lost out in a battle with the cassette and the Beta video system lost to VHS. Second, 'the same technology may have very different "effects" in different situations' (p. 6).

On the basis of the discussion so far, it is difficult to sustain the thesis of clear or simple technological determinism. However, as MacKenzie and Wajcman point out, this does not mean that technology is not important, and they point to three areas where technology can have decisive specific effects. First, technology can be political, as technologies can be developed and designed to eliminate certain social developments and encourage others. Thus the 'New York builder Robert Moses designed road systems to facilitate the travel of certain types of people and hinder that of others' (p. 7). Moreover, some technologies are more compatible with some social relations than others. Hence, it can be argued that 'basing energy supply around a nuclear technology that requires plutonium may enhance pressure for stronger state surveillance to prevent the theft of plutonium and help erode traditional civil liberties' (p. 7).

Second, technology can have long term specific effects. Thus, for example, once a road is built or sited in a particular place, it is difficult to alter it. Critics argue that the decision to build the M25 around London has had long term effects on the habits of car drivers and that it begins a process of expansion of the width of the road which is supposed to ease congestion, but which actually turns out to be self-defeating as more traffic uses it at each stage of expansion. Third, technology can have very significant environmental and ecological effects, as the debates over pollution, acid rain and nuclear power demonstrate so clearly.

In this argument, technology is not independent and directly determining, but one of a number of factors which interrelate to produce specific results. Other factors which MacKenzie and Wajcman (1985) draw attention to are economics, gender and the state. Thus technologies are invested in for particular reasons, often in the search for market advantage or profit. They are often related to particular conceptions of gender and the arrangement of households, and finally are sometimes financed by the state for miliary reasons among others.

Williams (1983) argues that technological determinism can often mesh with, and influence, forms of cultural pessimism, where, along with other factors, the development of new forms of technology is held to lead to forms of cultural decline. Thus the increasing development of computer technologies and games is thought, by some commentators, to lead to a decline in the ability of school children to concentrate on books, especially the sorts of book which are held to be of high standard. In the area of music it has been suggested that the introduction of new technologies leads to a decline in forms of previously established and valued standards of musicianship.

The discussion so far has raised a number of issues for consideration in the examination of technology and pop music. It is necessary, first, to define the sorts of technology being discussed; second, to consider whether some accounts slip into a sort of simple technological determinism, where technology is seen to change social arrangements on its own; third, to consider the specific effects of technology; and fourth, to examine the other factors which are affecting social and technological change. A complete examination of the relations between different technologies and pop is a long way beyond the scope of this book, and a useful general and historical account can be found in the work of Steve Jones (1992). Rather, the focus here is on some important dimensions of current technological change.

The extract from Jeremy J. Beadle's book, *Will Pop Eat Itself?* (1993), in box 8, details the sort of new technology now available and how it can be used in the construction of contemporary music, and points to the creator's lack of detailed musical or electronic knowledge.

In an important article also discussed in chapter 1, Andrew Goodwin (1992) identifies the key new technologies: the sequencer, the digital sampling music computer – the sampler, and MIDI (Musical Instrument Digital Interface). Sequencers:

> automate the process of music making, allowing drum patterns, keyboard bass-lines, arpeggios, melodies, and so forth to be entered in 'real time' a musician actually hits pads, electronic drum surfaces, or a synthesizer keyboard) in which the music is entered simply as information (with values such as the quarter note, for instance, or perhaps numerically constituted). The music can then be played back by the machine. It can also be manipulated by changing tempo, accuracy ('quantizing'), sequence, and sometimes timbre. (p. 78)

A sampler, as its name suggests, is used to 'sample' sounds which can then be altered in different ways, as the extract in box 8 shows. MIDI allows the interconnection of different machines so that they can interact.

There are pessimistic, optimistic and more balanced views of these technologies and the ways they can be used. Pessimistic accounts suggest, sometimes in a technologically determinist fashion, that they will inevitably have negative effects, leading to the decline of musicianship, the end of true musical creativity and the development of a kind of 'programmed' music, perhaps along the lines

Box 8   Making a record with the new technology

THE equipment which was used in the process I'm going to describe was: an Akai S1100 digital sampler (there was an Akai S900, an earlier less-swish model in there somewhere, too, acting as a separate store-house for spoken word samples); a mixing desk; Yamaha DX100 electronic keyboard; and an Apple Macintosh computer. The sequencer software package we used was Pass-port Mastertracks. Also helping things along was an Opcode Studio 3 Synchronizer and Midi Interface. I don't mention these names for reasons of commercial sponsorship, or because they were at the time of writing the last word in up-to-the-minute state of the art (which they weren't). In some ways we were operating relatively primitively . . . The material I wanted to turn into a dance masterpiece included a bass-line and rhythm culled from the twelve-inch mix of a British pseudo-soul hit of 1987, as well as the drum rhythm from the same disc. This second element turned out later to be too inflexible (a polite way of say-ing just too boring) and Rex elbowed it in favour of one of the most popu-lar beat samples in the business (Bobby Byrd). I also had on my cassette of breaks and beats and other things a weedy but catchy synthesizer figure from a mid-1980s gay-club favourite . . . and some chords from another high-energy floor filler of that time, 'Ti Sento', by the Italian group Matia Bazar. These later choices were fairly un-imaginative – early 1970s funk would have been much more useful. But the four truly distinctive ele-

ments I had to hand were: a Wagne-rian tenor singing the four-note '*Blutbruderschaft*' motif from the second act of *Götterdämmerung*; a three-note horn blast from the same source; a line of football commen-tary taken from a video of the TV coverage of the 1991 Spurs v. Porto match; and, best of all, a cartoon cat with the creepiest voice you ever heard enouncing the line 'But the third bowl of porridge was just right' . . .

Putting a track together differs from eating in many respects, but in this case the most significant was that the porridge had to wait until the end of the day. You start – well, we did – with the rhythm. And so the first rhythmic phrase I'd recorded was fed from the cassette into the sampler (in exactly the same way you'd record on to a cassette in the first place). There's always too much of what you record; as I've said, two bars of most beats or breaks is an extravagance. But this is where the sampler performs the first of its magic tricks, as an editing machine. In this case the bass figure was al-lowed to run twice before being chopped into two discrete phrases running alternately (so that the sec-ond could be made subtly different from the first in a way that it wasn't in its original form).

To help in editing, to make it virtually perfect and rhythmically exact (vital with 1990s techno-dance music), the sampler has its own small visual display, which portrays the sound as a graph. This display means that you can locate the pre-cise beginning of each measure much more easily than by manipulating a reel of tape. You can see exactly what you're editing and be sure of precisely what you're doing. Recorded sound is reduced to basic, visible, separable units, and can be worked on almost the way you'd make a drawing more accurate or graphic. Even figures played on the Yamaha keyboard can be reproduced visually through another display produced through the sequencer, so that you can augment or diminish your chords and rewrite your music as if you were dealing with something written on manuscript paper, rather than something you may have plucked out of your head. This graphic aspect means, conversely, that you need never write anything down, or make the effort to remember anything you've played.

Once the figure is edited precisely it is retriggered on the sequencer. The result of this is that loop-like effect of endless repetition of the figure is achieved. I say 'endless', but in fact the sequencer is programmed to take the figure through 120 measures initially.

As you're editing, apart from sheer precision with the start and finish of beats, you also have the option of varying the tempo of the figure you're working on. For convenience, we opted for the standard 120 beats per minute (the usual 'four on the floor' tempo), but this is no way necessary. Varying the tempo raises or lowers the pitch.

There is another visual display involved which I've already mentioned – that produced on the computer VDU by the sequencer. Generally this display lists each track line by line, identifying each track – each element or figure that's been fed into the sampler – by name (a name

which the producer/performer can assign according to his or her whim). After the sample has been fixed and played through, the display follows the tracks through all 120 measures, showing by means of a series of blocks whether or not each track is active in that measure – a black or filled block indicates that there is, a white or empty block that it isn't. This display is particularly helpful when editing the track (in the sense of song or number) as a whole, allowing you to work in unlooped variations in the various figures that have been sampled. After all, it's the unpredictable elements that tend to make even the most mundane of dance tracks memorable. But the elements which make up the rhythm track also need to have some kind of predictability about them to make dancing possible. Dance records with shifting rhythms have a limited appeal. The commonest and most effective way of putting variety into a rhythm track is to eliminate part of it momentarily, to take out the steady pulse of the beat for a measure or two so that only incidental percussion keeps the rhythm going in that time.

In the package that we were using, certain pre-sampled percussive sounds were available, saving us from the need to feed them into the sampler from outside. Many samplers come with a library of such sounds, or offer the capacity to retain such regular percussion features as bongos or tambourines on the machine's permanent hard-disk memory. There are, of course, separate digital drum machines, pioneered by Roger Linn (a standing joke on many Stock, Aitken and Waterman releases is that the drummer credit will go to 'A. Linn'). Such an instrument did not, however, feature in this day's work. When, after three beat samples had been fed in and doctored according to the method above, Rex felt that something lighter but sharper was needed to underline the beat, the percussion was added and edited like the other samples.

The keyboard turned out to possess power beyond my wildest dreams. Some of the time we used it simply as a synthesizer keyboard, and through it fed several 120-measure performances on to their own separate tracks. These tracks encompassed four completely separate styles, with varying instrumental sounds: rhythmically repeated minor triads, very common in much house music; frenetically repeated single notes, which form ideal complements to the triads; descending scales and similar figures; and finally the melodic line from the opening of Mozart's Piano Concerto No. 24 in C Minor, K.491, which is, after all, well out of copyright. The discrete keyboard performances were all separately edited. It turned out that the bottom notes of some of the triads had acquired, more or less by accident, a hollow tone, rather like the sound you get on a piano when one or two of the strings on a note have gone. This accidental sound was so pleasing that the bottom lines of the triads were separated out on to their own track, to give a separate sound timbre which could be used on its own. The triads and repeated notes had been recorded using a piano simulator (although the result didn't sound much like a piano to me, not even a fortepiano as beloved by the advocates of period instruments); the rest with a distinctly synthesized sound, to capture

the 'techno' feel so popular in 1991 and 1992.

However, the keyboard had much more going for it than its role as a synthesizer. It also had its part to play in doctoring what had been fed into the sampler. At the simplest level, a note on the keyboard was designed to trigger the sample, particularly useful when editing the rhythm tracks. But this quality really came into its own when the two Wagnerian samples where thrown into the grand scheme. The sound of the hefty Wagnerian tenor crying 'Blutbruderschaft' ... after it had been edited down to those simple four notes, was fed into the keyboard with the result that when you played the keyboard in certain designated areas, you got that note as though sung by the tenor in question backed by the Orchestra of the Met., with each group of four notes producing in turn each of the vowel noises of 'Blutbruderschaft' in the correct sequence. Obviously there was some electronic distortion on this ...

After the tenor had been subjected to this treatment, the same thing was done with the three-note horn blast. This time I was more cautious at the keyboard, and in the end the horn blasts were used only singly or in groups of two and only towards the end of the track to provide some further unpredictable element of variety ...

... to a computer-literate generation, this technology simplifies the concept of music-making. However much the punk ethos despised musicianship, it wasn't possible to get very far if you couldn't manage a few rudimentary chords on your guitar ... But even though you use keyboards which look something like the traditional piano/organ keyboard, in all this process you don't have to possess any knowledge of how to play it for real. It's just a way of controlling other people's music which you have fed in there. Again, real musical knowledge is an advantage but not necessary, providing you're not profoundly deaf. But if you edit properly, it's a question not of whether you passed Associated Board exams, but of whether you pressed the right buttons at the right time, with the right element of imagination. Music-making made supremely easy, if not supremely cheap . . .

Back in the studio, Rex decided to add some more 'pure' music to the proceedings, and plugged his guitar into the set up. The guitar figures he produced at strategic points as the whole track played back weren't put in the sampler. Having twiddled around at the guitar to his heart's content, he then ruthlessly edited what he'd played using the sequencer's graphic masterplan on the Apple Mac's

monitor. Again, the point of the guitar was variety, surprise, so to keep it going all the way through would have been otiose and marred the impact . . .

At last it was time for the porridge. I'd been told . . . that it was possible to feed straight from the soundtrack of a video into a sampler, simply by plugging the video and TV into the general system . . . Once the phrase 'But the third bowl of porridge was just right' had been captured inside the machine it could be edited and then messed around with like everything else. Although with a spoken phrase like this which was to recur at certain but by no means necessarily regular intervals, we used from a separate unit offering certain studio effects the tool of digital delay – the device which creates a stuttering effect with selected syllables or notes.

This was the first day's work.

Source: Beadle (1993:131–8). From *Will Pop Eat Itself?* Faber and Faber

adumbrated by the theories of Adorno which were examined in chapter 1. However, such accounts are difficult to sustain owing to the general problems of technological determinism identified earlier: the technology is somehow seen as independent of society in the first place, and technologies can have different effects in alternative social situations.

A far more complex, pessimistic account has been provided by Theberge (1989), who argues that the development of new technologies of musical production has led to increasing rationalization in the studio. This process is guided by the twin desires on the part of the producers for 'economic efficiency' and 'technical control'. Theberge maintains that this process involves the rationalization of music production along the Weberian lines outlined in chapter 1. The producer and the engineer take control of this overall rationalized process and 'enter directly into musical practice' (p. 101). The producers do not engage in a dialogue with the musicians or carry out their wishes but are increasingly moving towards a situation where they are in control of the process, by which finished recordings are created from multi-tracks in the studio. As Goodwin argues:

> Theberge sees the process of multi-tracking, then, as deeply ideological, creating an illusion of community and interaction, where in fact there is only a simulation created by the manipulation of separate, rationalized elements. These elements are apparently fused, partly through stereo imaging and the application of electronic reverberation (which can be used to construct the illusion that the individual parts were recorded in the same acoustic space) in the final mix. (1992:82)

This pessimistic account expects music to be increasingly rationalized, programmed and controlled. More optimistic accounts suggest otherwise, arguing that the development of these new technologies can lead to more creativity (of the type shown in the account in box 8 perhaps) as difficult operations become easier to perform. Further, it has been argued that there is a form of democratization involved in the process whereby the wider availability of these technologies leads to the possibility that more people can be involved in musical creativity. Goodwin (1992), in a more balanced assessment, enters two reservations about this sort of celebration. First, he suggests that there is a wide variation in the quality of the new technologies. The sorts of versions of these machines that are put into record studios are very different from those which are used by budding music makers in their bedrooms. It might be that such differences parallel those between the guitars often used by beginners and the quality instruments possessed by established rock stars. Second, Goodwin argues that more celebratory accounts tend to be gender blind, neglecting the point that it is men who are in control of such technologies.

Goodwin's conclusion is important, as he suggests that:

> There are clearly dangers in thinking about music as though it were a free-floating mystery, a social practice unconnected to actual conditions of production. As students of pop we need to know exactly how the means of musical production impact upon the sounds themselves. But in undertaking *that* task we have to recognize also that the definitions of *music* and *musician* can change. The new technologies

of pop music have not created new music. But they have facilitated new possibilities. (p. 97)

Such an approach suggests the need for complex sociological investigation, which locates the technology in context, and echoes the view of Steve Jones (1992) that there are new roles developing in the production of music. These involve a shift from the relationships and interaction between the musician, the producer and the recording engineer, which have characterized music production in recent years (and which will continue to exist in many areas), to those relationships which obtain between performers, programmers and performer–programmers (p. 12).

Summary

This chapter has considered:

- some important studies of jazz musicians which point to issues of art and commerce in their lives;
- evidence of the interconnections between art and pop music making;
- some important dimensions and accounts of music making at the more specific and everyday level;
- The nature of some of the most significant parts of the pop production process, including the increasing emphasis on promotion and marketing, the changing role of the producer, and the organization of the studio;
- The interactions between technology and pop production.

PART II

TEXT

4

History, Politics and Sexuality

This chapter is the first of three to focus on the texts of popular music. It begins the move away from the direct consideration of the production dimension of the production – text – audience framework outlined in chapter 1. However, in accord with the sociological orientation of this book, these texts are set in context. The chapter aims: first, to provide an account of the recent development of pop and rock music which locates the wider meanings of these forms in different political and economic contexts, developing some of the analysis from earlier chapters by including descriptive material on the development of contemporary pop music; second, to take up some of these wider meanings through an analysis of the inter-connections between pop and political action and meaning; third, further to consider some of these political and social meanings through discussion of pop's relations to gender and sexuality.

The chapter also introduces some themes which continue to reso-nate in the discussion of pop music. These include considerations of the value of pop music and why it is that some forms are valued more highly than others; and the extent to which forms of pop music are an authentic expression of individuals or social groups.

The development of rock and roll

Richard Middleton (1990) has located the development of rock and roll since the mid-1950s in a wider historical context of musical and cultural change. He suggests that there have been three 'moments' of important social change in music as a whole which have occurred in Western societies, though at different times in different societies. The first of these, which Middleton calls a 'bourgeois revolution', occurred in Britain between the late eighteenth century and the middle of the nineteenth. During this period, a music industry developed which was dominated by the commercialism of the capitalist, or bourgeois, class and 'most musical production is in the hands of or is mediated by commercial music publishers, concert organizers and promoters, theatre and public house managers' (p. 13). By the mid-1850s, there was a 'congruence across a range of different musical practices, resulting in a not exactly homogeneous musical field but one clearly dominated by a bourgeois synthesis' (p. 13). As Middleton explains:

> With variants, this relative congruence of musical technique, repertoire and practice stretched across light opera, bourgeois domestic song, the brass band and mass choral movements and the now more rationally organized music hall; it even penetrated the broadside and orally transmitted song genres of the industrial areas. Street music was gradually banished, political song pushed into tight proletarian enclaves, and the musical avant-garde characteristic of earlier in the century was either marginalized or assimilated, as brass bands played Wagner and parlour singers juxtaposed Schubert and Schumann with more commercial products.

The second period of change began by the 1890s, when new forms of mass culture, generated by the new monopoly capitalism, appeared. Large corporations became more important in international marketplaces, and American forms like ragtime and early jazz became more popular and showed a tendency to overshadow national musics. Middleton locates the third period of change after the Second World War, especially with the beginnings of rock 'n' roll, and argues that this was the 'moment' of 'pop culture'. At this point, there were the beginnings of increasing corporate domination, which coexisted with more local initiatives often based on particular sectors of the population. There were technological changes based around electronic systems, and young working-class people became significant movers in musical creation. This system became relatively stabilized by the late 1960s when:

> new social patterns, technologies and musical styles had been substantially assimilated into a reorganized music-industrial system: a transnational oligopoly of vast entertainment corporations, supplied

Up to 1958	rock 'n' roll
1958–1964	rock and roll
1964–	rock

Figure 4.1 Periodization of the development of rock
Source: adapted from Gillett (1983)

1 'northern band rock 'n' roll' (for example, Bill Haley)
2 'the New Orleans dance blues'
3 'Memphis country rock (also known as rockabilly)'
4 'Chicago rhythm and blues'
5 'vocal group rock 'n' roll'
All 'depended for their dance beat on contemporary Negro dance rhythms'

Figure 4.2 The five styles of rock 'n' roll
Source: Gillett (1983:23)

to some extent by 'independent' producers; serviced by mass audience radio and TV channels (with some 'minority' shows and channels), by a symbiotically pliant music press and by related leisure-products businesses; and directing itself at a series of separate audiences whose distinctness is less subcultural than a creature of market researchers' consumer profiles (Middleton 1990:15)

This view suggests that contemporary music is dominated by the large corporations discussed in chapter 2. Small or independent companies feed the larger ones. However, as was also noted in chapter 2, some writers have argued that 'independent' companies based in specific locations were central to the development of rock and roll. To consider such approaches it is necessary to examine the context in which rock developed. Gillett (1983) periodizes the development of rock in the way shown in figure 4.1. This periodization and terminology reflects a critical judgement of worth on Gillett's part which values the 'roughness' of rock 'n' roll over the later, blander, rock and roll. Rock 'n' roll is a hybrid which developed out of previous musical forms, most importantly black music, country music, folk music and previous pop forms (Frith 1983:12–38). According to Gillett, it contained a number of different styles, which are listed in figure 4.2.

This diversity in rock 'n' roll reflected the internal diversity of some of its source materials. Thus, in discussing black music (a topic more fully explored in chapter 5), Gillett points to the number of different types of rhythm and blues music, which itself is an all-encompassing label used to categorize the music produced for the black market. It replaced the earlier description of 'race music'. The different types of rhythm and blues music discussed by Gillett (1983) are the 'dancehall blues', the 'club blues', 'bar blues', gospel and what he calls the 'group sounds'. Detailed discussions of these different styles can be found in Gillett's book.

The pivotal figure in rock 'n' roll is Elvis Presley. Gillett (1983) interprets the relationship of Presley with other musicians and the producer, Sam Phillips, in a way that brings out the creative roles of the participants in the new rockabilly or Memphis country rock. Some extracts from Gillett's interpretation appear in box 9.

So far, this brief consideration of the development of rock 'n' roll has centred on the transformations within the music itself; how it related to earlier, source, material; and some of the processes which occurred at its creative moment. However, it is important to consider the social context in which rock 'n' roll developed in more detail. A key piece of work on this topic has been written by Peterson (1990).

Peterson asks the question 'why 1955?', that is, why was there such a fundamental shift in the nature of American popular music between 1954 and 1956? He suggests that previous analyses have tended to point to three main types of factor: first, the role of particular creative individuals, such as Elvis Presley; second, changes in the nature of the audience for popular music, in particular the influence of those individuals born after the Second World War; and third, changes in the media industries themselves.

Peterson criticizes both the first and second of these explanations. He argues that the first accords too great a role to the creative genius of particular individuals (though he does not suggest that these individuals were without talent). Rather, he maintains that at particular times certain individuals come to the fore because of a specific set of social conditions, which operate as a kind of pattern of selecting mechanisms. Peterson argues, therefore, that there are always more talented artists in existence than those who come to the fore at any one particular time. Peterson's argument against the second mode of explanation is more straightforward. He points out that in 1954 'the oldest of the baby-boomers were only nine years old and half had not been born yet' (p. 98). This leaves Peterson

Box 9   The development of rockabilly in Memphis

PRESLEY was the most commercially successful of a number of Memphis singers who evolved what they themselves called 'country rock' and what others, record collectors and people in the industry, have called 'rockabilly'. Country rock was basically a Southern white version of 12-bar boogie blues, shouted with a minimum of subtlety by ex-hillbilly singers over an accompaniment featuring electric guitar, stand-up bass, and – from 1956 – drums, still taboo in Nashville. The style evolved partly from the imaginative guidance of a Memphis radio station engineer, Sam Phillips, who entered the recording business by supervising sessions with local blues singers and leasing the masters to a number of independent companies (Chess in Chicago, owned by the Chess brothers, or Modern/RPM in Los Angeles, owned by the Bihari brothers). The success of some of these singers, notably B. B. King and Howlin' Wolf, encouraged Phillips to form his own label, Sun, and two of the singers he recorded for his own label, Little Junior Parker and Rufus Thomas, had hit records in the Negro market.

The Memphis blues singers used small bands which featured piano, guitar, and saxophone. No particular dominant style linked them all, but common to many of their records was a kind of intimate atmosphere created by the simple and cheap, but unorthodox, 'tape delay echo' recording technique of Phillips. The singers invariably made their personal presence felt on the records, menacingly in Howlin' Wolf's case, impatiently in Junior Parker's. These recordings, and other more traditional blues, and rhythm and blues records issued by Sun, were known to a substantial number of white youths through the South, and presented a source of song material and stylistic inspiration that was in

many ways more satisfactory than the orthodox country and western culture.

Jimmie Rodgers sang the 'white blues' in the twenties but Elvis Presley was the first to make it work as pop music. According to the legend of his recording debut, his discovery by Sam Phillips was casual and lucky. Presley is said to have attracted the attention of Phillips when he used Sun's studios to cut a record for his mother's birthday present; Phillips encouraged him to make a record with proper accompaniment, and the two men were rewarded with a local hit from one of the sides, 'That's All Right'.

The story of Presley's discovery has the elements of romance, coincidence, and fate that legends need, and in fact seems to be true, but it is likely that if Phillips and Presley had not met, two other such people would soon have done what they did – merge rhythm and blues with country and western styles and material, and come up with a new style. In the panhandle of west Texas, in Arkansas, in north Louisiana, and in Memphis there were other singers whose cultural and musical experience were comparable to Presley's; indeed, some of them followed him into the Sun studios, while others tried studios in Nashville and Clovis, New Mexico.

It is difficult to assess how great a part Sam Phillips played in influencing his singers – among other things, by introducing them to blues records – and how much they already knew. Presley told one interviewer:

I'd play [guitar] along with the radio or phonograph, and taught myself the chord positions. We were a religious family, going round together to sing at camp meetings and revivals, and I'd take my guitar with us when I could. I also dug the real low-down Mississippi singers, mostly Big Bill

Broonzy and Big Boy Crudup, although they would scold me at home for listening to them. 'Sinful music', the townsfolk in Memphis said it was. Which never bothered me, I guess.

In the same interview, Presley stressed the importance of Phillips:

Mr. Phillips said he'd coach me if I'd come over to the studio as often as I could. It must have been a year and a half before he gave me an actual session. At last he let me try a western song – and it sounded terrible. But the second idea he had was the one that jelled. 'You want to make some blues?' he suggested over the 'phone, knowing I'd always been a sucker for that kind of jive. He mentioned Big Boy Crudup's name and maybe others too. I don't remember.

All I know is, I hung up and ran 15 blocks to Mr. Phillips' office before he'd gotten off the line – or so he tells me. We talked about the Crudup records I knew – 'Cool Disposition', 'Rock Me, Mama', 'Hey Mama', 'Everything's All Right', and others, but settled for 'That's All Right', one of my top favourites. . . .[4]

What Presley achieved was certainly not 'the same thing' as the men he copied. On 'That's All Right' and 'Mystery Train' (written and first recorded by Junior Parker for Sun), he evolved a personal version of this style, singing high and clear, breathless and impatient, varying his rhythmic emphasis with a confidence and inventiveness that were exceptional for a white singer. The sound suggested a young white man celebrating freedom, ready to do anything, go anywhere, pausing long enough for apologies and even regrets and recriminations, but then hustling on towards the new. He was best on fast songs, when his impatient singing matched the urgent

rhythm from bass (Bill Black) and guitar (Scotty Moore). Each of his five Sun singles backed a blues song with a country and western song, most of them already familiar to the respective audiences; each sold better than its predecessor, and increasing numbers of people discovered Presley either through radio broadcasts or through his stage appearances.

But Presley did not reach the mass popular music audience with his Sun records, which sold mainly to audiences in the South and to the minority country and western audience elsewhere. Only after Presley's contract was bought by RCA-Victor did his records make the national top ten, and the songs on these records were not in a country rock style. At Victor, under the supervision of Chet Atkins, Presley's records featured vocal groups, heavily electrified guitars, and drums, all of which were considered alien by both country and western audiences and by the audience for country rock music. Responding to these unfamiliar intrusions in his accompaniment, Presley's voice became much more theatrical and self-conscious as he sought to contrive excitement and emotion which he had seemed to achieve on his Sun records without any evident forethought.

Presley's success for Sun, and later for RCA-Victor, encouraged Phillips to try other singers with comparable styles and material, and attracted to his studios young southerners with similar interests. Carl Perkins and Warren Smith from the Memphis area, Roy Orbison from west Texas, Johnny Cash, Conway Twitty, and Charlie Rich from Arkansas, and Jerry Lee Lewis from northern Louisiana brought songs, demonstration tapes, and their ambitions to Phillips, who switched almost completely from black singers to white singers once the latter became commercially successfull.

Source: Gillett (1983:26–9)

free to develop an argument which stresses the place of contextual factors in the development of rock. In general, he has been associated with the 'production-of-culture' perspective which argues that there are six kinds of factor which 'shape' the development of culture: 'law, technology, industry structure, organization structure, occupational career and market' (p. 98). In the main body of his article, he explores how these factors influenced the events of 1955.

He begins with law and technology, which are thought to have a significant role in defining the ways in which the other factors operate. With respect to law, he identifies three important aspects: copyright, patent law and Federal Communications Commission (FCC) regulation. Peterson argues that the main copyright collecting agency for public performance, the American Society of Composers, Authors and Publishers (ASCAP), which had controlled the reproduction of music to ensure that only certain forms were allowed on the radio, for example, was challenged by a rival organization, Broadcast Music Incorporated (BMI), which had been formed by the radio networks, when they had failed to agree over licensing fees. Because of ASCAP's control over more traditional radio-type material, BMI utilized other types of music which had previously been excluded from radio airplay. Thus, a struggle over rights revenue (see further, chapter 2 of this volume) is seen as one of the contributing factors to the development of rock. However, this conflict occurred in the early 1940s so it does not explain the outbreak of rock on its own. In terms of patent law, Peterson examines the struggle between different companies over the ownership of different record formats which led by the early 1950s to the existence of the long-playing $33\frac{1}{3}$ rpm and the 45 rpm record. The latter was particularly important as it was aimed at the pop market and was far more robust than the fragile 78 rpm. disc which it replaced. Thus, the 45 rpm record could be distributed much more easily by smaller record companies. Finally, in terms of FCC regulation, there was a great increase in the number of radio stations that were licensed to broadcast.

The introduction of the 45 rpm record was a form of technological innovation. Peterson draws attention to two other important forms of technological innovation: the introduction of television and the development of the transistor radio. Television is important, in the main, for its effects on radio. The big networks that had previously controlled radio moved into television, which they have continued to dominate in the USA, where local television stations are affiliated to NBC, CBS or ABC. Smaller, more specialized radio stations were set up. Much of the traditional radio programming (for example, soap operas) moved over to the new television medium. Second, there was the introduction into America of cheap, portable, radios from Japan.

In discussing industry structure, organization structure, occupational careers and the market, Peterson draws comparisons between the situation in 1948 and 1958. He provides much detail, in describing a movement over this ten-year period from the control of the industry by a small number of companies who produced, distributed and manufactured musical products to a relatively more diverse and 'entrepreneurial' situation (see also the discussion of these developments in chapter 1 of this book). As Peterson (1990:113–14) summarizes:

> In the early 1950s, the music industry was blind to the large and growing unsatiated demand for greater variety in music and deaf to the efforts of musicians that might have satisfied that demand. The music industry was financially as well as aesthetically committed to the big band-crooner style of popular music of the time, and, because of its oligopolistic control of the production, distribution and marketing of new music, was able to thwart the marketing of alternative styles.
>
> Then with the transfer of network radio programming to television, radio turned to playing records as the cheapest effective form of programming. The arrival of cheap transistor radios and the development of the Top 40 radio-as-jukebox format meant that a much larger number and far wider range of music was exposed to the audience. Using the new durable 45 rpm records, and taking advantage of the developing network of independent record distributors, numerous independent record companies experimented with a wide range of new sounds in an effort to tap the unsatiated market demand. In a matter of two dozen months between late 1954 and early 1957 rock was forged in this caldron of entrepreneurial creativity.

Peterson provides a very important and illuminating sociological account of the social context of the development of rock in the United States. However, it is important to note two problems with this approach. First, it is not always clear whether Peterson is contextualising the development of rock or explaining its development at a particular moment. At the beginning of his article he stresses the explanatory. However, as the piece develops, he becomes more involved in drawing comparisons across time, which are not, in themselves, explanations, as it is not clear precisely what effects the factors are thought to have. Second, Peterson's focus is on the United States and his account is not necessarily very helpful in explaining the development of rock in other societies, such as Britain.

The latter has been examined by Bradley (1992) in the context of the 'composite account of rock 'n' roll'. His clear summaries of what he sees as myths about the development of rock are reproduced in box 10. Bradley identifies a number of problems with the 'composite account', which are also of general relevance to work on the history and meaning of rock. These are:

1 Many accounts neglect 'the problem of understanding and explaining the phenomenon of white kids responding to black styles' (p. 14). This is an area which is explored in chapters 5 and 7 of this book.
2 There is a tendency to neglect the phenomenon of the development of the group. Bradley suggests that the idea of a small group of musicians playing together is a new departure for white music in the 1950s.
3 There is a gender blindness in many of the standard accounts which neglects or plays down the 'maleness' of rock 'n' roll.
4 The accounts do not pay enough attention to the nature of amateurism in rock music production and the development of local pop music making in the 1950s.

Aspects of these sorts of criticisms have been dealt with in some of the more recent work on rock and pop which is summarized and examined at other points in this book. However, the discussion so far illuminates two significant factors which will continue to be developed through the rest of this chapter. First, there is the value placed upon particular textual forms of popular music by critics and commentators. As we have seen, Gillett conveys approval of a particular form through his use of the term rock 'n' roll and his denigration of the more 'sanitized' rock and roll. In this account, rock 'n' roll somehow stands for freedom and expression and rock and roll for constraint and manipulation. We shall see how rock came to have a particular meaning in the 1960s with connotations of opposition and resistance, especially when compared to pop music. Thus, definitions of textual types or genres are not just of academic interest but convey meaning to a much wider audience. This is often connected with politics in the broadest sense.

Second, there are the interconnected issues of gender and sexuality.

Box 10   The composite account of rock 'n' roll

IT is possible to construct a sort of standard composite account of the main events and developments known as 'rock 'n' roll', based on the main texts discussed above and other similar books. It consists of a list of factors on which they more or less all agree, and on which they confer major causal status in relation to the rise of rock 'n' roll and beat music. It also involves a starting definition or delimitation of the body of musical artists, and records, radio and TV shows, which make up the phenomenon of rock 'n' roll and beat music.

The USA

The following is a summary of what might be called the standard view, the agreed wisdom, or the prevalent *myth* about early American rock 'n' roll.

1 'Popular music' already exists in the early and mid-1950s as an industry, with its 'major' and 'independent' recording companies, publishing houses, radio stations, etc. 'Live' venues exist in most towns and cities, while for records a whole infrastructure of distribution and sales outlets, as well as large chains of juke boxes, are well established. Trade magazines, magazines for listeners, and the charts or hit parades all serve promotional functions. The popular music audience already includes almost the whole population. Profits are high and, consequently, plant and other investments are expanding; this is especially true of record production, which, having all but died during the Depression and the war years, is growing dramatically, on the basis of improved and still improving materials (vinyl replacing shellac) and technology (hi-fidelity and, later in the 1950s, transistorization of radios).

2 'Popular music' also exists already as a *tradition* familar to virtually all American listeners and musicians. Certain styles are nationally established as 'popular', others are more locally based (country music), or are excluded, to some degree, from the national popular charts ('race' music, as gospel, blues and rhythm and blues were then called), though they are closely related to popular music, in being often catered for by the same companies, and in providing numerous popular artists. There are also several varieties of jazz, from 'traditional' to 'modern', each of which is less than fully familiar but by no means unknown to the 'mass' of the listening public. Both modern jazz and country music enjoy 'booms' in the late 1940s and early 1950s, but these are not on the scale of the rock 'n' roll developments which follow.

The presence of a black, working-class population in every major city of the USA by 1950, a result of migrations mainly from the First World War onwards, means that local radio stations and record stores almost everywhere reflect, to a significant degree, the tastes of these communities. And since neither radio-dial-twiddling nor shopping-around can be censored, despite the industry's compulsive categorizing, young white people in ever-increasing numbers do listen to the music which is becoming known as 'rhythm 'n' blues' and 'rock and roll' (or rock 'n' roll) in these years. Those local DJs, juke-box operators and independent record store and record label owners who are close to this development take note, and begin to consciously promote this music for white listeners.

Most of the authors agree, to some extent, that the 'boring', 'bland', 'sentimental' state of the nationally popular (among whites) music of the early 1950s, as a whole, contributes to the defection of these young white listeners, but they all argue this in a very generalized, sweeping way, and all argue for different exceptions. Their problems with regard to verbalizing musical meaning are clearly displayed in this difficulty or weakness which they all share.

3 A 'post-war boom' in the USA is the economic background to new scale of working-class and middle-class 'affluence' in the 1950s. Both pocket money and widely available part-time work swell the disposable income of 'teenagers' at high school, while wages are often relatively high in the first years of work, in comparison with the 1930s and 1940s. The overall effect is to create a large group, throughout the country, of independent young or 'teenage' consumers, of relatively high spending power, even despite the rise in numbers staying on longer at school.

Most of the rock histories use the term 'teenagers' uncritically, ignoring the fact that it was a neologism of the late 1940s or early 1950s, replete with many new connotations. The connotations which are clearly retained in the rock historians' appropriation of the term are (a) a style of *leisure*, and of *consumption*, found among 'kids' from the ages of 13–14 to the early 1920s, (b) a certain exuberance or rowdiness, which can become a threatening wildness, and which includes (c) a foregrounding of sexual practices (dating, going steady, courtship in general, and the 'threat' of 'sex before marriage'). Behind these implications of the term, we can also see clearly that the standard notion of 'the teenager' is usually of a boy, not a girl, and that the 'threat' of sex is a threat *of* boys *against* girls, as seen *by* parents, teachers, etc. These things, sadly, remain unsaid in the rock histories.

4 The search for 'novelty', derived from the competitive economic character of the pop industry, and in particular from attempts by 'independent' record companies to outflank 'majors', leads to 'cover versions' of dance blues and vocal group successes from the 'race' market, being offered on the mainly white pop market as a whole. In a sense, this is merely the equivalent of the raids on jazz and on country music of the same years, but partly it is also the result of an 'authentic' pressure from existing teenage audiences, as spotted by adventurous DJs and independent studio producers. These 'cover versions' are normally produced by 'acceptable' white artists, and involve some

changes in musical style, and some cleaning up of lyrics on occasions, but none the less they have the side-effect, when successful, of arousing some interest in the originals, and the longer-term effect of familiarizing the white pop audiences with some of the conventions of the black styles. Some groups of white musicians actually begin to specialize in a 'half-way' style, notably Bill Haley and the Comets, whose 'Shake Rattle and Roll' is a cover version of a rhythm 'n' blues hit, while 'Rock around the Clock' is an original number modelled on the work of black artists to some extent.

5 A cluster of media events combines to shoot the Haley style, and that of some others, into national prominence, notably the use of the music in the sound track of 'Blackboard Jungle', a successful film about 'wild' adolescents, and subsequently the appearances of Elvis Presley on the Nashville TV show 'Grand Old Opry', and later on the nationally screened 'Ed Sullivan Show'. Later come other films, such as 'Rock around the Clock' and 'The Girl Can't Help It'.

6 At this point, the competitive logic of the industry once again influences developments, producing a race to imitate the initial successes and to promote the music with all the resources available. In particular, again, the 'independents' see their chance to compete on more equal terms with the 'majors', since both are relatively new to the style, and neither is very sure at first of how to predict who and what will be successful. Literally dozens of young artists are signed up, especially by independent companies, to produce rock 'n' roll; others are converted overnight, from aspiring crooners or country singers into imitation Elvises.

The very over-production and financial chaos which result help to ensure that this situation cannot last, and by about 1958–9 in the USA, the initial 'explosion' of production of, and enthusiasm for, rock 'n' roll is over. However, the consequences of this period of upheaval are that one or two independent companies do indeed establish themselves as small majors, that a new generation of producers, artists and song writers becomes established in the industry, and also that some black rhythm 'n' blues artists share in the explosion, singing their own music more or less as they would be doing anyway, but reaching young white audiences. Fats Domino, Little Richard, Chuck Berry, Jackie Wilson, Lloyd Price, Larry Williams and the Coasters are among those who owe their wider success to this upheaval.

Britain

Each of the rock histories devotes a section to Britain (though not normally to any other country), tracing the story of the impact of rock 'n' roll (and of the home-produced 'skiffle') and placing these events, usually, as 'background' to the Beatles and the 'beat-boom' years of 1963–6. I would argue very strongly that the view which sees the period 1955–63 in Britain as a mere 'background' to later beat, and other later styles, is heavily distorted by an a most fetishistic attention to the charts (i.e. the successes of the Beatles, etc.), and that, sales of records notwithstanding, the development of a 'youth culture' in Britain, and of a music *of* that youth culture, can only be understood by reversing that emphasis. In a very real sense, there is an element of *myth* in the way rock histories skip from one commercial peak to another, or from one 'great artist' to another, ignoring almost totally the social roots of both the music making and the listening, which ought to be among their objects of study. None the less, the main points of a composite account can again be enumerated, this time relying, however, on a slightly different list of books.

1 The pop industry is already international. American music already features strongly in British record stores, and on Radio Luxemburg, while the BBC allows a little of it into the major popular radio shows. British artists 'cover' most big US hits themselves. Equally, and very importantly, American films are readily available at British cinemas. Any BBC resistance to 'American trash' is out-flanked by the rise of records and by films; and when ITV comes along, it exhibits no scruples in adding to this trend with its pop shows. In any event, pop music coverage on radio and TV is on a very small scale in these years, by 1990s standards, and young listeners rely heavily on record buying and jukeboxes.
2 The Teddy boys already exist, chiefly in London, before rock 'n' roll arrives in Britain. They probably originate (according

to Hebdige) in the traditional working-class areas of South and East London in the early 1950s. Their style of dress is, in part, an imitation of the Edwardian man about town, but in other respects, they imitate American models. The interest in unusual clothes itself is odd (and new?) among male, working-class Londoners, as is the responsiveness to rapid change in fashions of music which follows in the mid-1950s. Hebdige calls this style 'a focus for an illicit delinquent identity' and points out its connection to a fantasy of America. The phenomenon apparently needs only publicity to spread: only later does commercial exploitation of the style move in.
3 The absence of a large black community with its own musical life (though this was beginning to take shape in the major cities), and also the resistance to pop and rock in general, and American pop and rock in particular, which is maintained by the BBC, combine to give the films which feature rock 'n' roll a greater importance in Britain than in the USA. The film 'Rock around the Clock', and its title song, are adopted by Teds in particular and teenagers in general all over Britain in 1955–6: various 'riots', and the occasional destruction of cinema seats to make room for dancing, gain the music and the audiences much notoriety, orchestrated by the newspapers into a full-scale 'moral panic'. This reaction tends to make rock 'n' roll a sort of badge of defiant identity, rather than just another fad of taste, for the kids involved.
4 Skiffle, a musical style taken initially from traditional jazz

bands, coincides with this early rock 'n' roll enthusiasm and, being slightly more respectable in origins, is accepted as a quaint offshoot of jazz or folk music, even by the BBC, who launch '6/5 Special' as a TV pop show specializing in skiffle. One of the important things about this style is that its great simplicity, and the cheapness of using home-made instruments, lead to a wave of amateur and semi-professional imitations by the kids themselves. (What almost every account omits to mention, but is none the less true, is that it is *boys*, specifically and almost exclusively, who take up playing skiffle.) This craze lasts from 1956 to 1958 or so, after which amateurism continues, but now mainly in imitation of American rock and post-rock musics.

5 At the same time as amateurism becomes firmly established among teenagers, by about 1957 or 1958, the 'real' rock 'n' roll records from the USA dry up, and post-rock 'balladeers' and British artists exhibiting little or no rock influence come to dominate record sales and radio and TV shows, Tommy Steele, Marty Wilde and Cliff Richard perhaps being the most rock-influenced of these. Some of the new 'rock-pop' records lack the prominent beat of rock 'n' roll, and most are also highly 'arranged' products; on both counts they are not seen as good models by the teenage amateurs, who aim chiefly for a lively dance music. The result is that young audiences seeking live dance music turn away from the charts, just as some American teenagers did in the early 1950s. A live dance music style which becomes known as 'the big beat', and later as 'beat', develops, as does a standard group format of lead and bass guitars, sometimes a third ('rhythm') guitar, drums and vocalist(s), sometimes with a piano or organ, or a harmonica. This beat music thrives most strongly in the provincial British cities where the hit-making, and indeed, record-making, machinery is virtually non-existent (Liverpool, Birmingham, Glasgow, Manchester, Newcastle).

6 A somewhat more self-conscious movement of rejection of the charts leads to the British 'rhythm and blues' movement, chiefly in the colleges and universities and their milieux. Though this has much in common with the earlier and later jazz booms, in being mainly middle class and often idealistically anti-commercial, it also resembles beat and rock 'n' roll in many ways: it is performed by small groups (four or five members, with guitars and drums the chief instruments), it uses electrical amplification, and it includes a lot of dance music with a strong beat. The Rolling Stones, the Animals and the Zombies are among many representatives of this movement who become pop successes, while other more 'uncompromising' groups have less success in the early and mid-1960s but strongly influence the later 'British blues', 'underground' and 'heavy' rock developments (John Mayall, Alexis Korner's Blues Incorporated, etc.)

Source: Bradley (1992:9–14)

Bradley (1992) comments on the maleness of many of the accounts of the development of rock. Related to this is the way in which pop music has often been seen as 'immature' or superficial because of its implied audience among young women. The femininity of pop is something implicitly problematic for male writers. Such themes can be explored as we take the story of the development of pop rather more up to date (see also, Chambers 1985).

Rock and pop in the 1960s and 1970s

The conventional account of the development of rock and pop sees a bland period between the late 1950s and 1963. This is the period where, according to Gillett, the excitement of rock 'n' roll is replaced by standardized music industry products such as Fabian in the United States and Cliff Richard in Britain. A perceived shift occurs with the rise to fame of the Beatles in 1963 in Britain and 1964 in the United States. While in many respects the Beatles were partly located within more 'conventional' forms and packaged in a show business sort of way, their reappropriation of black music styles opened the way for a series of developments during the 1960s. Partly they are important for the way in which they brought together different forms, integrating forms of black soul with more rock and roll-orientated material. They acted as a bridge between the rock 'n' roll of, for example, Chuck Berry, and more pop-orientated material. It is possible to say that they integrated pop and rock and led the field in producing a kind of unified audience which was to exist for a good part of the 1960s. The suggestion here then is that there is normally recognized to be a difference between rock and pop musics which runs through the development of the forms since the 1950s. However, at particular point these forms are intertwined. Indeed, some writers such as Grossberg (1983) have argued that in detail it is actually very difficult to separate them. In part this has to do with the role of more detailed analysis of the actual nature of the sounds themselves. This is an issue taken up in chapter 6.

The Beatles opened the space for the development of rock music in the 1960s. There were many different strands of this. In Britain there were a number of groups that utilized blues-based themes and structures and a continuing appropriation of black American forms. Sometimes Black Americans developed the styles themselves, Jimi Hendrix being the most notable example of black American musician who played in r 'n' b groups in America in the early 1960s, before coming to Britain in 1966 to team up with two white musicians to form the Jimi Hendrix Experience.

Rock music sold in large quantities and was often seen by its producers and audience to involve the communication of authentic artistic consciousness and to have important things to say about contemporary events. At this time, there developed an audience for rock which seemed open to a number of different styles. Of course, this is not to say that there were not different tastes within the audience and different types of rock. There clearly were. However, by comparison with the polarization between different forms in the early 1960s and the increased separation of forms in subsequent years, these differences were not so clear cut. There were perhaps more divisions in the United States, though it is possible to argue that forms of fragmentation of the rock pop audience really begin to appear around 1968, between West and East Coasts and forms such as 'folk rock (1965–6), largely a phenomenon of New York and Los Angeles, and its wandering son, the San Francisco sound (1966–7)' (Heylin 1993:3) and the embryonic East Coast scene centred around the Velvet Underground.

Throughout the 1960s in Britain there had been differences between the influence of more contemporary black sounds in the form of soul, and earlier forms, like blues, which fed the more guitar-orientated rock bands. In the early to mid-1960s these could be integrated, as the extract from the journalist Cliff White's diary from 1964 in box 11 shows. However, by the end of the 1960s and the early 1970s a greater degree of fragmentation had set in.

Looking back from the 1990s, it is possible to see the beginnings of forms which were increasingly to separate as time went on. It has become increasingly common to date the beginnings of the genre of Heavy Metal to the work of Black Sabbath, Deep Purple and Led Zeppelin in the late 1960s and early 1970s (Weinstein 1991; Walser 1993). Also, the 'pomp' or 'classical' rock of groups like ELP, Yes and Genesis can be clearly identified, as can the influence and popularity of some forms of British folk rock, such as Fairport Convention. While the followers of all these forms might now see them as separate types they might not have been seen in such a separated manner in the early 1970s, when it was perfectly possible to be a fan of all three.

What did open up in a clear way in the late 1960s and early 1970s was a new divide between what was perceived to be the more serious and, somehow more 'authentic' rock music, and 'commercial'

Box 11   Cliff White's 1964 Diary

Fri	Oct 30	Jimmy Reed, Sugar Pie De Santo, The Dixie Cups on Ready, Steady, Go.
Sat	Oct 31	Saw Jimmy Reed at Club Noreik. Had to miss John Lee Hooker at Flamingo.
Mon	Nov 2	Saw Carl Perkins, Tommy Tucker, The Animals at Gaumont State. Had to miss Jimmy Reed at Flamingo.
Wed	Nov 4	Martha & Vandellas on Top Of The Pops.
Fri	Nov 6	Martha & Vandellas, Kim Weston on RSG.
Mon	Nov 9	My birthday. Still alive.
Tues	Nov 10	Martha & Vandellas on Pop Inn.
Fri	Nov 13	Saw The Isley Brothers at East Ham Granada. Had to miss The Soul Sisters at Flamingo.
Sat	Nov 14	Perkins, Tucker etc. at Finsbury Park Astoria.
Mon	Nov 16	Down to The Scene with the mob as usual.
Wed	Nov 18	Saw Jimmy Reed at Flamingo. Chatted with him for about an hour backstage. Great bloke.
Thurs	Nov 19	Took some records up to Jimmy's hotel and had breakfast with him. Geezer called Al Smith from Vee Jay was there. Nice enough bloke but seemed more keen to talk about Betty Everett than Jimmy.
Fri	Nov 20	Jerry Lee, Marvin Gaye, The Stones on RSG.
Sat	Nov 21	Saw Jerry Lee at Club Noreik.
Sun	Nov 22	Load of us went down to Brighton to see Jerry Lee again.
Mon	Nov 23	Saw Jimmy Reed at British Legion Hall, South Harrow. Had to miss Jerry Lee at Eltham Baths.
Thurs	Nov 26	Saw Howlin' Wolf and Hubert Sumlin at Marquee.

Source: C. White, sleeve notes for Jimmy Reed: *Upside Your Head*, Courtesy of Charly Records CRB 1003, 1980

---

pop music. Devotees of rock could be scathing in their attacks on pop and commercialism, and the criticism of groups 'selling out' became exceptionally shrill. This accusation, which continues to this day, was regularly hurled at musicians like Marc Bolan who moved from being a hero of the so-called underground to mass-selling single records. It had of course been made against Bob Dylan when he moved from acoustic to electric instruments in the mid-1960s. Pop was singles and chart success, rock was albums and serious. It is important to recognize that the distinction was not necessarily built around the size of the audience. The rock groups sold lots of albums, but their 'serious' intent and content seemed to protect them from the criticism of 'selling out'. The criteria of values did not depend on sales. There are issues around politics here which are considered in more detail later in this chapter.

There were forms which bridged this increasing divide between rock and pop in the early 1970s, in particular the association of different artists under the heading of glitter rock. Some of these bands were clearly seen to be pop groups orientated to top-twenty success, examples including the Sweet and Gary Glitter; however, others straddled, and in lots of ways reconstructed, the divide between rock and pop, most notably David Bowie and Roxy Music. Both of these showed the influence of the later forms of connection between art and pop influence considered by Frith and Horne (1987) as discussed in chapter 3. This crossing and breaking down of the barrier which had been erected between pop and rock was to be influential on developments in both Britain and the United States in the mid- to late 1970s, where art, pop and rock intertwined to produce punk rock.

There has been some rather nationalistic debate on the origins of punk. This was certainly an issue at the time when various factions wanted to claim punk as their own. However, it is more useful to see American and British punk as intertwined and interacting forms and to leave aside rather pointless debates about originality and ownership. The beginnings of American punk can be traced through from the forms of East Coast rock art collaboration of which the Velvet Underground are the clearest example (Heylin 1993). Such collaborations, in combination with the influence of glitter rock and the pub rock movement of the mid-1970s combined to produce the punk and new waves of 1976 and 1977 (Laing 1985; Savage 1991). These often explicitly attacked the rock values which were seen to have been corrupted through the 1970s as rock stars became richer and more detached from their audiences. However, most important for the present chronicle was the way in which punk attempted to draw on black forms, most notably the Jamaican one of reggae, in the production of something that was neither pop or rock, or which attempted to integrate the two. Thus initially, punk went against the album ethic of the rock bands and the kind of Top 20 promotion strategies of the pop groups. Singles became important again, but they were to be produced in an 'independent' and amateur manner, though as was discussed in chapter 2 there are clear difficulties with the notion of independence used here. This integrative moment did not last very long before a new and qualitatively different (on some accounts) form of fragmentation occurred in the 1980s and 1990s.

Rock and pop in the 1980s and 1990s

It is possible to see the punk period as a watershed. It represents an attempt first, to regain the spirit of the early days of rock 'n' roll, in its desire for independence and the short three-minute song; and, second, to reintegrate the pop and rock forms which had increasingly split during the 1970s. It also marks the beginning of the fragmentation that was rapidly to develop during the 1980s and 1990s. Thus in Britain, the early eighties saw both the integration of punk and reggae in the Two Tone movement which updated sixties Jamaican Ska with a punk framework, and the development of new pop as represented initially by the groups labelled as the 'New Romantics'. Slightly later came the new 'rock' bands such as Big Country and, more enduringly and popularly, U2. Heavy metal reasserted itself during the later stages of the punk period, in a new wave of heavy metal bands in Britain and subsequently, during the 1980s, in the United States, where it has been argued that Heavy Metal moved to the centre of the popular music field (Walser 1993).

As the 1980s progressed other forms like hip hop from America increased in importance and influenced white musics in different ways. There has been the continued existence of the so-called independent or Indie sector, though, as has been noted at several points so far, it is not always easy to specify what this is independent of or from. All this has led to a fluidity between the different types of music where it has become, argue many commentators, more and more difficult to sustain the sorts of definition of rock and pop which seemed to have some analytic purchase in the sixties and seventies. There has been a breaking of barriers, it is suggested, where it is possible for Michael Jackson to employ 'heavy metal' forms as associated with Eddie Van Halen on his *Thriller* album of 1983. Furthermore, it has been argued that fragmentation into lots of different forms of music and the interactions between such forms represent postmodernism in popular music. At this point it is necessary to examine this concept in more detail.

Pop and postmodernism

Postmodernism is a disputed term, which has been the subject of some of the most convoluted argument in the social sciences and humanities over the past fifteen or so years. From its beginnings as

---

'1 the breakdown of the distinction between culture and society
2 an emphasis on style at the expense of substance and content
3 the breakdown of the distinction between high culture (art) and
   popular culture
4 confusions over time and space
5 the decline of the "meta-narratives"'

Figure 4.3 Elements of postmodernism
Source: Strinati (1992)

a categorization of new forms of architecture which broke from the
regularity of the modern block of glass, 'postmodernism' has been
applied to diverse cultural forms, intellectual activities, and the nature
of society itself. An introductory account of 'Postmodernism and
Popular Culture' (Strinati 1992) has suggested that there are five
main characteristics of postmodernism. These are listed in figure 4.3.

In this account, postmodernism entails a new fluidity between
culture and society. Culture is not in some way separated from
society or reflecting parts of it. Indeed, society cannot be defined
without taking account of cultural factors. Style is central. It is not
added on to an essential content as a secondary matter, but is often
foregrounded over the meaning of a cultural form. Moreover, it may
be argued that it is impossible to separate style from content. In
earlier periods, it is maintained, such essential content to culture
or art could be isolated, and style was less important and seen as
secondary. There is a new fluidity between forms of popular culture
and high culture, which has led to difficulties in defining precisely
what these different forms of culture actually refer to. For example,
in the late 1960s, the artist Andy Warhol collaborated with the rock
band the Velvet Underground, which itself included a classically
trained musician in John Cale and the more pop-orientated writing
of Lou Reed. The resulting product is difficult to classify in high or
popular culture terms.

Further, there has been a breakdown of old feelings and experiences of time and space. People are less located in one place. They
travel more and have wider experiences of other cultures. They can
see events as they are happening on live TV, as in the reports on the
bombing of Baghdad during the Gulf War, and find the products of
other societies for sale in local supermarkets and shops in a way that
would have been unthinkable only twenty years ago. Finally, there
are arguments that the grand narratives or ideas by which people led

Modernism

- 'aesthetic self-consciousness and reflexiveness'
- 'a rejection of narrative structure in favour of simultaneity and montage'
- 'an exploration of the paradoxical, ambiguous and uncertain open-ended nature of reality'
- 'a rejection of the notion of an integrated personality in favour of an emphasis upon the destructured, dehumanized subject'

Postmodernism

- 'the effacement of the boundary between art and everyday life'
- 'the collapse of the hierarchical distinction between high and mass/popular culture'
- 'a stylistic promiscuity favouring eclecticism and the mixing of codes'
- 'parody, pastiche, irony, playfulness and the celebration of the surface "depthlessness" of culture'
- 'the decline of the originality/genius of the artistic producer and the assumption that art can only be repetitious'

Figure 4.4   Comparison of modernism with postmodernism
Source: derived from Featherstone (1988)

their lives have increasingly broken down. For example, Marxism, the official ideology of state communist societies, or a form of socialist ideology in the West, has collapsed, and alternative religions compete with more established or state-recognized ones. Some commentators maintain, therefore, that there has been a distinct shift in values in contemporary societies.

The discussion of postmodernism so far has been rather general, in that it is held to be a concept which applies across a range of developments in society, culture and philosophy. The term is also used in a more specific sense, to examine the nature of artistic change. Some writers have suggested that postmodernism is an explicit break from those forms of culture grouped under the heading of modernism which have been so influential in the arts during the twentieth century. Examples of modernism would be the paintings of Picasso and the novels of James Joyce. Some of the specific differences between modernism and postmodernism in the arts are summarized in figure 4.4, which complements the general account of Strinati. Through this discussion, Featherstone (1988) illuminates clear differences between modernism and postmodernism. Postmodernism is more playful than the serious modernism, it uses popular culture forms and is unafraid of suggesting that the artist is not a genius. Modernism tended to foreground the importance of the author and to separate high and popular culture.

There are difficulties with these general characterizations in that they often blur the specific development of particular forms of art and the differences between them. Thus it may be that postmodernism in the novel is rather different from postmodernism in painting, or that modernism in the novel developed at a different time from modernism in architecture. However, it has been suggested that postmodernism has now become a 'cultural dominant' (Jameson 1991). If this is the case, it would affect popular music. Thus, it has been suggested by some analysts that the breaking of the boundaries between previously separated genres of popular music evidences the development of postmodernism. Likewise, the break with the narrative of the conventional song in forms of hip-hop and rave music could be argued to be postmodern. A related case has been made for the interconnection of music and image in contemporary music video which some have seen as a postmodern form.

The important point to consider at the moment is the extent to which the seemingly increasing fragmentation and interconnection of pop and rock musics in the 1980s and 1990s is an example of postmodernism, which can therefore be connected to other developments in different cultural and social areas (such as the post-Fordism discussed in chapter 2). There is a certain amount of dispute around this issue and this can be followed up in the work of such as Stratton (1989), Redhead (1990) and Goodwin (1991). We shall return to some of issues involved in the case study of Madonna at the end of this chapter. However, it is important to note that the debate on the nature and relevance of the concept of postmodernism has tended to take place at a high level of generality. Moreover, examples from different areas of culture are used as examples of postmodernism. The danger is that broad cultural changes are identified and examples then found to fit the overall characterizations. Furthermore, the focus on modernism and postmodernism obscures the continued importance of realism in popular culture in general and popular music in particular. The relations between these textual forms are considered at greater length in chapter 5. However, the potential benefits of a concept like postmodernism are that it illustrates the linkages and parallels between different areas of culture, which may be influencing each other, and facilitates the identification of overall trends in society and culture, showing in broad outline how society is changing.

The debate around postmodernism has often raised issues of politics. In some accounts the playful, anything goes, tendency within postmodernism is conservative, or deflects attention away from opposition to dominant groups through the celebration of individual actions. This raises more general issues of the connections between popular music and political intervention.

Pop and politics

Pop music has been seen as an important social force in many different ways. In this section attention is drawn to the connections between pop and politics along two different dimensions. First, there is the way in which pop or rock is seen as in some way oppositional to established values in the broadest sense. Second, there are the interconnections between rock and politics, as understood in a more conventional way, as concerning political parties, the government, the state and so on.

As has been discussed above, the development of rock 'n' roll in the 1950s is often presented as a kind of liberation from the dullness of American and British life of the period. It is seen to have opened up new possibilities for self-expression and to have broken down the conventions and stuffiness of everyday life. Rock was vibrant and something that authority did not like. In this account there is something inherently oppositional about rock. In the 1960s ideas about the oppositional status of rock were entailed in its characterization as the music of protest, the 'movement' or the underground. A clear version of this argument has been expressed by Bradley (1992), who argues that rock music is a 'collective, collectivizing, communal phenomenon' (p. 118). Rock is produced in a communal fashion, in groups and bands for example, and is consumed communally at concerts, in clubs and so on. For Bradley (p. 96), it was primarily the music of youth and:

> youth culture involves a resistance to atomization and massification, and to the boredom, the loneliness, the fear and the experiential vicariousness they produce. The unique position of post-war teen- agers, physically adult yet excluded from adult roles and respons- ibilities, with considerable disposable cash, and familiar from early childhood with the products of the modern mass media, healthy, well-fed and energetic, yet involved in less hard physical work than many of their ancestors – this privileged, new position seemed merely

to throw into sharp relief for them the limitations, frustrations and oppressiveness of their existence in other respects, and to give them the opportunity to respond in new ways to these conditions. Music-use became one of the main chosen instruments of their response.

In Bradley's account, rock music, therefore, is resistant. In its connections to youth culture, it resists and relates to feelings, about the family, school and the media. Further, it is connected to issues of boredom and the attempt to overcome the mundane nature of society. Rock also resists the atomization or individuation of contemporary life in its construction of communities, which are often to exclude the adult world. All in all, in Bradley's phrase, rock involves a 'resistant communality' (p. 131). Other aspects of the relation between rock and youth groups will be discussed in chapters 7 and 8.

This sort of stance concerning the oppositional character of rock developed rapidly during the 1960s. However, the decline of some of the ideals of that period and the sorts of activities of rock stars which led them to be perceived as a part of a capitalist commercial activity threw the idea into crisis. In lots of ways, punk was built on that crisis and attempted to renew the idea that rock was an active political force. This occurred specifically through the activities of organizations like Rock against Racism in the late 1970s (Widgery 1986; Frith and Street 1992) and in a broad sense through the opposition of some of the new groups to the established record industry by the ethic of do-it-yourself which punk spawned. These raised expectations about the inherent oppositional nature of rock have often somewhat paradoxically given rise to some of its strongest criticisms. Authors who believed strongly in rock's oppositional stance, become disillusioned and then point to the role of the rock industry in the corruption of the original ideal. Thus, much rock criticism sees innovation and opposition as being bought off by big record companies and their agents. The writing on punk was no different as the extract from Burchill and Parsons (1978) in box 12 shows.

The problem with this sort of approach is that it is difficult now, and indeed it may always have been difficult, to suggest that rock or pop was ever outside of the structures of the record industry and capitalism. If the arguments of Negus (1992) that the record industry is a web of connections between the small and the large, which were examined in chapter 2, are taken seriously, it is difficult to see where the pure spaces for creation outside the context of commercial

Box 12   The plastic nature of punk

ASHES

You, kid! Come here . . .
    You wanna 'Capital Radio' EP?
You wanna black bag EMI 'Anarchy'? You wanna A & M 'God Save The Queen'? You wanna French 12-inch 'Anarchy'? You wanna 'Anarchy In The USA' bootleg? You wanna collect butterflies?
    Very fulfilling, collecting things . . . very satisfying. Keep you satisfied, make you sated, make you fat and old and cold, queueing for the rock and roll show.
    In 1978 every record company is waking up to find a somewhat superfluous punk combo on its doorstep. Supply and demand? But you can't supply something that there's no demand for.
    Never mind, kid, there'll soon be another washing-machine/spotcream/rock-band on the market to solve all your problems and keep you quiet/off the street/distracted from the real enemy/content till the next pay-day.
    Anyhow, God Save Rock And Roll . . . it made you a Consumer, a potential Moron . . .
    IT'S ONLY ROCK AND ROLL AND IT'S PLASTIC, PLASTIC, YES IT IS!!!!!!

Source: Burchill and Parsons (1978:96). From *The Boy looked at Johnny*, Pluto Press

relations exist. Further, the debate around postmodernism, discussed above, which argues that the boundaries between art and commerce are increasingly breaking down, also suggests that commercial relationships are unavoidable, but this does not necessarily make musical products corrupt, inauthentic or valueless.

There is another version of rock and the record industry which suggests that it was always a capitalist con-trick or part of an industrialized society anyway. Some of these sorts of general account have also been considered in chapter 1, where some problems with them have been identified. It is important to point out again that the examination of the politics of rock need to take place in a more specific context where the assertions are of a less general nature.

Grossberg (1983) has carried out an investigation of this kind. Building on a framework developed by Raymond Williams (1973), he argues that rock can produce three types of boundary between its followers and dominant culture: oppositional, alternative and independent (he also identifies the way in which rock can be co-opted, which he examines at greater length in his book *We Gotta Get Out of This Place* (Grossberg 1992a). He defines these boundaries in the following way; 'Oppositional rock and roll presents itself as a direct challenge or threat to the dominant culture', whereas alternative rock 'mounts only an implicit attack on the dominant culture'. 'Independent rock and roll does not present itself as a challenge, either explicitly or implicitly, to the dominant culture although it may function as such' (Grossberg 1983:110). Grossberg shows that there are crucial differences between different forms of rock with regard to their critical potential. This leads into the second part of this discussion of pop and politics.

The direct connection of rock with politics in the case of Rock against Racism in the late 1970s has already been mentioned. In the sixties rock was often seen as the music of protest continuing those 'folk' forms which had been connected with the working class, often by middle-class intellectual members of revolutionary political parties (Harker 1980). There have been various other direct connections between pop music and political activism, for example the free festival movement in the seventies (M. Clarke 1982) which continues in the struggles around the festivals and activities of so-called new-age travellers in the nineties. Groups on the right have also connected their politics to rock music. In the late 1970s the fascist right in Britain founded a group known as Rock against Communism and the Oi Skinhead Rock of the early 1980s is also often related to fascist activity. Rock and pop have been connected in rather different ways to politics in the 1980s and 1990s through a number of charitable concerts such as Live Aid in 1985 and in more direct ways around the Nelson Mandela concerts in London.

Garofalo (1992b:26–35) discusses four potential functions that such events may have: fundraising, consciousness raising, artist activism and agitation. According to Garofalo, Live Aid in 1985 raised $67 million. Such events might raise the consciousness of the public about issues and political figures such as Nelson Mandela. Furthermore, they could deepen artist involvement in politics and contribute, perhaps indirectly, to political change.

In discussing such events, it is important to consider the issues and outcomes in a specific way. This has been done in other accounts of rock and politics, and some of the most interesting connections drawn in the context of events in Eastern Europe in the late 1980s.

Recent work by Wicke opens up the issues in a clear manner (see also on this topic and the politics of rock more generally, Street 1986). Wicke (1992a, though see also, for example, Wicke 1992b and Wicke and Shepherd 1993) suggests that rock music played a significant role in the disintegration of East Germany in 1989. During

September of that year musicians issued a statement which argued, from a leftist position, for greater democracy in East Germany. This had been prompted by the exodus of young people to the West via Hungary which had been going on through 1989, and which the East German authorities had tried to conceal, though the information was freely available from the Western media. The musicians' statement was read out at numerous state-sponsored performances held to celebrate the fortieth anniversary of the foundation of the German Democratic Republic on 7 October 1989. The attempts to prevent this by the State Security forces led to conflict with audiences which continued after that date.

The fact that rock music could have such effects was based on three preconditions. First, East Germany's rock musicians had been organized by the state under the Committee for Entertainment Arts. This represented an attempt 'to render the musicians susceptible to forms of state-imposed discipline' (Wicke 1992a:201). Second, the performances of the musicians provided a clear space for debates on political ideas, not least because other media were closed to such discussion. Third, the authorities interpreted lyrics in political terms, 'finding nearly every lyric to be politically disruptive' (Wicke 1992a:201). Audiences interpreted songs in this way as well, finding their own politically disruptive messages in them. Through these processes, rock music had become politicized by the state, the performers and the audiences.

Wicke argues that the state had been worried about the potential for opposition expressed by rock music since the middle of the 1960s, at first trying to argue that it had no place in a socialist society. This strategy was altered in the early 1970s to one which tried to incorporate rock music under the umbrella of state organization. However, this proved very difficult to sustain and by the mid-1970s the state was forced into a number of public struggles with rock musicians. By the late 1980s the state was attempting to split the musicians between the younger and older elements, in a strategy of 'divide and rule'. Thus, the state's own attempts to incorporate rock, to neutralize the threat that it was perceived to pose to the state, had actually led to the further politicization of the music, and indeed provided mechanisms for the expression of opposition from within state umbrella organizations themselves. Furthermore, once the state had fallen, the way was open to the influx of Western bands which has eliminated the indigenous rock music scene, showing the linkages between this form of rock and the state itself. In Wicke's words:

But just as East German rock music was born and lived as an oppositional cultural and political force during Honecker's years in power, it is now in the process of dying with him. With the fall of the Berlin Wall has come a radical change in the music scene in the former communist territory. Having achieved their revolutionary cultural and political goals, German musicians from the East have for the most part been quickly (and sadly) forgotten in the flood of commercial popular culture that has swept in from the West. (1992a:206)

Pekacz (1994) has argued that accounts such as Wicke's have overestimated the role of rock music in political change in Eastern Europe and the extent to which it opposed the established regimes. She argues that, in fact, the government in such societies was much less monolithic and doctrinaire than is suggested by Wicke, and that rock music entered into a number of everyday accommodations with it. Below the level of state rhetoric, rock musicians and state functionaries often shared common frames of reference. In sum, Wicke, in this view, romanticizes the oppositional role of rock partly by overemphasizing the unity of the structures it confronted. This is rather similar to those 1960s accounts of the oppositional status of rock which saw it as fighting an all-pervasive 'system'.

To evaluate the political significance of rock it is important to consider the way in which the different forms of music operate within specific constellations of political forces. The conclusion then is that it is difficult to have, or develop, a *general* account or theory of the political nature of rock music. This reinforces the critical comments on general accounts of rock discussed in chapter 1. Such accounts are further complicated when the relations between rock, gender and sexuality are considered.

Rock, gender and sexuality

It has been suggested earlier that the more conventional accounts of the development of rock point to its initial power and resistance (in rock 'n' roll) which was transformed as the music industry moved in (producing rock and roll). Further, there was a clear barrier built between rock and pop at a later date. It has been suggested that these accounts reflect hierarchies of gender in popular music and society. The most influential case for this interpretation has been made by Frith and McRobbie (1990).

Frith and McRobbie's initial suggestion is that rock music cannot be analysed as either simply a product of the culture industry, and hence as a commodity which acts ideologically to incorporate its consumers, or in its subcultural consumption by different audience groups. Frith and McRobbie argue that rock's meanings, especially in the construction and representation of sexuality, are more complex than these rather general accounts allow.

Frith and McRobbie further suggest that male domination of the music industry leads to representations of masculinity in contemporary pop music. They identify two main types of pop music which they label 'cock rock' and 'teenybop'. Cock rock is 'music-making in which performance is an explicit, crude and often aggressive expression of male sexuality', its 'performers are aggressive, dominating, and boastful, and they constantly seek to remind the audience of their prowess, their control', the 'image is the rampant male traveller, smashing hotels and groupies alike. Musically, such rock takes off from the sexual frankness of rhythm and blues but adds a cruder male physicality (hardness, control, virtuosity)' (p. 374).

Teenybop, according to Frith and McRobbie, is consumed mainly by girls, whose teenybop idol's 'image is based on self-pity, vulnerability, and need'. This finds a different form of musical expression from cock rock. They argue that:

> In teenybop, male sexuality is transformed into a spiritual yearning carrying only hints of sexual interaction. What is needed is not so much someone to screw as a sensitive and sympathetic soulmate, someone to support and nourish the incompetent male adolescent as he grows up. (p. 375)

There are artists who seem to fit fairly clearly into these categories (many heavy metal groups have been seen as examples of cock rock and singers such as Jason Donovan as teenyboppers), though Frith and McRobbie point out that there can be important crossovers between the two. Frith and McRobbie argue that these textual and performance types connect to different audiences. Boys, as the consumers of cock rock, are active. They attempt to follow guitar-playing idols into the music industry and attendance at the cock rock concert is active. Furthermore, suggest Frith and McRobbie, this attendance is collective. Boys are in and form groups. The female fans of the teenybopper are, by contrast, relatively passive and individual. They consume as individuals. Their aims as performers are to be singers, or else face the kind of exaggeration of aggression associated with such musicians as Janis Joplin, with the attendant dangers of self-destruction. In addition, Frith and McRobbie suggest that teenybop idols can be used in different ways by the girl audiences as a form of collective appropriation and resistance to school norms, and aspects of this will be considered at later points in this book.

In Frith and McRobbie's view the conventional narratives of the decline of rock 'n' roll are actually accounts of its feminization (p. 383). Furthermore, they begin a process of attempting to look beyond the lyrics of a song to investigate its gendered meaning in musical terms. The vehicle for this is a comparison of Tammy Wynette's 'Stand by Your Man' with Helen Reddy's 'I Am Woman', which values Wynette over Reddy:

> The lyrics of 'Stand by Your Man' celebrate women's duty to men, implore women to enjoy subordinating themselves to men's needs – lyrically the song is a ballad of sexual submissiveness. But the female authority of Tammy Wynette's voice involves a knowledge of the world that is in clear contrast to the gooey idealism of Helen Reddy's sound. 'Sometimes it's hard to be a woman,' Tammy Wynette begins, and you can hear that Tammy Wynette knows why – her voice is a collective one. 'I am woman,' sings Helen Reddy, and what you hear is the voice of an idealized consumer, even if the commodity for consumption in this instance is a package version of women's liberation. (p. 385)

In this article, Frith and McRobbie address a number of important themes. These include:

1 their idea that it is important to go beyond a focus on the rock industry or the consumption of rock;
2 their characterization of the music industry as male dominated;
3 the characterization of the different forms of masculinity entailed in 'cock rock' and 'teenybop';
4 the interconnections between these textual and performance forms and audiences;
5 the attempt to move beyond lyrics in the characterization of the worth of songs;
6 the argument regarding the feminization of rock 'n' roll.

In a subsequent critique of this piece, Frith (1990) suggests that in 'a jumble of good and bad arguments', there was a confusion of 'issues of sex and issues of gender'. Sex was somehow seen as an essence, rather than something which, like gender, was subject to forms of construction. This argument rejects the idea that there is a core to sex, which was simply expressed in music. Music plays a significant part in the construction of gender and sexuality. However, Frith suggests that 'the most misleading of our original arguments was the distinction between male activity and female passivity when, in fact, consumption is as important to the sexual significance of pop as production' (Frith 1990:422). The original article tended to emphasize the ways in which music was produced at the expense of its consumption. This is an important theme. The first chapter of this book has suggested that it is as important to examine audience appropriations of texts as their production, and this is discussed at length in chapters 7 and 8.

Another problem with Frith and McRobbie's argument is that it was written before the developments in pop music during the eighties and nineties, and in the next section I want to examine some of these through a brief discussion of the most discussed pop figure of the period: Madonna.

Madonna: pop, politics, gender and sexuality

The Madonna phenomenon raises issues in the three areas which have been discussed in this chapter: the distinction between rock and pop; the politics of pop music and its connections with power; and gender and sexuality. These three areas will be considered in turn (for extended examination of Madonna, see, for example, Schwichtenberg (ed.) 1993, which contains a number of important papers which contribute to the discussion here).

First, there is the relationship between rock and pop. Early interpretations and accounts of Madonna tended to focus on her implication in the pop industry. She was seen as an inauthentic product of the culture industry who was involved in the exploitation of others for the gain of that industry. Madonna was sometimes contrasted with another popular woman singer of the early and mid-1980s, namely Cyndi Lauper, whose work was seen to be more thoughtful and authentic. However, as time has passed these debates have been reconstituted. Partly in connection with the increased salience in popular culture of the debates around postmodernism, there has been a heightened recognition of the problems of the definition of authenticity, and what this can mean in an increasingly commercialized, commodified, and media-saturated society. Hence, while Madonna seemed to have started from what would normally be seen as pop beginnings her work, in some accounts, has been at the forefront of the breaking down of this particular barrier. Further, this could be seen as breaking the divisions between art and commerce in a way consistent with the development of postmodernism. However, Madonna has sometimes asserted her own rights and authenticity as an individual artist. An example of this occurs in *In Bed with Madonna* when she argues against the censorship of her show on the grounds of artistic freedom, using a notion of individual authenticity close to that expressed by rock artists (and expressed by the jazz musicians studied by Becker), which itself derives from earlier conceptions of the nature of the artist. However, an alternative interpretation would stress that this is in itself a kind of pose for particular purposes, which has little to do with what Madonna really is, even if there is any point in exploring such an issue.

Second, there is the issue of politics. If Madonna can be seen by some as transcending debates about authenticity, she also connects to new ideas about a form of politics based in ideas of play, the 'freeing' and reconstitution of identity, again in ways connected to the advocates of postmodernism. In an introductory discussion, Hall (1992) distinguishes three concepts of identity: 'Enlightenment', 'sociological' and 'postmodern'. The Enlightenment concept rested on notions of there being an essential core to identity which was born with the individual and unfolded through his or her life. The sociological concept argued that a coherent identity is formed in relations with others and thus develops and changes over time. The postmodern subject is thought to have no fixed or essential identity. In postmodern societies identities have become 'dislocated'.

It can be suggested that earlier forms of politics could be related to the search for new forms of identity as the oppressed or dominated threw off those forms which implicated them in the operation of power. These forms of identity could be seen to be relatively stable and to enable the new identity to be expressed in new oppositional forms. In such accounts, one identity which colluded with oppression was replaced by a new one that opposed the dominant order. Thus, the standardized identity of the pop consumer as characterized by Adorno, might be replaced with the more sophisticated identity of the follower of serious music, who would recognize the way in which the culture industry used pop music to reproduce inequalities. This sort of politics can be seen to rest on a sociological concept of identity, where the subject can be changed, or switched over, as social conditions change.

Some more recent forms of politics, however, suggest that the stability of such identities is problematic in that they freeze the fluidity of contemporary identities and indeed often involve the privileging of one construction of identity over another. Thus, talking of a working-class identity might neglect the different identities of black and white workers, and, for example, subsume the black identity in the white one. Similar arguments have been made against forms of feminism which do not take account of the different identities of black and white women. In some recent forms of politics, there is a celebration of the idea that there is not a true or real identity but a multiplicity of identities which operate in different circumstances. In these respects Madonna has, it is argued, caught the notion that there is no real identity, no authentic way of being, and has become involved in the play of masks and surfaces, rather than in a search for the truth and the underlying reality.

Third, in relation to gender and sexuality, Madonna is held to have exhibited a form of play with gender roles which overcomes the privileging of one form of gender as that to be emulated and which represents a form of freedom from straitjackets. Furthermore, the sense that she is in control of her own destiny and image has projected the idea of her being a strong woman who is generally in control, rather than someone who is manipulated by the men who dominate the pop music industry. In terms of sexuality, Madonna has connected to forms of culture and politics which value the transgression of established sexual norms concerning violence and pornography. It is argued that her videos and books like *Sex* bring forms of sexual representation, which had been hidden, into the mainstream. This process makes visible forms of sexuality which had been hidden away, or denigrated by the mainstream culture. This may lead to greater tolerance of those who engage in what have been described as 'perverted' practices.

Furthermore, there has been consideration of the way in which Madonna is a hero to younger generations of women (the 'wanna bees') who are tired of the older forms of politics and of the sterility of their everyday lives. However, there are also members of the audience who reject these ideas which value Madonna. As Schulze, Barton White and Brown (1993) found in their audience study, there are those who hate Madonna for a variety of reasons. In their descriptions of the views of Madonna haters, these authors point to four critical accounts of Madonna: as the lowest form of culture, as 'the lowest form of irresponsible culture, a social disease'; 'the lowest form of the feminine'; and, 'as the antithesis of feminism'. They also suggest that these readers of Madonna feel that they are going against the dominant ideas of Madonna as a 'good thing': they are, in the phrase of Schulze et al., 'resistive readers'.

This debate about the worth of Madonna and her connections to postmodernism has carried through into more academic debate, where for example the merits of boundary breaking, transgression and play have been much debated, often in relation to gender and race. This debate throws into sharp relief many of the issues examined in this chapter. First, the distinction between rock and pop has often entailed judgements of value, and assumptions about gender. For example, the valuation of rock has often involved the privileging of masculinity. Second, general arguments about the relation between pop and politics need revision, if the ideas associated with postmodernism are taken seriously, as more needs to be made of the specific contexts in which political practices occur. Arguments about politics need to be considered with respect to particular cases, as the extended discussion of the East German situation in the 1980s showed. Third, while the approach pioneered by Frith and McRobbie is still illuminating in certain respects, contemporary gender relations and feminine identities are far more complex (McRobbie 1993). Issues of gender and sexuality need discussion in a way which recognizes such complexity.

Summary

This chapter has considered:

- the development and meaning of various types of popular music, pointing to the location of the beginnings of rock and roll in a complex social context, and how the consideration of the contemporary trajectory of popular music involves examination of the debates about postmodernism;
- discussions of the distinction between rock and pop and some of the implications of this;
- the politics of rock music in general and specific senses, raising issues of the extent to which pop music opposes a dominant culture and the connections of rock with the state;
- the interconnections between gender, sexuality and pop music, using early work by Frith and McRobbie to provide a springboard for debate;
- the Madonna phenomenon in terms of the issues raised by the chapter.

5

Black Music

This chapter develops some of the themes introduced in chapter 4, as ascriptions of value and claims about authenticity have run through debates about the implications and wider resonances of black music. The chapter opens with a discussion of the important issue of how 'black music' is actually defined. This is important in itself as it raises concerns about the extent to which an 'essence' of black music can be defined in musical or sociological terms. Furthermore, it introduces issues concerning the political implications of black music, and the ascription of the label of 'black'. This is followed by an examination of the development of blues and soul which is used to point to some important sociological dimensions of the evolution of these forms. The discussion of the reggae tradition which follows elaborates on these themes, in a way which connects the discussion to the debates about modernism and postmodernism introduced in chapter 4. The implication of this section of the chapter is that the development of specific forms of reggae can be understood through the utilization of ideal types of textual forms, which are themselves to be understood in social context. This theme is followed through into a discussion of rap and hip-hop culture, which reviews some of the debates about this form, which have centred on ideas of resistance, racial segregation and gender.

Defining black music

The concept of 'black music' has sometimes been used in an unreflective way, where it is assumed that it is the music performed by black people. However, there are several questions to be posed to such a view. First, would a black musician performing a song by Lennon and McCartney count as black music? Or a black opera singer performing a piece from the European classical tradition? (Oliver 1990) Second, how is a black person actually defined and recognized? In some accounts of black music there is a danger of running into stereotypes of natural racial difference. From such an angle, black people are held to have natural abilities in music-making or dancing and so on. However, as Oliver explains:

> To follow this argument through one has to confront the problem of genetic admixture through intermarriage and cross-fertility between races. The outcome of miscegenation between people of different racial stocks over generations inevitably leads to the diminution of some genetic traits and the dominance of others. They're expressed most visibly and physically in, for instance lightening of skin hue, or differences in hair section and hence, changes in hair growth. If abilities *are* genetically related, the diminution or dominance of some would also seem to be the inevitable result of such racial cross-breeding, but the vast literature on race does not bear this out. Nor does common experience: in the jazz field, for instance, dark-skinned Louis Armstrong, Bessie Smith or Charlie Parker are not rated as being the musical superiors (or inferiors, for that matter) of light-hued Jelly-Roll Morton, Billie Holiday or Lester Young; at least, not on account of the presumed 'blackness' of their genes.

Furthermore, as Hatch and Millward (1987:117) have argued, blackness varied according to legal definition between different states in the United States:

> Legally speaking, the definition as to what constituted a black person varied from state to state under the 'Jim Crow' laws. In Alabama, Arkansas, and Mississippi, anyone with a 'visible' and/or 'appreciable' degree of 'Negro blood' was subject to segregational laws as a black person whereas in Indiana and Louisiana the colour line was drawn at one-eighth and one-sixteenth negro blood respectively. Clearly, then, it was possible to change one's status – and therefore legal rights – by moving from one state to another.

On the basis of the argument advanced by Oliver and Hatch and Millward, it is difficult to maintain that there is a genetic, or bio-logical base to 'black music' which marks it off from other forms. A similar point has been made by Tagg (1989) who also suggests that it is difficult to find common features in what has conventionally been classed as black music. He argues (p. 288) that four musical characteristics are often used to define 'blackness': 'blue notes', 'call-and-response techniques', 'syncopation' and 'improvisation'. Tagg maintains that none of these characteristics can be used to identify a discrete category of black music, and argues that the term black music should not be used. He concludes (p. 295) by noting that his:

> scepticism towards the supposed pair of opposites 'black' or 'Afro-American music' versus 'European music' has two main grounds: (1) musicological because no satisfactory definitions of any terms are provided and (2) ideological. The latter is particularly important because not only does the implied dichotomy pre-ordain certain sets of feeling and behaviour for one race and deny them to the other, it also turns the overriding question of class into a matter of race or ethnicity.

Tagg argues for a position which can be seen as 'anti-essentialist' (Gilroy 1993) in that he rejects the idea that there is an essence to black music. Despite such criticisms, some writers have continued to argue that the concept of black music has some importance. According to Hatch and Millward (1987) the music made by black people is related to their oppression in the United States, and they point out that these oppressions and inequalities are often cut across by class, locality and so on. They argue for a pluralistic account of pop music, which rejects the idea that some forms are more authentically black than others. This allows that study of the complexity of the relations between different textual forms of music and the inputs into them without prior suggestions that one is more 'true' or authentic than another. Thus, on Hatch and Millward's account, 'pop music has always depended upon the interaction between white and black traditions' (p. 120), and they show the importance of such in the development of forms like the blues. Hatch and Millward do not take this position to reduce the importance of black musicians to the development of pop music: something which they want to recognize. However, they suggest that there is no need to oversimplify and consider one form of music to be authentically black.

Oliver (1990) also uses a pluralistic notion to form the basis for the investigations which make up his edited collection of articles on *Black Music in Britain*. He argues that:

> 'black music' is that which is recognized and accepted as such by its creators, performers and hearers . . . encompassing the music of those

who see themselves as black, and whose musics have unifying characteristics which justify their recognition as specific genres: peculiar
patterns of 'sonic order' in John Blacking's phrase. (p. 8)

In this sort of view, black music is that which is socially defined as
such. This is a form of sociological approach which emphasizes the
actor's own point of view, rather than adopting some 'objective'
standard of judgement. However, there are problems with such an
account, as there may be different or competing definitions of what
black music is. Thus, the current music of Michael Jackson might
be seen as black by some and not by others. However, it may also
be argued that in sociological terms such disagreements over 'blackness' are relatively fruitless as they will run into the sorts of difficulty
already outlined above. More important, it may be suggested, is an
examination of the complex roots of Jackson's music and how it is
produced and consumed in particular ways. This is not to say that
the attribution of blackness has no effect. However, this is most
important in the discussion of how particular forms of music articu-
late and connect to political issues.

It can also be suggested, therefore, that context and political meaning are important in the discussion of 'black' music, and that some
of the more relativistic arguments might tend to neglect this. Consider, for example, the account of attending *Porgy and Bess* by Maya
Angelou (1985) reproduced in box 13. Here, a clear expression of
the pleasure in a 'black' performance can be seen, in a way which
conveys Angelou's eyes being opened up, with the implication that
a form of commitment to black culture and expression may develop
from it.

The discussion so far has the following implications. First, that it
is difficult to sustain the idea that black music is based in biological
factors. Second, that in the development of many forms of popular
music, the interaction between black and white has been crucial.
Third, that this does not necessarily denigrate or undervalue the
contribution of black people to popular music. As Hatch and
Millward (1987:116) argue, 'those designated as black have made
the major contribution to the development of pop music from its
earliest origins'. Fourth, that some, more relativist, writers have
concluded that the term black music should not be used as it tends
to imply the existence of a black musical or racial essence. Fifth,
sociological investigation into the development of those forms which
have been designated as black needs to examine the complex social
contexts and locations which have led to the development of such

Box 13   Maya Angelou at *Porgy and Bess*

IF *New Faces of 1953* excited the pulses of San Franciscans, *Porgy and Bess* set their hearts afire. Reviewers and columnists raved about Leontyne Price and William Warfield in the title roles and praised the entire company. The troupe had already successfully toured other parts of the United States, Europe and South America . . .

I went to the theater ready to be entertained, but not expecting a riot of emotion. Price and Warfield sang; they threaded their voices with music and spellbound the audience with their wizardry. Even the chorus performed with such verve that a viewer could easily believe each singer was competing for a leading part.

By intermission I had been totally consumed. I had laughed and cried, exulted and mourned, and expected the second act to produce no new emotions. I returned to my seat prepared for a repetition of great music.

The curtain rose on a picnic in progress. The revelers were church members led by a pious old woman who forbade dancing, drinking and even laughing. Cab Calloway as Sportin' Life pranced out in cream-colored suit and tried to paganize the Christians.

He sang 'It Ain't Necessarily So,' strutting as if he was speaking *ex cathedra*.

The audience applauded loudly, interrupting the stage action. Then a young woman broke away from a group of singers near the wings. She raced to the center of the stage and began to dance.

The sopranos sang a contrapuntal high-toned encouragement and baritones urged the young woman on. The old lady tried to catch her, to stop the idolatrous dance, but the dancer moved out of her reach, flinging her legs high, carrying the music in her body as if it were a private thing, given into her care and protection. I nearly screamed with delight and envy. I wanted to be with her on the stage letting the music fly through my body. Her torso seemed to lose solidity and float, defying gravity. I wanted to be with her. No, I wanted to *be* her.

In the second act, Warfield, as the crippled Porgy, dragged the audience into despair. Even kneeling, he was a large man, broad and thick-chested. His physical size made his affliction and his loss of Bess even sadder. The resonant voice straddled the music and rode it, controlling it.

I remained in my seat after the curtain fell and allowed people to climb over my knees to reach the aisle. I was stunned. *Porgy and Bess* had shown me the greatest array of Negro talent I had ever seen.

Source: Angelou (1985:126–7). Copyright © Maya Angelou 1976. Published by Virago Press 1985

- ■ 'a critique of productivism: work, the labour process and the division of labour under capitalism'
- ■ 'a critique of the state revolving around a plea for the disassociation of law from domination, which denounces state brutality, militarism and exterminism'
- ■ 'A passionate belief in the importance of history and the historical process. This is presented as an antidote to the suppression of historical and temporal perception under late capitalism'

Figure 5.1   Core anti-capitalist themes in black expressive culture
Source: Gilroy (1987:199)

forms. Sixth, that such investigation will often lead to consideration of the political meaning and roles of such forms, in both the general and specific variants identified in chapter 4. In a seeming paradox, this may lead to the reassertion of the importance of the ascription of the label of black music. One of the strongest arguments along these lines has been made by Paul Gilroy (1987, 1993).

Gilroy suggests that many discussions of black music play down its political importance and he argues that 'There are three core themes around which the anti-capitalist aspects of black expressive culture have been articulated' (1987:199). These are detailed in figure 5.1.

He further suggests that there is a core to black culture, and argues for an approach called 'anti-anti-essentialism' (1993:102), which recognizes that a biological or natural core to black culture and black music cannot be found, but which argues against attempts to suggest that, because of this, it is impossible to use a category of black culture. Such black culture is based in social practices and social definitions, though the process of call and response is seen as central to the structure of black music by Gilroy (p. 78). It can be argued then that the identification of categories of black culture and black music is intimately connected to a range of social and political issues.

Further to examine these issues, and those concerning the ascription of cultural value and authenticity, this chapter traces the development and meanings of blues and soul in the United States; the rise of ska and reggae in Jamaica; and the implications of rap and hip-hop culture. This will involve the elaboration of the discussion of modernism and postmodernism introduced in chapter 4.

The focus of this chapter is on Afro-American and Afro-Caribbean musics. It is important to note that there are many other forms of black music, which have been relatively neglected in the sociological study of pop music or implicitly not recognized to be 'black'. An important exception to this trend is the collection edited by Oliver (1990) where the contemporary development of styles like bhangra is considered (Banerji and Baumann 1990). However, this does not overcome the fact that writing on black music, often by white people, has implicitly constructed a black tradition around particular styles while excluding others. This has been highlighted by the contemporary success of performers like Apache Indian, whose work foregrounds interconnections between different ethnic groups. Some have argued that rap and hip-hop music facilitates such developments, as will be examined later in the chapter.

Blues and soul

In chapter 4 it was noted how rock 'n' roll developed in part from r 'n' b. Following Gillett (1983), five forms of r 'n' b can be identified in the post-Second World War period. These were:

1 dancehall blues
2 club blues
3 bar blues
4 gospel
5 group sounds

Gillett's distinctions illuminate the diversity of r 'n' b, which encompassed a variety of different types of music, and the connections between these forms and particular social contexts. Gillett suggests that there are a number of musical characteristics of the blues or r 'n' b. First, all the forms of r 'n' b had a dance rhythm, which distinguished the form from post-war jazz 'which was rarely recorded as dance music and which could therefore dispense with the convention of maintaining a particular beat throughout a song' (pp. 122–3). Second, Gillett suggests that:

> In rhythm and blues, the soloists were generally more 'selfish', concerned to express their own feelings, depending on the rest of the band to keep the beat going and the volume up while they blew their hearts out and their heads off. In jazz, there was usually more interplay

between musicians, more exploration into melody and harmony, less reliance on the emotional force of the musician's tone. (p. 123)

Third, in Gillett's view, the blues entailed the communication of character on the part of the performers.

Having thus identified the common features of r 'n' b Gillett examines the nature of the five categories in some detail. He identifies three subtypes of the dancehall blues: 'big band blues; shout, scream and cry blues; and combo blues' (p. 124).

The dancehall blues were, as the name suggests, performed for large audiences as a backdrop to dancing. The large dance bands often contained a main singer and a saxophonist, whose roles became more important with the passage of time. The 'jump combos' were particularly important in the development of rock 'n' roll leading to the popularity of performers like Bill Haley, Chuck Berry and Fats Domino. In Gillett's account, the jump or combo blues was an exuberant music, which 'served to express whatever confidence people felt on the West Coast during and after the war, the quieter club blues expressed the more dominant mood there, one tinged with despondency' (p. 142). One of the first to play in this style was Nat 'King' Cole.

The bar blues developed in the cities as rural blacks migrated. In particular much of what is familiar as the electrified blues which fed into rock 'n' roll in the 1950s, influencing rock music in the 1960s, was associated with the movement of black performers from the Mississippi Delta in the South to cities like Memphis in Tennessee and especially to Chicago. As Guralnick (1992:46) explains, 'the blues came out of Mississippi, sniffed around in Memphis and then settled in Chicago where it is most likely it will peacefully live out the rest of its days'. This Delta style was distinctive, as Palmer (1981:44) suggests:

> The Mississippi Delta's blues musicians sang with unmatched intensity in a gritty, melodically circumscribed, highly ornamented style that was closer to field hollers than it was to other blues. Guitar and piano accompaniments were percussive and hypnotic, and many Delta guitarists mastered the art of fretting the instrument with a slider or bottleneck; they made the instrument 'talk' in strikingly speechlike inflections.

The originators of the style tended to play and record for local audiences throughout the South, often living in a hand-to-mouth manner. They recorded their music for the local black market, though they were also recorded in a more anthropological way by 'field researchers' as representatives of a kind of 'folk music', which placed a particular connotation of 'authenticity' on music which was often commercial in its aims and context. The musicians entertained, and developed their skills, at parties and social gatherings on large Southern plantations.

The style originated with Charley Patton and was developed by such figures as Son House, Robert Johnson and perhaps most famously by Muddy Waters. Waters was born in 1915 in the Mississippi Delta, grew up in Clarksdale and played at fish fries for local audiences. He left the country to move north to Chicago in 1943. He recorded for a label called Aristocrat in the late 1940s which had been formed by the Chess brothers, who were immigrants from Poland. The label was subsequently renamed as Chess and in 1950 Muddy Waters had his first 'hit', which:

> meant you sold probably 60,000 copies in the race market and almost exclusively around Chicago, Gary, St. Louis, Memphis and the South. There was no distribution on the coast, there was no radio air play, and the money that was involved would certainly seem small by today's inflated standards. Even so it was enough to make Muddy Waters a star. (Guralnick 1992:69)

Waters continued to have hits through the 1950s, though his star waned as the fifties progressed. His work continued to influence white musicians and he was 'rediscovered' at many points subsequently. His career is important as it illustrates a number of social processes: first, the origination of a style in a particular local setting, though the style may have been developed out of commercially available recordings; second, the way in which the music was performed in social contexts for the local market; third, the movement of the music to a different, more urban, social setting; fourth, the recording of that music for the local market; fifth, the wider taking up of the music at various points by different international markets. These are common processes in the development of black music, and they will be further considered in the discussion of reggae below.

Gillett's characterization of the nature of the blues as a musical form was introduced above. Other writers have suggested that it is less easy to define its essence than might be thought. Thus Guralnick (1992:41) asks:

What is blues then? Well, it's a lot easier to keep on saying what blues is not. It isn't necessarily sad music. It doesn't tell a story. It neither makes nor alludes to minor chords. It is for the most part self-accompanied. It follows certain basis progressions (I–IV–V–IV–I or tonic, subdominant, dominant chord patterns). It is not a music of particular technical accomplishment. In the end you come back to the familiar conundrum; if you have to ask, well then you're just not going to understand. Because blues is little more than a feeling. And what could be more durable or more fleeting and ephemeral than just that?

These difficulties are also brought out by the more detailed discussion of the musical structure of the blues in the extract from Hatch and Millward (1987) reproduced in box 14.

The fourth and fifth forms of r 'n' b discussed by Gillett (gospel and group sounds) fed into the development of soul music during the 1960s. As Guralnick (1991:21) suggests, 'the story of soul music can be seen largely as the story of the introduction of the gospel strain into the secular world of rhythm and blues'. Soul was, in Guralnick's account, 'Southern by definition if not by actual geography' (p. 6) and centred in three main cities: Memphis in Tennessee, Macon in Georgia, and Muscle Shoals in Alabama (p. 8). A similar story can be told for soul as for the blues, with a movement from the local to the wider international market over a very short space of time, so that figures like Otis Redding, James Brown and Aretha Franklin became international stars whose work remains enduringly popular.

As with other forms there are a variety of different soul styles, though some commentators such as Guralnick (1991:7) have pointed to common features. He suggests that 'soul music is a music that keeps hinting at a conclusion, keeps straining at the boundaries – of melody and convention – that it has imposed upon itself'. However, of importance from Guralnick's account is the following:

The one other irreducible component of Southern soul music was its racial mix, and here, too, opinion remains divided about its precise significance. To some it is just one more variation on the old racist story: black workers, white owners. I have spoken earlier of my own confusion and my ultimate conviction that here was a partnership. But it was a partnership with a difference: the principals brought to it such divergent outlooks and experiences that even if they had grown up in the same little town, they were as widely separated as if there had been an ocean between them. And when they came together, it

Box 14 Blues as a musical type

AS a musical type the blues is not easy to describe. Traditionally, writers on the subject take the other, emotional, meaning of the term too seriously in attempts to delineate the genre. Yet for its fans the music is immediately recognizable, but via its structure rather than through its supposedly 'sorrowful' qualities. In fact, as a music the blues is no more sorrowful than, for instance, popular, art-music, hillbilly, or many 'folk' musics. Hillbilly music in particular, and especially the modern 'country and western' variety, has a far stronger tradition of overt expression of sad and sorrowful themes, in the manner of the 'tear-jerker'. Like most songs, blues reflects human life in general, though concentrating on the experiences relevant to the singer/composer and immediate audience. Blues songs are thus, not surprisingly, concerned with such topics as sexual relations, travelling, drinking, being broke, work and the lack of it, etc., etc. If there is one central emotional attitude typical of the music it is that of *irony*. And whether this represents a cathartic method for overcoming the 'blues', as many writers, including Southern (1983:331), claim, is mere psychological speculation. For the number of psychological states involved in blues singing may well be as many as there are performers. Some undoubtedly did it for the money, a normal motivation for professional entertainers. Still others quite obviously saw themselves as 'artists' with something important to give to the world (among these we would count at least Skip James, Robert Johnson and Muddy Waters).

The ironic qualities of the music have always been enhanced by the prevailing musical structure of the blues: though this has very often been described as being, wholly or partly, in a 'minor key', that is, really not an adequate representation of the music's structural properties. The melodic patterns of blues very often look like minor tunes, particularly when transcribed. Yet the aural effect, which is far more important, is one closer to harshness than to the traditional minor effect of 'sad' sounds. Thus many European and Anglo-American 'folk' songs which contain minor intervals in their melodies often look, on paper, similar to blues songs, yet when heard they sound very different. In fact many of the musics, including country and western, which do specialize in sorrowful sounds, use certain major key melodic patterns to achieve the required 'sad sound'.

The 'harsh' tonality in blues is particularly apparent in what Robert Palmer, following Muddy Waters, calls the 'deep blues', i.e. those with their roots in the Delta. These have a structure based on the 'blues pentatonic'. This mode is composed of the first, fourth and fifth tones of the scale plus 'altered' (or 'accidental') thirds and sevenths. The altered thirds and sevenths constitute what have come to be known as the 'bluenotes'. Though the 'bluenote' phenomenon is difficult to describe within the terminology of western musical theory, it constitutes a tone in between minor and major tones. That is, the major tone is 'leant on', flattening it somewhat, or the minor is sharpened in the same manner. On the guitar this can be done by bending the strings with the left hand; and on the piano an equivalent effect can be obtained by means of 'crushing' the notes (that is by playing adjacent notes at the *same time*, so blending them). The techniques required for the vocal expression of the mode are more difficult to master than many people seem to realize, and little more than a handful of those who have been recorded can be considered virtuosos. Prominent among those are Bessie Smith, Robert Johnson, Muddy Waters, Elvis Presley, Ray Charles and Aretha Franklin.

As these and a few other artists have illustrated, blues singing requires vocal range, intensity and the most delicate control. But it also requires the ability to provide subtle melodic and rhythmic improvisation. Bessie Smith's 'Gulf Coast Blues' (1923) is a wonderful demonstration of these qualities, as is Robert Johnson's 'Come On In My Kitchen' (1936), in which he shows to perfection the technique of using the guitar as a 'second voice' by matching the tones and textures of voice and guitar. And Muddy Waters's recording of 'Long Distance Call' (1951) exhibits beautifully the subtlety of vocal mannerisms involved in all the most accomplished blues singing. This is especially apparent in the first line of the final verse, as he sings

Hear my phone ringing, sounds like a long distance call,

sliding effortlessly between the major and the 'blue' tones, with just the right mixture of hope and bitterness in his voice.

Elvis Presley may seem a surprising, even a perverse, choice to anyone who has yet to listen closely to his best work in the blues field, though few would deny the awesome qualities of his voice. Despite Presley's well-established brilliance on his *Sun* recordings, perhaps his most convincing performance as a blues vocalist is on his version of the Lowell Fulson number 'Reconsider Baby' (1960), cut during the sessions immediately following his army release.

Ray Charles and Aretha Franklin are better known as soul singers. Yet unlike many of the gospel-trained vocalists who stuck closely to the major scale in their secular performances, as in the case of Sam Cooke, Charles and Franklin have often recorded songs with melody lines based upon the blues pentatonic. Charles' 'What'd I Say' (1959) and Franklin's 'I Never Loved A Man' (1967) are perfect examples of this aspect of their work.

The melodic structure is the basic *musical* component of the country blues song. Of the three fundamental song components, *lyrics*, *melody*, and *harmony*, it is the last named that is of least importance to the genre. For country blues are typically constructed so as to maximize the compatibility of their lyrical and melodic components. Thus the central 'logic' of the music is that of 'horizontal' (i.e. melodic) rather than that of 'vertical' (i.e. harmonic) coherence. It is a particular feature of Delta blues, for instance, that vocal and guitar parts are sung and played in unison, especially in the case of recordings where the vocal part is accompanied by 'bottleneck' style guitar, wherein the voice and guitar 'echo' each other. Harmony in country blues is an embellishment, secondary to the melodic line, which has become more important as blues have increasingly been played in bands.

An all too common method of describing the 'fundamental' musical structure of blues, particularly by writers with a jazz or popular music background, is that proposing a 'typical' chord sequence. It is ubiquitously given as:

```
1st line   ------ / ------ / ------ / ------ /
chord symbols I       I        I        I
2nd line ------ / ------ / ------ / ------ /
chord symbols IV     IV       I        I
3rd line ------ / ------ / ------ / ------ /
chord symbols V      IV       I        I
```

Thus the 'typical, twelve-bar' blues is commonly described, in shorthand, as being of an AAB, I–IV–V–IV–I, form (wherein the AAB shows that the first, lyrical, line of the stanza is repeated).

However, the descriptive outline given above seriously distorts the structure of country blues. For not only does it imply that a particular harmonic progression is a crucial part of the music's structure; it also ignores the phenomenon of 'bluenotes' in the music. The more enlightened commentators at least include in such outlines symbols such as I^{7dim} and IV^{7dim} to denote the use of diminished chords. Without the addition of diminished chords the outline resembles a boogie progression rather than that of a blues. And even as an outline of boogie progressions it is little more than a very basic, practical, guide, providing a simplified 'musical map' for those who wish to strum out a boogie pattern, for instance.

Given the fundamental *melodic* nature of blues structures, the outline does not even give an adequate guide to (chordal) guitar accompaniment. Country blues often begin on the dominant (i.e. Vth) tone of the scale. Furthermore, the actual chord position used to 'cover' the vocal line can be one of several, including that of the Vth chord, confined in the outline to the third stanza. Many Delta and Chicago 'downhome' blues commence with a diminished seventh (^{7dim}) tone. These include the Muddy Waters recording of 'Long Distance Call', in respect of the stanza quoted above (p. 61). A chord progression which conforms to the verbal part, as appearing on the record, could be:

chording: $I^{7dim \frown 7maj.}$ IV $IV^{7dim} \frown IV \frown V$
vocal: Hear my   phone ring——ing——
chording: V   V $\frown$ IVIV $IV^{7dim} \frown I$ I
vocal: Sounds like a long dis——tance call
(See Appendix A for transcription and analysis.)

Beginning the verse on the diminished seventh, as Muddy Waters does here, is a common feature of Delta, and Delta-derived blues. Moreover, the melodic structure of the whole line is typical of that blues strain. Thus the tune of the first two lines of the verse is noticeably similar to those of, for instance, B. B. King's 'Rock Me Mama' (1961) and Robert Johnson's 'Rambling On My Mind' (1936). The line is composed of two musical phrases the progressive structure of which conform to typical phrases of Delta blues. And the construction of blues songs by means of stringing together a number of lyrical and musical phrases has always been the basis of both continuity and change in that music.

Source: Hatch and Millward (1987:59–63). From *blues to rock*, Manchester University Press

may well have been their strangeness to each other, as well as their familiarity, that caused the cultural explosion. (p. 10)

This returns the discussion to the theme considered at the beginning of this chapter, concerning the difficulties of clearly defining and separating black and white musics. However, this section has been concerned to demonstrate some particular points. First, that forms of black music have tended to develop in particular local and commercial contexts (for example, dances and bars) where a number of influences were brought together, in performances for black audiences. Second, that such forms have then been transmitted to wider audiences where they are then developed in other ways. Third, that it is possible though often relatively difficult to convey the precise musical texture of these forms of music. These are themes to be taken up in the next section on ska and reggae.

Ska and reggae

Reggae developed in the 1960s in Jamaica from two previous related forms: ska and rock steady, which had themselves grown out of music popular in Jamaica earlier in the fifties and sixties. These were mento, the drum musics particularly associated with country-based Rastafarian religious groups, and the American r 'n' b sounds which were available in Jamaica from radio stations based in the Southern states of the USA (S. Clarke 1980:57–8; Hebdige 1987:23–70; Jones 1988:18–23).

Ska and rock steady, like reggae, addressed themes of importance to the everyday life of the oppressed in Jamaican society. For example, in the 1960s there was a cycle of songs whose lyrics debated the rights and wrongs of the rude boy phenomenon. Musical argument about the rude boys of the West Kingston ghetto considered their morals and ethics as well as the extent to which their law-breaking could be seen as an expression of political and social protest, or whether they should be seen as murderers and thieves who were simply hurting their own people. Lyrics of the current songs took different positions on these issues.

Reggae as a specific form developed from rock steady. As Clarke (1980:96) explains:

In its formation, rock steady began to express the specifically Jamaican experience as diversely as possible. Political protest was on the increase, but songs speaking of other themes were also part and parcel of the music scene. By 1968 rock steady was evidently being overtaken by another type of rhythmic invention, reggae which was faster and a synthesis of both rock steady and ska.

By the late 1960s reggae existed as a distinct musical form. At this point it began to address in a direct fashion themes articulated in Rastafari. There were many precursors to the development of Rasta, but perhaps the most important, and the most celebrated in the 1960s and 1970s, was the work of Marcus Garvey, a black Jamaican who formed the Universal Negro Improvement Association (UNIA) in both Jamaica and the USA in the early part of this century. Garvey and his organization stressed black pride and ideas of repatriation or return to Africa. He formed a company called the Black Star Line which was to purchase ships to take those who had been forcibly removed by whites back to their African homelands.

Garvey is significant for his iteration of many themes which were to become part of Rastafari, such as black pride and the idea of Africa as a homeland. However, his direct significance is on a different level. As Clarke (1980:38) states: 'Garvey's main contribution to the birth of Rastafari, however, was his prophecy to "Look to Africa, when a black king shall be crowned, for the day of deliverance is near".' The coronation of Ras Tafari (Head Prince) as Haile Selassie I of Ethiopia in 1930 was seen as the answer to Garvey's suggestion, though as Clarke (1980) notes, Garvey might have known rather more about the political and social situation in Ethiopia and Africa and the likely imminence of this event than some of those who subsequently followed his words.

Some of the key themes and features of Rastafari are listed in figure 5.2 (see further: Owens 1979; Gilroy 1987). Rasta themes were increasingly articulated in reggae in the late 1960s and the 1970s. However, it is important to recognize that there were different styles of reggae. Three different forms can be distinguished: the vocal group style; the DJ/talkover form; and the dub form. The vocal group style is the most familiar form of reggae, perhaps its most well-known exponents were the Wailers and the subsequent work of Bob Marley. The vocals are foregrounded, either those of the main vocalist or the harmony of the small group. The DJ/talkover style, where the DJ talks over the basic rhythm track, originated in the sound systems of Jamaica where the record producer who controlled the sound system, providing the music at dances, produced a particular rhythm which the DJs talked over at the dance, supplying

---

1 The belief in the divinity of Haile Sellassie I. The Rasta term for God is Jah, which some commentators see as derived from Yahweh.
2 The characterization of white-dominated society as *Babylon*. There are obvious biblical reference points. Babylon can stand for different conceptions of white society, ranging from the society as a whole to its manifestations in particular oppressive agencies such as the police.
3 The centrality of Africa, though there has been debate about whether repatriation to Ethiopia or Africa in general actually means physical repatriation or whether it can be seen on a more spiritual plane, connected to other movements of Pan-Africanism.
4 The use of marijuana (ganga) as an aid to discussion and 'reasoning'. Marijuana is a sacred or religious plant, and is used as part of the cleansing of the body.
5 Dressing in particular ways including the growth of dreadlocks for males, the wearing of headscarves by women. Also important is the display of the red, gold and green colours of Ethiopia.
6 The following of a specific diet. A taboo on pork is important as the attempt to follow what, in other cultures, might be termed an 'organic' diet.
7 A particular system of language, including the use of I-words. Thus, 'I and I' used to mean we, with a notion of the individual consciousness within the collectivity being stressed. There are a large number of I-words. Other examples include stressing the 'I' at the end of Rastafari.
8 A division of gender roles. The 'elevation' of the woman as the 'Queen'.

Figure 5.2 Some key features of Rastafari

words addressing individual and social concerns. These were then subsequently recorded and issued as records in their own right. This form alerts us to the central importance of the sound system and the live experience in this form of Jamaican music, in a similar way to which the blues functioned in black communities in the southern states of the USA. In the dub form the basic rhythm track is doctored by the producer, so that electronic tricks can be played with it. Again, this points to the importance of the record producer in Jamaican music.

Rasta themes were brought to wide prominence by the work of Bob Marley, though the mass circulation of reggae has been interpreted as another form of white exploitation of an indigenous black form. Thus Clarke (1980:168) quotes from an interview he conducted with a black record producer:

> Now, all this heavy Reggae music sells a lot in Africa, but who gets the money? Virgin, Lightning . . . There are millions of pounds that come out of Afrika, but whose pockets does it go into? The same white man that these Reggae artists sing about, that they are gonna cut his head off, down with colonialism, and up with Rastafari. Those white companies enjoy that, man, because they are using those same words to sell you and me (i.e. black people)!

Reggae and ska had been popular with young white people in the late 1960s in Britain (see further, chapter 7), and the more developed, politicized and Rasta-influenced reggae was popular in the late 1970s with the followers of punk. Early ska records were reinterpreted by the 2 Tone bands in the late 1970s and early 1980s, a process which led to the blurring of the edges between punk and reggae. Thus, a form produced originally in a black local context achieved wide circulation. The implications of this require further consideration. This means elaborating some of the categories introduced in chapter 4.

Realism, modernism, postmodernism, folk culture and reggae

Chapter 4 introduced the concepts of modernism and postmodernism, and in this section these are supplemented by ideas of realism and folk culture. Realism can be defined as consisting of three elements (Abercrombie, Lash and Longhurst 1992). It offers a window on a world, mobilizes a particular kind of narrative and conceals the process of its own production. First, realist cultural forms offer a window on some kind of world. This does not have to be 'our' world and, indeed, very often it is not, but it is a world that has plausibility for us and is coherent in everyday ways. Characters have familiar motivations. Often the constructed world is related in some way to our own world. However, popular fictions construct their own world, which relate to ours and within that world there is both coherence and plausibility. Second, realist narrative is constructed through cause and effect, which often consists of a beginning, a middle and an end. Thirdly, realism conceals the fact that it is a fiction. The audience is often encouraged to think that they have dropped in on a world, which exists independently of them and the producers of it. We 'suspend disbelief' in the common phrase.

There are many different realisms which have developed on the basis of this essential structure. For example, in a discussion of the American television soap opera *Dallas*, Ang (1986:45) identifies an emotional realism which she contrasts with 'empiricist' and 'classical' realism. However, the basic structure of realism can be contrasted with modernism and postmodernism.

Modernism exposes a different world. Rather than acting as a window it focuses or refracts to show different elements of a world in a new light. The familiar world is made strange, a deeper reality of a different kind is alluded to, or explored. As Featherstone (1988) in the discussion reviewed in chapter 4 explains, narrative is fractured and the familiar patterns of cause and effect are shattered or self-consciously set in juxtaposition to other forms. Modernism is authored in an important sense. The author is central as the manipulator of the language of the representation and may be central as a site for the exploration of consciousness. Language and the play of language are central. Modernism in its classical development was a creature of high culture and the late nineteenth century, related to the city and particular forms of new 'border crossing' experience (Williams 1989).

As was explained in chapter 4, modernism differs from postmodernism. Postmodernism does not offer a window on a separate world, or encourage the search for a different reality, rather it suggests that the world itself consists of images and discourses which cannot be known in an independent fashion. Further, it may be argued that the world has lost meaning, or is simply the site of a clashing of incommensurate discourses which can only be juxtaposed and not ranked in order of importance. There is no truth or reality to be found. Narrative may be fragmented or move in the direction of a 'knowing', self, or other-textually (for example, to another film, book or record), referring narrative. Different elements from different discourses or genres are placed together in one work of art. Jim Collins (1989:62) discusses the novel *The Name of the Rose* by Umberto Eco as a postmodernist text in this manner, explaining that:

> the Sherlock Holmes story is only one of a wide range of discourses invoked by the text. Eco intersperses A. Conan Doyle with Roger Bacon, William of Occam, and a host of diverse medieval works,

along with frequent 'flash forwards' to contemporary figures (e.g. the monastery's chief librarian Jorge of Burgos, or, Jorge Borges). But the single most important intertext is 'fictional' and ironically serves as the justification of the interpenetration of detective and philosophical discourses. The key to the mystery within *The Name of the Rose*, responsible for so much murder and mayhem, is Aristotle's legendary 'lost' study of comedy, and it is this fictive text which serves to accentuate the power of discourse in and of itself.

Further, postmodernism *plays* with ideas of production and authorship. An example of this is David Byrne's film *True Stories*, a fictional documentary about a Texan town. Byrne (who led the group Talking Heads) appears as narrator of the documentary, implying control over the narrative on his part. However, he often undercuts this by foregrounding his own lack of understanding of events or by forgetting information that he wanted to convey to the audience. At points the film appears realist, but is revealed to have been produced by utilizing devices like having Byrne step through a scenic backdrop. Authorship and production are revealed in a joking manner.

At any one time these forms (or ideal types) of culture may be in conflict with each other and a final form of culture to which it is important to pay consideration. This is the concept of folk culture which has been used in diverse ways in the study of music (Middleton 1990:127–54). In the current discussion, folk culture refers to forms of culture which are tightly linked to particular social groups and which are not subject to mass distribution, even if they are electronically reproduced. In many respects they are not realist as they do not open a window on a world, do not use conventional narratives of cause and effect and do not conceal the production process. The reggae tradition can be examined through these categories, which are summarized in figure 5.3.

The pre-ska forms identified above were essentially folk forms. This does not mean that they were unchanging, 'traditional', or 'authentic', but rooted in particular social groups and specific localities. Ska was important as it began increasingly to address social and political issues in Jamaican society. The music itself was distinctive with a new 'jerky' sound. In this form can be found the beginnings of the social realism in music in Jamaica, for example, concerning rude boys and criminality which was to be so important during the 1960s. This direct, documentary and declamatory realism was to continue to run through Jamaican music. Themes of love and

	Folk	Realism	Modernism	Postmodernism
World	'bounded' or local supernatural or religious	clear window secular	strange opaque	discursively structured
Narrative	episodic	cause and effect Beginning–middle–end	fragmented	cause and effect with incorporation of other texts
Production	immediate – performance based	concealed	foregounded	playful + problematic

Figure 5.3   Ideal types of folk culture, realism, modernism and postmodernism
Source: elaboration of Abercrombie, Lash and Longhurst (1992)

romance were increasingly played down by contrast with the earlier American R & B-influenced forms (S. Clarke 1980:72). This social realism was to become increasingly pronounced in the mid-1960s. At this point the audiences for these forms were predominantly local or in the black Jamaican communities overseas, in particular in Britain. At this point ska and Jamaican forms did begin to have a certain wider impact. For example, Chris Blackwell set up Island Records and Millie Small had a number-one hit in Britain. However, despite this success, the main audience was not ultimately to be found in white audiences but among blacks and in particular working class blacks. The music addressed some of the struggles of these groups directly: against the police, the upper class forces in Jamaica and gang leaders who preyed on the community.

The music was not 'owned' by the sorts of people who played it or were its main audience, as it was controlled by entrepreneurs who produced the records and employed the musicians in an exploitative manner. Within this context the role of the male record producer as entrepreneur and businessman was paramount. The musician was an employee. The musicians themselves may have recognized their own skills and looked to the great figures of black American jazz for their inspiration but their own social position resembled that of an underclass of employees with little hope of considering themselves as 'artists' in the 'romantic' or 'classical' sense. Their own struggles were with their employers to whom they had to sell their labour power. One of the essential problems for the musician, that of earning a living, was solved through a clear set of industrialized social relationships.

As has already been suggested, sound systems were also important. The latest sound was prized (as it still is), as a means of establishing a distinctive or novel feel and reputation. Through the concealment of the source of the sound, there was often an attempt to prevent quick mass distribution, though, of course, record sales were important and could be stimulated once a following for a particular track had been developed at dances. At this point, while there had been some success in Britain, this was still a folk form in the way defined above, though the transition to realism was well under way.

The realist tradition in reggae developed during the 1960s. Importantly, the sort of social realism already discussed continued to develop as ska turned into rock steady and then into reggae. The reggae that was popular in Britain in the late 1960s was essentially a familiar sort of form. The lyrics tended to address themes of love and loss, the instrumentals were rather simple, if danceable, tracks which held few surprises. Themes deriving from Rastafari also increased in importance. In the early 1970s these different aspects of the form were combined in the work of the Wailers and most importantly in the figure of Bob Marley (Davis 1984; T. White 1984).

Marley and the Wailers brought together many of the different aspects so far discussed. In developing what can be called an 'international' style of reggae, the Wailers drew on Rastafarian themes and imagery, addressed social issues such as the illegality of marijuana, police harassment and the conditions of slum dwellers, and were concerned with love and romance. They represent the high water mark of reggae realism.

The Wailers' music opened a window on a particular, coherent world, centred in black Jamaican life, rested on narratives about oppression, exploitation and love and increasingly concealed the manner of its own production, through more sophisticated recording techniques. The latter was aided by the process of international success. The smoothing off of the rough edges of the Wailers music after they were taken up by Chris Blackwell and Island Records is well documented and is sometimes seen as a typical dilution of the music's power for commercial purposes. However, it can also be described as an essential part of the perfection of the realist reggae form. Furthermore, the music was packaged in a way to make it more acceptable to those who were used to the form and content of Anglo-American rock, which had itself moved through a realist phase in the 1960s (Goodwin 1991:178).

A further important aspect of this process should be noted.

Increasingly, Bob Marley was marketed as an international star, which no doubt precipitated the split of the original Wailers, as the other two original members (Peter Tosh and Bunny Wailer) were left behind. This process rested on the promotion of Marley as an artist in a way which was relatively unfamiliar in the reggae tradition up to that point. Marley was seen as the creative genius behind the originality of the Wailers' music. This constructed ideas of the artist, within the reggae tradition, which paralleled those used in Western art traditions. During the 1970s various other artists were promoted in this way, which can be seen as central to the strategies of the international music industry as described in chapters 2 and 3, though many seemed rather uncomfortable in the role (for further discussion of the construction of pop music stars through video, see chapter 6).

By the mid- to late 1970s, reggae had taken off as a recognized international style, or a form that would be 'marketed internationally as reggae' (Gilroy 1993:95) was particularly successful. It had moved into the album market and was integrated into the white mainstream. Its own concerns and focus were developed to the highest realist point. The texts sought to open a window on a particular world, utilized narrative lines which were structured by conventional understandings of cause and effect and which reached conclusions or closure, and which seemed to be produced in a seamless manner, concealing the complexity of production.

Such developments leave those who wish to innovate with two main options: either to carry forward the realist strategy which had been so successful for Marley, or to do something rather different. Some acts were promoted in ways which approached the former strategy, but innovators tended to move in the latter direction, extending developments which had been happening parallel to the consolidation of realism in reggae.

During the 1970s and into the 1980s various reggae artists developed modernist forms. These were often based in some aspects of the forms which predated the realist phase. From the centrality of the sound system developed the two forms which encapsulate the modernist movement in reggae: dub and the DJ/talkover.

In the dub style there is play with sound itself. Rather than being smooth and developing in a familiar fashion the music became disjointed and 'difficult' in ways that parallel similar developments in art forms like the novel and 'classical' music. Attention is directed to the form itself. The familiarity of the reggae sound is made strange, and the role of the producer in the production of such strangeness is called attention to. It is the artist as expert with sound who is important rather than as the commentator on romantic or social issues. Artistic experiment with the form is valued for its own sake: like modernist art it is the form that is the focus.

The second style did similar things, though the focus was on the *voice* rather than the sound. The toaster would follow his or her inclinations in voicing over the often familiar rhythm track. These words possessed a degree of narrative, but key phases were often repeated and drawn attention to. Language itself became important rather than being a means to represent something else of political or emotional importance.

Within both of these styles, a world is not constructed or represented in a clear fashion, and the previous worlds constituted by reggae were dismantled and made strange in important ways. Narrative was broken and cause and effect of the rational kind downplayed. Production and the role of the sound or language artist moved to the forefront.

Modernism in reggae does not simply follow on from realism in a straightforward sense, as variants evolved simultaneously. However, it is important to recognize the role of social and cultural struggle in these processes. The reggae artist, like all cultural producers, needs money to continue in operation and, above all, requires an audience to sustain a flow of finance. There are different strategies available to gain money and an audience. One way is to try to do something different from that which is already being done. However, in some respects innovation has to be based on what already exists. In the case of modernist reggae this includes the resources of the tradition itself, the growing dominance of realist reggae, and technical resource, such as the increasingly sophisticated recording technology. The modernist forms set themselves against the dominant realist tradition, by using assets from the (folk) past including key vocal phrases, biblical imagery, mythical themes filtered through the new technical developments. At this point a reggae avant-garde developed which took forward the claims of reggae as experimental. It could then be claimed, as a form of legitimation, that this was a more *real* form of reggae than the increasingly mass-accepted international style popularized by Marley and the Wailers. In this way the notion of the real might be used to ground a form which was increasingly moving away from the currently popular realist conventions.

The 1980s and 1990s have seen have seen a mixing of reggae styles with soul (Hebdige 1987:153–6) and with rock, not in a way which integrates them harmoniously but in a manner which allows the different discourses they entail to intertwine. It would be possible to analyse records like Smiley Culture's *Cockney Translation* (Hebdige 1987:149–53; Gilroy 1987:194–7), which plays with the relationship between white cockney speech and black patois, in a manner similar to Jim Collins's (1989) consideration of *The Name of the Rose* cited above. Increasingly, discourses clash and 'mix' without one being the master or claiming dominance in a straightforward fashion (Collins 1989). The world has taken on a new complexity and an external view is not constructed; the music is within discourses which do not reflect the determination of cause and effect, but which are multiplied and multi-accented. Different ideas are juxtaposed. Production is not directly revealed, or consciously elaborated, but is not concealed in the manner of realism either. Rather there is a play with production which is almost taken for granted. As the audience has become more aware of the process by which texts are put together, there is more fun to be had by playing on that knowledge. The consideration of this mixing of discourses can be developed through the examination of the development of rap music in the 1980s and 1990s.

Rap and hip-hop

Rap music came to wider prominence in 1979, though its roots can be found in other black musics (Toop 1991). Rap was a part of hip-hop culture in New York which included particular modes of dress, language and so on. The music developed from DJs' merging different records and sounds together in a way which seemed startling at the time but which now has become a part of everyday pop music, especially as it has been facilitated by the sorts of technology described in chapter 3. Experiments in sound and voice occurred in rap as well, in part influenced by the Jamaican developments (Cross 1993:15). However, one of the things which is distinctive about rap is the eclectic mix of elements. Toop (1991:65–6) quotes one of the pioneers of the style, Afrika Bambaataa, on his mixing strategy in the illuminating passage reproduced in box 15.

Rap had been developing through the 1970s before the first commercial records were released in 1979. These were a surprise to those at the core of the hip-hop scene who were themselves quickly taken up by record companies and had their own records released. One of the key records which exemplified the hip-hop cut-up style was 'The Adventures of Grandmaster Flash on the Wheels of Steel' by Grandmaster Flash from 1981. As Toop (1991:106) explains, this is:

> a devastating collage of Queen, Chic, The Sugarhill Gang's '8th Wonder', The Furious Five's 'Birthday Party', Sequence and Spoonie Gee's 'Monster Jam' and Blondie's 'Rapture'. It also overlaid a Disney-sounding story, the source of which Flash is keeping a firm secret.

The sources of much of the material used in these records could be surprising. However, Toop (p. 115) suggests that the strategies involved elaborated black traditions:

> An underground movement indirectly inspired by a Cliff Richard percussion break might give the impression of a lemming-like abandonment of black traditions, but in a perverse way these cut-ups of unlikely records, whether by the Monkees or Yellow Magic Orchestra, were a recreation of the forthright emotion that at times looked like becoming a rarity in the mainstream of black music. They were a way of tearing the associations and the pre-packaging from finished musical product and reconstructing it, ignoring its carefully considered intentions and restitching it into new music. As the process of recording music became increasingly fragmented in the 70s – a drum track laid down in Muscle Shoals, a back-up vocal in California, a lead voice in New York – so the implication began to exist that consumers might eventually be able to rejig a track according to their own preferences.

At the same time as these experiments in sound and voice were taking place, there was a direct address to political issues in rap. As the name suggests, these were often raps about issues such as the denigration of black history and the current exploitation of black people (Gilroy 1987:182–7). These twin directions have continued as the form has developed into the 1990s, when hip-hop from Los Angeles became more prominent (Cross 1993), though it has been the lyrics of rap which have led to a range of controversies, especially over the way in which rap records have been held to promote violent solutions to black problems, exhibit a kind of gang worldview, and to denigrate women. This has led to widespread news coverage of the music and the sorts of story reproduced in box 16.

More recent serious consideration of rap music have suggested that it raises some significant and complex issues. Stephens (1992) has argued that rather than advocating a kind of black separatism,

Box 15   Afrika Bambaataa's mixing strategy

WHEN I came on the scene after him I built in other types of records and I started getting a name for master of records. I started playing all forms of music. Myself, I used to play the weirdest stuff at a party. Everybody just thought I was crazy. When everybody was going crazy I would throw a commercial on to cool them out – I'd throw on *The Pink Panther* theme for everybody who thought they was cool like the Pink Panther, and then I would play 'Honky Tonk Woman' by the Rolling Stones and just keep that beat going. I'd play something from metal rock records like Grand Funk Railroad. 'Inside Looking Out' is just the bass and drumming . . . rrrrrmmmmmmmm . . . and everybody starts freaking out.

I used to like to catch the people who'd say, 'I don't like rock. I don't like Latin.' I'd throw on Mick Jagger – you'd see the blacks and the Spanish just *throwing* down, dancing crazy. I'd say, 'I thought you said you didn't like rock.' They'd say, 'Get out of here.' I'd say, 'Well, you just danced to the Rolling Stones.' 'You're kidding!'

I'd throw on 'Sergeant Pepper's Lonely Hearts club Band' – just that drum part. One, two, three, BAM – and they'd be screaming and partying. I'd throw on the Monkees, 'Mary Mary' – just the beat part where they'd go 'Mary, Mary, where are you going?' – and they'd start going crazy. I'd say, 'You just danced to the Monkees'. They'd say, 'You liar. I didn't dance to no Monkees'. I'd like to catch people who categorize records . . .

In the who-dares-wins delirium of the house parties, Bambaataa mixed up calypso, European and Japanese electronic music, Beethoven's Fifth Symphony and rock groups like Mountain; Kool DJ Herc spun the Doobie Brothers back-to-back with the Isley Brothers; Grandmaster Flash overlaid speech records and sound effects with the Last Poets; Symphonic B Boys Mixx cut up classical music on five turntables, and a multitude of unknowns unleashed turntable wizardry with their feet, heads, noses, teeth and tongues. In a crazy new sport of disc jockey acrobatics, musical experiment and virtuosity were being combined with showmanship. Earlier in black music history the same potent spirit had compelled Lionel Hampton to leap onto his drums, Big Jay McNeely to play screaming saxophone lying on the stage and the guitar aces – T Bone Walker, Earl Hooker. Johnny Guitar Watson and Jimi Hendrix – to pick the strings with their teeth or behind their heads.

Source: Toop (1991:65–6, 105)

Box 16 Murder rap

He's armed and he's dangerous: Ice Cube's lyrics are about race hate, the Los Angeles gangs and the glory of the gun. He's America's worst nightmare. And he's over here.

Caroline Sullivan

RAPPER Brings Message of Hate to Britain, howled a headline in the London Evening Standard. The accompanying story warned that the Los Angeles hip-hop baron, Ice Cube, famed for raps apparently condoning misogyny and extreme violence, was coming to the UK for three concerts. 'He is accused of glorifying rape,' the piece continued, concluding with the observation that four people leaving a recent Ice Cube gig in Seattle had been machine-gunned in a drive-by shooting.

Cube's third album, The Predator, sold 1.5 million copies in America within a month of its release last December. That makes him a big star – as big, in relative sales terms, as Madonna. His immense popularity dovetails with white America's perception of him as its worst nightmare made heavily-armed, foul-mouthed flesh.

Cube (born O'Shea Jackson in the Compton district of Los Angeles in 1968) owes his notoriety to 'gangsta rap', a hip hop variation that is the musical equivalent of aggravated assault. Gangstas, or 'gangbangers', are America's indigenous terrorists – the drug dealers and gang-thugs whose lawlessness has made the inner cities fearsome no-go zones. Gangsta rappers are the oral historians, chronicling the life in graphic street-language.

The first gangsta raps were recorded in Los Angeles in the mid-1980s, by a reformed burglar called Ice T (whose name was derived from Iceberg Slim, a pimp and jailhouse novelist). The genre came to wider attention in 1986, with the formation of the Compton hip hop crew, Niggaz With Attitude. Before Ice T and NWA, rap had been an East Coast phenomenon. 'Where New Yorkers would rap about parties and clubs, I would rap about car chases and guns and the shit I was living through,' Ice T has said. As NWA's main lyricist, Cube was responsible for tunes such as Gangsta Gangsta and Fuck Tha Police. Both were on NWA's epochal debut LP, Straight Outta Compton. Gangsta Gangsta found Cube snarling: 'Do I look like a motha-fuckin' role-model?' The al-

bum's multi-million sales made it clear that America's teenagers had decided he was.

That record and its 1991 successor, Efil 4 Zaggin (Niggaz 4 Life), charted the group's version of the Compton life cycle: from a bleak childhood in the streets of South Central Los Angeles (where the 1992 riot would occur) to 'living large' to, inevitably, prison or a violent death.

Several themes run through all Cube's lyrics: women exist to be abused (a typical verse: 'Tucked her in/pulled out my third leg, pumped it in/she said will you call me? yeah. I'll call you a bitch or a ho'): all police are white and racist: men are judged by the fire power they wield. Guns figure in most songs, along with an array of vivid synonyms for 'to kill', such as 'dusting', 'smoking', 'wetting' and 'burning'. AKs and 'gats' are not just symbols of machismo but the means of evening the odds against the white establishment. 'I'm a nigger gotta live by the trigger,' runs one song.

For all his evident toughness. Cube (the name refers to his impassive demeanour) had a fairly cushy upbringing. His was a middle-class home with a strict father who steered him away from the gangs. 'I was more scared of my father than I was of the niggers on the street,' he has said He earned a certificate in architectural drawing but, enterprising to the core, saw rap as a quicker and more satisfying route to success.

He began writing lyrics in his teens. He did not lack inspiration. 'Some of the people I grew up with, they're straight-up killers . . . the hardest motherfuckers have seen, or are going to see, many of their homeboys die. Boom, boom, boom.' Dead Homiez, considered one of his more compassionate tunes, is about the funeral of a friend who fell victim to the gang warfare that once plagued South Central. (A truce has been observed since the riots.)

In 1990, Cube left NWA. He and the group's manager, Jerry Heller, were in dispute about money. Cube claimed he had been done out of royalty and tour profits – after a US tour grossing $650,000 he received a pay cheque of just $23,000. Heller, a white Jew (this is an important dis-

tinction, given persistent rumours of Cube's anti-Semitism; he denies it), declared that Cube was merely jealous of his fellow NWA rappa, Eric 'Eazy-E' Wright, who had made a platinum-selling solo album.

'I knew I had talent and I wasn't gonna stay there and get fucked out of my money.' Cube has said.

He released his first solo album, AmeriKKKa's Most Wanted, in the spring of 1990. The record confirmed that there was a social conscience under the belligerence. Laddish braggadocio was tempered with politically-charged observations on ghetto life and police brutality. Song titles like Once Upon A Time In The Projects and Endangered Species signalled a shift in Cube's preoccupations. The large-living gangsta had discovered Nation Of Islam minister Louis Farrakhan, and was in the process of becoming an outspoken campaigner for black rights. His music was adored by black teenagers for its ferocious condemnation of police harassment. White teenagers liked it because it intimidated their parents.

It took his next album, 1991's Death Certificate, to properly rouse white America's ire. Black Korea, a track inspired by the shooting by a Korean shopkeeper of an unarmed black girl, for which the killer received six months' probation, got Cube accused of incendiary racism. A coalition of groups, including the Southern Christian Leadership Conference and the Simon Wiesenthal Centre, called for a boycott of the album because of its 'outrageously violent and derogatory lyrics', which promote an attitude of racial hatred and violence'. A sample: 'Your little chop-suey ass will be a target.' Cube's UK label, Island Records, released Death Certificate without Black Korea and another controversial number, No Vaseline.

The same year, Cube made his film debut in John Singleton's Boyz N The Hood. His portrayal of a teenage excon won high praise and talk of an Oscar nomination. Violence in which one person died and 30 were injured marred the film's premiere. He returns to the screen here in May with Trespass, an all-actioner in which he and Ice T star as supremely unpleasant gangbangers. Cube's fee was said to be $1 million.

Which brings us to his new album. It opens with a prison body-search and ends with the shooting of a policeman. Cube is on typical form, raging against the society that disempowered his race and seems determined to keep it that way. The Predator is his inquest into the riots, which he regards as having been long overdue. 'I loved every minute of that shit. When it happened, I set my guns on the bed and waited.'

Cube is a powerful spokesman. His relentless aggression bludgeons you into seeing his point. The violence he depicts on his records is not titillation but a barometer of black anger.

It is a shame that Cube, so clever about other issues, is so stupid about women. Sorry, 'bitches'. Although he is happily married, his songs contain no hint of sensitivity or tenderness. The closest he comes on the current record is, 'Got a beep from Kim, and she can fuck all night.'

This attitude saturates hard-core rap. Quick as Ice T and Cube are to take umbrage at racial slights, they refuse to believe that their view of women is vilely offensive. Ice T chortles it off as feminist jealousy of 'feminine women'. He says: 'Girls don't have a problem with being called a bitch.' And gays? Cube knows where he stands: 'Trueniggas ain't gay/Ya fuckin' homo.' Well, that's that, then.

They get away with it because few interviewers are willing to contravene the code of right-on-ness and challenge them. Those who do, find the rappers intractable, unable to comprehend the other side of the argument. Yet Cube and Ice T are dedicated to 'the enlightenment and education' of African-Americans.

But their misogyny and homophobia are peripheral issues nowadays. Ice T is embroiled in a censorship controversy that has riven America. Last year his backing band, Body Count, recorded a song called Cop Killer. In the wake of the South Central riots, it was considered so inflammatory that police organisations pressed for a boycott of all Warner Bros Records products. The new York Patrolmen's Benevolent Association prepared to sell its $100 million investment in Time-Warner (the label's parent company) shares, and General Motors withdrew a $53 million investment. Warner Bros employees received death threats.

Citing the first Amendment, Time-Warner supported Body Count's right to free speech. Eventually the group voluntarily pulled the song from their album.

However, Ice T recently ran into more trouble. Warner decided not to release his fifth album, Home Invasion: it felt the cover artwork was contentious (apparently, it showed a white boy surrounded by rap records and armed black boys). Ice T refused to change it, and he and the label parted company in January. Home Invasion will now be released by Cube's label, Priority. As for Cube, he is white America's bogyman. It is a role he relishes. But he realises the importance of reaching the other side. 'White listeners are real important,' he says. 'Those kids that are listening to my records are going to be the mayors and senators until [blacks] get our act together.'

Reckless rhetoric of a fairy-tale gangsta

Playthell Benjamin

WHILE Ice Cube goes to great lengths to maintain his tough guy black militant persona, in reality he is taking advantage of the poetic licence allowed creative artists.

Cube is engaging in myth-making of a grossly self-aggrandising sort. He is neither a boy from the hood like Ice T, nor a militant activist organiser like Malcolm X. Cube is a poseur, a B-Boy Wannabe son of the black middle class masquerading as a street tough.

While Ice T recounts tales from his life on the mean streets of South Central, Cube must rely on artifice to compose his raps. Under ordinary circumstances, this would be a cause for applause; for it is in the nature of things that artists should rely on artifice. But in the case of hard core rappers, excessive reliance on artistic imagination is anathema, because authenticity is central to the legitimation of their views.

Hence a middle class black guy like Cube – (who has been called 'soft' by his former collaborators in NWA) – is almost compelled to go to extremes in order to prove how hard he is. Yet Cube is not alone in seeking to camouflage his true background to gain authenticity. The white rapper, Vanilla Ice's account of his hard life in the Miami streets has been exposed as a near total fraud.

Instead of frankly identifying the excessive posturing of hard core rappers like Cube for what it is – the testosterone-driven rhetorical aggressions of ego-manaical and intellectually under-developed young males) – legions of misguided pop music critics have become willing apologists for their transgressions against reason, manners and civility.

A persistent theme in the arguments of those critics who insist that hard core gangster and porn rappers are making an important contribution to the public discourse is that their listeners are not moved to act out the scenarios they hear on records. Greg Wilder, a writer for The Source, America's leading rap journal, makes a typical comment: 'People go too deep into things as far as I'm concerned. These rappers are just making records, just rhyming words that fit, that's all! I contend that not one of the millions of people who listen to these records is going to go out and try to do the things he hears on them.'

Many Afro-American psychologists disagree with this cavalier dismissal of the negative effects of the violent imagery and decadent values of some rappers. Psychological researchers like doctors Niam Akbar, Amos Wilson and Alvin Poussaint agree that violence-riddled raps like Cube's Gangsta Fairytale can influence young people to engage in anti social behaviour and even push those who may be inclined to violence over the edge.

There is a real tragedy here because there are real issues of injustice that cry out for redress lurking behind Cube's reckless rhetoric. But he has neither the intellectual equipment nor the disciplined organisational experience to offer any viable solutions.

On the contrary, considering some of the feelings he's expressed about the rap We Had to Tear This MF Up, a commentary on the Los Angeles riot, one could argue that he is part of the problem rather than the solution. 'I did a song called We Had to Tear This MF Up, because that's the only way that black people can get respect. We had to burn LA and put them out of business for three days and now they want to talk ... But, you know, I love that shit. Every bit of it.'

Source: The Guardian, 11 March 1993

rap actually creates a form of interracial dialogue. In Stephens's view, as whites and Latinos have become involved in rap-like forms there has been the creation of new languages and a form of multiculturalism (see also, Cross 1993). In Britain the increased prominence of artists like Apache Indian could be taken as an example of this phenomenon. In advancing an argument that music cannot be seen as racially 'owned', Stephens notes the way in which black rap has borrowed from white sources and the pride in 'multicultural identity' advanced by Latino rappers. Stephens offers a optimistic account of the development of the rap form, which sees it as a kind of 'transnational', or 'transcultural' form. His conclusion captures the essence of this argument:

> 'Black' music acts like a 'wave' at sporting events: once the wave starts rolling, you can't ask people not to stand up. When the call-and-response starts cooking, you can't pick and choose who's going to answer. It seems to me that instead of trying to draw colour lines around our music, we ought to be proud that black grooves are writing the basslines to a new multicultural song.
>
> In hip hop, white rappers like Third Base and Tony D, biracial rappers like Rebel MC and Neneh Cherry, Latino Rappers like Kid Frost, and black rappers like KRS-One, all use black music and liberation theory as a base. But they use this tradition inclusively. The outcrop can no longer be defined along colour lines. With this mutually created language, participants can engage in 'negotiation strategies' through which they can 'transcend the trappings of their respective cultures'. This dialogic discourse provides a model of our movement towards the cultural crossroads where we can truly come to know what diversity means. (1992:79)

In a much more critical discussion, Irving (1993:107) has argued that 'much black music, which works to construct a space for the self-dependent black male subject, has excluded spaces for the construction of alternative femininities. This is especially true of rap music.' Irving argues that rap's exclusivity, which does not completely exclude white men, works against women. She contrasts this American situation with that found in contemporary British black music, which she suggests is far more open to a 'multi-subjectivity'.

For Irving (p. 114), the sexist and misogynistic terminology used in rap enables white male critics to identify with the black male position: 'Over and over, rapping is described in violent and phallic terms and, amongst both critics and performers, the sexism is a deliberate ploy to keep women off the turf.' She argues that this sort of male exclusionary practice can and has been overcome through some female rap records, such as those by M. C. Lyte and Roxanne Shante, which construct different positions for women. Irving's paper is one of the most developed analyses of gender address and politics in this form of music.

In a rather more positive assessment of rap, Swendenberg (1992) argues that the form has been particularly successful in articulating a political message within the context of a mass-circulated form. In this argument, rap constructs and reconstructs a black community which reinterprets the pre-existing forms of culture, in a far more radical way than punk, in a widely circulating form of music. However, Swendenberg neglects the sorts of argument that have been made about gender identified above, as well the homophobia which he finds in much rap music, which he sees as 'shortcomings'.

The discussion in this chapter suggests that ideal types of different cultural forms can be used in the analysis of black music. The specific black forms were connected to social locations and social movements. In these locations, distinctive themes were often articulated which express, according to Gilroy (1987), some core aspects of black culture. Such themes can sometimes facilitate dialogue between different racial groups, thus leading to the generation of new musical forms, such as Asian rap. These forms tend to have value ascribed to them because of their authenticity. However, this does raise problematic issues concerning the extent to which any artist can speak for a community. The discussion has been predicated on *social* definitions of black, rather than essentialist ones, and has taken account of the wider social and political meanings of blackness. There remain problems with such descriptions. It may be that often-used categorizations of black slide over and eradicate important social and political differences between different racial and gendered identities. The examination of rap brings some of these matters to the foreground, prompting consideration, for example, of the relation between 'black' and 'chicano' and male and female identities. In this respect consideration of rap and the current fluidity of the relations between different musical forms further illuminates the discussion of postmodernism, politics and identity introduced in chapter 4 and exemplified through the discussion of Madonna. The valuation of the 'black' identities constructed for men by 'gangsta' rap may be problematic for women (of all races) illustrating the complicated interactions between ethnic and gendered identities in contemporary cultural politics.

Summary

This chapter has considered:

- the nature of 'black music' and some of the issues raised by the use of this concept;
- the textual development of blues and soul in the USA and the social contexts for these forms;
- the textual development of reggae in social context, utilizing distinctions between folk, realism, modernism and postmodernism, elaborating the arguments of chapter 3;
- the development of rap in its social context and some of the issues raised by this.

6

Texts and Meaning

This chapter is concerned with the ways in which pop music creates and conveys meaning. This means examining: first, *what* conveys meaning; second, *how* meaning is conveyed; and third, *who* conveys meaning. These threads run through the chapter, which begins with a consideration of how the established discipline of musicology has treated pop music. There then follows a discussion of the way in which concepts deriving from structuralism and semiotics have been used in the study of the texts of popular music. This leads into an examination of the relationship between words and music in the conveyance of musical meaning. Discussions of musical meaning have been complicated by the appearance of music video in the 1980s, a fact that is examined in some length in the chapter through contrasting the accounts of Kaplan (1987) and Goodwin (1993). The chapter concludes with briefer consideration of the role of the star in the creation of musical meaning.

Musicology and pop music

Several writers have pointed to the way musicology, because of its origins in the study of Western classical music, neglects pop music. Middleton (1990) suggests three areas where musicology has problems with the study of pop music. First, there is the terminology used in the musicological approach. According to Middleton, musicology uses value-laden terms like harmony and tonality to the neglect of ideas like rhythm and timbre. Furthermore, such terms are not used in a neutral fashion. In Middleton's view, a term like melody suggests something to be valued whereas tune suggests a everyday banal form. He argues that:

> These connotations are ideological because they always involve selective, and often unconsciously formulated, conceptions of what music is. If this terminology is applied to other forms of music [for example, non-Western or pop forms] . . . clearly the results will be problematical. In many kinds of popular music, for example, harmony may not be the most important parameter; rhythm, pitch gradation, timbre and the whole ensemble of performance articulation techniques are often more important. (p. 104)

Second, Middleton argues that there are problems with methodology, particularly in the use of notation in musicology. This leads to an emphasis on those parts of music which can be written down using conventional notation, however, many non-classical musics have features which cannot be expressed through the forms generated for the notation of European classical music. Furthermore, the focus on notation leads to the valuation of the score as representing what the music actually is. Again, this is not applicable in a direct way to other forms of music, where a score may not exist, or in the case of some pop music is created after a piece of music has been recorded and marketed.

Indeed, Middleton suggests that:

> Even in notated popular music – Tin Pan Alley ballad, music hall, vaudeville and minstrel songs, ragtime and nineteenth-century dances – the published sheet music, almost always for piano and voice and piano, sometimes 'simplified', acted to some extent as a prognostic device or a beside-the-fact spin-off. (p. 106)

The analyst who simply focused on the text of a pop song as written down with notes on a score would miss a number of the different ways in which such music creates meaning, including, for example, the nature of the performance given of the song. A number of these different dimensions to the creation of meaning are explored as this chapter progresses.

The third problem with musicology identified by Middleton concerns ideology. Musicology developed in nineteenth-century Europe to examine European classical music. While it has expanded its horizons somewhat, this is still its touchstone. Therefore, the claims of a particular kind of music are valued above others in a way which reproduces the tastes and practices of a particular powerful social group and marginalizes those of weaker social groups. The way in which other forms of music are judged against the classical European tradition, leads the latter to be valued in ways which props up established ways of thinking of music. This is a similar sort of point to that made by Middleton against Adorno, which was examined in chapter 1.

Given that 'The discipline of musicology traditionally is dedicated to the painstaking reconstruction, preservation, and transmission of a canon of great European masterworks' (McClary and Walser 1990:280), the prospects for developing a musicological study of pop music would not seem promising. However, in recent years a number of writers have attempted to elaborate approaches which recognize that an analysis of the music can contribute to the study of pop music. For example, Middleton (1990:117) suggests that the critique of musicology which he so clearly sets out should not be taken too far, because this would block the proper understanding of how pop music works as music. Moreover, it would specifically obscure the connections which exist between the European classical tradition and popular music. Thus, Walser (1993) has shown how heavy metal makes use of the baroque tradition from classical music. In general, Middleton (1990:122) argues that:

> The 'critique of musicology', then, should take aim not at 'art music' or musicology themselves – separating popular music off from them – but at a particular construction of musicology, based in on a particular subject, conceived in a particular, ideologically organized way. Once the musical field as a whole is freed from the distorting grip of that ideology, the ground is cleared for a useful musicology to emerge. The metaphor should be not one of opposed spheres, or of decisive historical breaks, but of a geological formation, long-lived but fissured and liable to upheaval: the task is to *remap the terrain*.

McClary and Walser (1990) also want to reconfigure the musical study of popular music, suggesting that it is important to study those aspects of the music which 'trigger adulation in fans' (p. 287) as these are central in the creation of meaning. Walser (1993) has expanded upon these points in his study of heavy metal music, where he argues that:

> The danger of musical analysis is always that social meanings and power struggles become the forest that is lost for the trees of notes and chords. The necessity of musical analysis is that those notes and

chords represent the differences that make some songs seem highly meaningful and powerful and others boring, inept, or irrelevant. (p. 30)

If this sort of argument is to be followed it is necessary to consider the ways in which it has been suggested that music conveys meaning and can be analysed as a textual form. These ideas are developed in the next section.

Aspects of musical meaning

Much recent writing on the way in which music creates meaning has been influenced by structuralism and semiotics (or semiology). One important source of structuralism was de Saussure (1857–1913), whose linguistic theories were developed in the 1960s by influential writers such as Althusser, Barthes, Chomsky, Foucault, Lacan and Levi-Strauss. Keat and Urry (1975:124–6) identify the following main features of structuralism:

1 Systems must be studied as a set of interrelated elements. Individual elements should not be seen in isolation. For example, in a set of traffic lights, green only means go because red means stop.
2 An attempt to discover the structure which lies behind or beneath what is directly knowable.
3 The suggestion that the structure behind the directly visible and the directly visible itself are both products of structural properties of the mind.
4 The methods of linguistics can be applied to other social and human sciences.
5 Culture can be analysed in terms of binary oppositions. For example, between good and bad.
6 The adoption of a distinction between synchronic (static) and diachronic (changing) analyses.
7 The attempt to identify similar structures in different aspects of social life. For example, the standardized structure of pop music may be the same as the standardized structure of society.

Semiotics or semiology is the systematic study of signs. To introduce some of the concepts and ideas associated with these approaches we can consider the photograph reproduced with its caption from *Vox* Magazine in figure 6.1. Certain features of this photograph can be identified immediately. It shows two white women standing next to each other, one with dyed blond hair wearing a white dress and the other with short black hair dressed in black. The blond woman is holding a baby's bottle and appears to be offering it to the other woman. The photograph appears to have been taken at some kind of public function as there seem to be people standing around in the background. In the language of semiotics, this is what the photograph *denotes*. We can understand, or *decode*, such meanings in a fairly straightforward manner, as they are relatively objective.

However, the possession of other knowledge may facilitate more detailed decoding of the photograph. Thus, the contemporary pop fan might recognize these women as Courtney Love from the band Hole and the Irish singer Sinead O'Connor. He or she might also be able to explain Love's possession of a baby's bottle from the knowledge that she has recently had a child. Further layers of meaning, or *connotations*, of this photograph are built up on the basis of this knowledge. These women are pop stars and the photograph conveys ideas or *discourses* about motherhood and nurturing.

Still further levels of meaning are generated when the photograph is considered in context with its caption. The caption both explains some other factors surrounding the photograph and conveys a joke. It explains that this is indeed Courtney Love and Sinead O'Connor and that the photograph was taken at the MTV Awards. It is assumed that the readers of the magazine from which this photograph is taken will understand what MTV stands for, though not everyone would know this. The joke depends on understanding that Love has a record of drug use which might be passed on through her milk. O'Connor is interpreted as ensuring that her health will be protected. It is likely the readers of *Vox* magazine will be aware of this aspect of Love's life as the magazine had previously published long extracts from a book about the band Nirvana, led by Love's husband Kurt Cobain, which contained extensive descriptions of the couple's drug use.

The discussion of this photograph has introduced several important points:

1 That any image or text can be said to contain different layers or levels of meaning. In particular there is a distinction between *denotative* and *connotative* levels.
2 That the nature of such meanings will depend on the context in

Here, this'll put hairs on your . . . er . . . head. Courtney Love extends her mothering instincts to an undernourished Sinéad O'Connor at the MTV Awards. 'It was *formula* milk, wasn't it Courtney? I mean, tell me, it was out of a tin wasn't it – *wasn't it???*'

Figure 6.1   Courtney Love and Sinead O'Connor, 1993 MTV Awards
© London Features International Ltd, photographer: Kevin Mazur/Lfi-UKM.

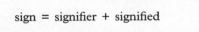

sign = signifier + signified

Figure 6.2 The structure of the sign

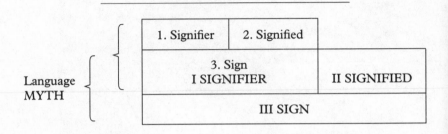

Figure 6.3 Language and myth

Source: Barthes (1976). Originally published in Britain by Jonathan Cape. Translated by Annette Lavers

which they are contained, or the surrounding circumstances. Meaning is *relational*.

3 That some of the levels of meaning or *codes* are relatively neutral, or objective, whereas others will be saturated with social meanings or discourses.

4 That the recognition and elucidation of these different meanings involves analysis or *decoding* which often depends on the nature of the knowledge and experience brought to the analysis.

Using the language of semiotics, the photograph can be said to be acting as a sign. The sign consists of two elements: the signifier and the signified. The signifier is a sound, printed word or image and the signified is a mental concept. This structure is represented in figure 6.2.

The semiotic approach, which was developed from the study of language by de Saussure, has been applied widely. Thus, the French theorist Roland Barthes (1915–80) argues:

> take a black pebble: I can make it signify in several ways, it is a mere signifier; but if I weigh it with a definite signified (a death sentence, for instance, in an anonymous vote), it will become a sign. (1976:113)

Barthes shows how different levels of meaning are associated. This is shown in figure 6.3. This demonstrates the relationship between

langue: a general Western music code, governing the territory, roughly
  speaking, of functional tonality (starting, that is, about the sixteenth
  century and still largely current today);
norms: e.g. the mainstream conventions *c*. 1750–*c*. 1900, or those
  governing the post-1900 period; within these
sub-norms: Victorian, jazz age, 1960s, etc.; and
dialects: e.g. European, Euro-American, Afro-American; within these
styles: music hall, Tin Pan Alley, country, rock, punk, etc.; and
genres: ballad, dance-song, single, album, etc.; within many of these
sub-codes: e.g. within rock, rock 'n' roll, beat, rhythm and blues,
  progressive, etc.; and
idiolects: associated with particular composers and performers; within
  these
work and performances.

Figure 6.4   Musical codes
Source: Middleton (1900:174)

the denotative or connotative levels of meaning. Barthes also writes
here about the distinction between language and myth. For Barthes,
myths shore up existing structures of power, which favour the bourgeois class. Myths make what is historical or changeable appear to
be natural and static.

Signs are organized into systems which convey meaning, these
systems are often called codes in structuralist and semiotic approaches
(Fiske and Hartley 1978:59). Middleton (1990) suggests that there
are a number of different levels of code which structure popular
music. These are given in figure 6.4. Thus, if an track by Bruce
Springsteen was analysed in these terms, we could see that it contained characteristic figures of speech (or idiolects) in Springsteen's
vocal for example. We might argue that it was a rock song and in
this context it might be a ballad or a rocker. It might be Euro-
American and be seen as a typical product of the 1980s, when rock
took a particular direction and so on working up through the levels
of code.

This sort of categorization can be used to inform discussions
around the idea of competence. Middleton shows how Stefani distinguishes between 'high' and 'popular competence' or ability in the
understanding or decoding of the code. High competence 'treats
music as highly autonomous' suggesting that there are a set of
distinctive skills which are needed to understand it properly. In

contrast, 'popular competence appropriates music in a more global, heteronomous manner' (Middleton 1990:175), perhaps connecting it more directly with everyday life. Furthermore:

> Popular competence can attach itself to *any* kind of music – though musics themselves coded in an analogous way are the most likely. Similarly, popular *music* can be listened to according to *high* competence principles (as is sometimes the case with professional performers). But a *preponderance* of popular music listening does seem to be of a popular competence type.

This suggests, for example, that a piece of classical music could be decoded for its melody, but this would neglect other features that would be identified through the use of high competence.

The idea of musical code has been used in other ways by recent writers on popular music. For example, Bradley (1992) draws a broad distinction between the 'tonal-European code' and the 'Afro-American code', which he suggests are merged in the development of rock 'n' roll (see further, chapter 4). In identifying these codes, Bradley draws upon the work of Chester (1990) who distinguishes between the *extensional* nature of classical music and the *intensional* structure of rock and other non-European musics. Chester (p. 315) argues that in extensional classical music:

> Theme and variations, counterpoint, tonality (as used in classical composition) are all devices that build diachronically and synchronically outward from basic musical atoms. The complex is created by combination of the simple, which remains discrete and unchanged in the complex unity. Thus, a basic premise of classical music is rigorous adherence to standard timbres, not only for the various orchestral instruments, but even for the most flexible of all instruments, the human voice.

By contrast, in intensional music:

> the basic musical units (played/sung notes) are not combined through space and time as simple elements into complex structures. The simple entity is that constituted by the parameters of melody, harmony and beat, while the complex is built up by modulation of the basic notes, and by inflection of the basic beat.

Another use of the idea of code can be found in the work of Sheila Whiteley (1992) who mobilizes the idea of 'psychedelic coding' to study 1960s progressive rock. According to Whiteley, such coding of the music, which included 'the manipulation of timbres (blurred, bright, overlapping), upward movement (and its comparison with psychedelic flight), harmonies (lurching, oscillating), rhythms (regular, irregular), relationships (foreground, background)' conveyed 'the hallucinogenic experience' in music (p. 4).

The concept of style has been deployed in musicological discussion of rock by Moore (1993) who argues that it is possible to distinguish a general rock style, which includes a number of common features in areas such as rhythm and the voice, and a variety of different and specific styles within this general category of rock style.

The discussion so far has examined the ideas of sign and code, as they have been used in semiotics. Middleton (1990:214–20) suggests four dimensions along which music can be considered in structural terms, which develops the structuralist approach. He sees each of these as a continuum. The four continua are:

1 generative
2 syntagmatic
3 paradigmatic
4 processual

Generative structure refers to the continuum between the deepest levels of the structure and those at the surface. This is similar to the idea of there being a hierarchy of codes as considered above. Middleton's classification of generative levels is given in figure 6.5.

Syntagmatic analysis refers to the ways in which different musical units are combined to produce sequences of sounds. Thus a pop song may be made up of a series of instrumental passages, verses, choruses, bridges and so on. Likewise, to take another example, a meal may be thought of as a syntagmatic chain. In Britain, this might consist of a first course or starter, a main course and a pudding. Discussion of the precise contents of the different courses means moving the analysis on to the paradigmatic level, as this refers to the alternatives which can be substituted into the different components of the syntagmatic chain, thus a choice might be made between fish or meat for a main course.

Finally, Middleton considers the 'processual continuum'. He suggests that 'all musical events relate forward (through expectation and implication) and back (through memory), and their function and meaning change as the processual dynamic unfolds' (1990:219).

1 General cognitive processes. Here, methods relating to the schemes of sensorimotor-affective organization and symbolic-behavioural logic would be appropriate (for example, principles of same/different, strong/weak, up/down, and of proportion, grouping, contour and gesture).
2 Culturally determined applications of (1), specific to *musical* materials (for example, note-frames, time-frames, patterns of tonal and harmonic relationship). Generative theories come in here.
3 Style-specific syntaxes constructed from (2) (for example, available scales, intervals, rhythms, parameter relationships; preferred formulae, modes of combination). Distributionist, commutational and paradigmatic approaches are appropriate at this level.
4 Intra-opus patterns: the individual piece in all its uniqueness.

Figure 6.5 Levels of generative structure
Source: Middleton (1900:214)

For Middleton, a full structural analysis has to consider the inter-connections between these different dimensions.

An issue which has come under close scrutiny in much recent con-sideration of the creation of musical meaning is the relationship between words and music. At this point, therefore, the chapter moves away from the examination of themes deriving from structuralism and semiotics to focus on the issues raised the examination of this relationship.

Words and music

Much analysis of pop music has focused on the meaning of the words or lyrics. Early attempts to study pop music often considered the lyrics as a form of poetry suggesting that certain pop writers could be seen as poets. Much analysis of Bob Dylan was carried out along these lines. Lyrics have also been studied in other ways. In some cases the focus has been on the *content* of the lyrics. Thus, in his book-length study of punk rock, Laing (1985) shows the differ-ence in subject matter between punk and Top 50 pop songs through content analysis, as shown in table 6.1.

Punk songs were less concerned with romantic and sexual relations

Table 6.1 The subject matter of the lyrics of five punk groups

	Punk	*Top 50*
Romantic and sexual relationships	21% (13)	60% (31)
Sexuality	15% (9)	–
First person feelings	25% (16)	3% (2)
Social and political comment	25% (16)	4% (2)
Music and dancing	7% (4)	18% (10)
Second and third person	7% (4)	3% (2)
Novelty	–	8% (4)
Instrumental	–	4% (2)

Figures in brackets denote the actual number of songs in that category.

Source: Laing (1985:27); source for Top 50: *Star File* 1977

than pop songs and focused more on the nature of sexuality. Social and political comment was far more commonplace in the punk song than in the pop song. Content analysis involves six steps:

(1) selecting a topic and determining a research problem; (2) selecting a documentary source; (3) devising a set of analytic categories; (4) formulating an explicit set of instructions for using the categories to code the material; (5) establishing a principled basis for sampling the documents; and (6) counting the frequency of a given category or theme in the documents sampled. (Ball and Smith 1992:21–2)

As with all forms of content analysis it is important to see how the different categories of content are defined, to consider the basis on which the sample has been arrived at and so on. Further details on these matters can be found in Laing's book. However, as Laing recognizes, content analysis is a rather crude form of analysis. It tends to abstract the specific content from its context and does not pay much attention to the detail of the modes of expression in the lyrics.

In an attempt to overcome some of the problems of content analysis some more recent analysis of the lyrics of songs has studied different modes of expression in lyrics and the ways in which the listener is addressed by them. One of the most consistent writers in this vein is Barbara Bradby (e.g. 1990, 1992), whose work is a form of discourse analysis. She suggests that lyrics and music construct and refer to discourses in songs which have much wider significance. In the discussion of Madonna's *Material Girl*, which is reproduced in figure 6.6,

[The figure] transcribes the lyrics of 'Material Girl', as actually performed on the record, which differs considerably from the neat verses reproduced on the inner sleeve of the album *Like a Virgin*. In addition, I have indicated the parts sung by the different voices in the performance, as follows:

Madonna as solo singer	= ordinary typeface
Madonna as girl-group, or female chorus, i.e., using her own voice as backing vocal	= *italics*
MADONNA + MALE CHORUS OF THREE BACKING VOCALISTS	= CAPITALS
Madonna's voice as interrupting response	= {lyrics}
prominent electronic echo effects	= lyrics

Madonna, 'Material Girl', discourse analysis

	Lyrics	Discourses	Pronouns
Intro.	(4 lines rhythm alone, then 4 lines with prominent melody in the bass)		
Verse 1	Some boys kiss me, some boys hug me	maternal/romance	– me
	I think they're OK	everyday	I – they
	If they don't give me proper credit	money/school	they – me
	I JUST WALK AWAY	everyday	I
Verse 2	They can beg and they can plead, but	romance	they
	They can't see the light, {That's right},	religious/everyday	they
	Cos the boy with the cold hard cash is	money/	
	ALWAYS MISTER RIGHT	romance	
Chorus 1	Cos we're *living in a material world*	material	we
	And I am a material girl	material	I
	You know that we are *living in a material world*	material	you, we
	And I am a material girl	material	I
Verse 3	Some boys romance, some boys slow dance	romance	
	That's all right with me	everyday	me
	If they can't raise my interest then I	money	they, I –
	HAVE TO LET THEM BE	everyday	– them
Verse 4	Some boys try and some boys lie but	teaching maternal	
	I don't let them play, {No way},	maternal	I – them
	Only boys that save their pennies	maternal/money	
	MAKE MY RAINY DAY	everyday	
Chorus 2	Cos we're *living in a material world*	material	we
	And I am a material girl	material	I
	You know that we are *living in a material world*	material	you, we
	And I am a material girl	material	I
Chorus 3	Cos we're *living in a material world*	material	we
	And I am a material girl	material	I
	You know that we are *living in a material world*	material	you, we
	And I am a material girl	material	I

authority, anti-parental videos, which took a variety of different forms. Second, there were videos which concerned American foreign policy or 'specific social injustices, such as poverty' (1987:75). These sorts of video were shown far less frequently than some of the other types. Examples include Bruce Springsteen's video for *Born in the USA* as a critique of post-Vietnam America, and the Sun City video by Artists Against Apartheid. The third theme in the socially conscious category addresses 'women's oppression and the possibilities for female solidarity' (p. 87). Thus, Kaplan argues that some videos address the problems faced by women in society and attempt to represent and construct forms of female solidarity. This theme has been developed by Lisa Lewis (1993), who identifies forms of gender address to women in video. She argues that such videos use two distinct types of sign in particular ways. Thus: 'Access signs are those in which the privileged experience of boys and men is visually appropriated. The female video musicians textually enact an entrance into a male domain of activity and signification' (p. 136). Discovery signs, by contrast: 'reference and celebrate distinctly female modes of cultural expression and experience. Discovery signs attempt to compensate in mediated form for female cultural marginalization by drawing pictures of activities in which females tend to engage apart from males' (p. 137). Lewis finds evidence of these modes of address in videos by Cyndi Lauper, Madonna, Pat Benatar and Tina Turner. However, Kaplan maintains that these sorts of video are relatively few and far between.

Kaplan relates the *nihilist* type of video to the 'originally anarchic positions of recent punk, new wave and heavy metal bands' (1987:60). On MTV this is mainly the province of heavy metal bands. These videos often feature live concerts or recreations of them. They rely on musical and visual shock. Sadistic and masochistic themes are often present, as are concerns with hate and destruction.

The *classical* video often relies on a more conventional, realist, narrative structure. However, they are also classical in 'retaining the voyeuristic/fetishistic gaze towards women as objects of desire that feminist film theorists have spent so much time analysing in relation to the classical Hollywood film' (p. 61). Women are located in these videos to be looked at by men, both within the video itself and by the male spectator for the video. A second type of classical video takes on and uses classical Hollywood film genre, which moves it more towards postmodernism.

The *postmodern* form of video involves a large element of play with images. When we watch them we often feel that we have lost a clear position from which to view. They do not put forward a clear 'line' or point of view, or positions are advanced at one point of the video which are then undercut later. While elements of this are present in all videos there are exhibited to a far greater extent in this form.

Kaplan's account is one of the most detailed examinations of music video. However, there are some problems with it, the most important of which revolve around three issues: first, the nature of music video as promotion; second, the place of music in music video; and third, the nature of the audience.

The first point concerns the nature of the video as a promotional device. While Kaplan opens her book by examining the commercial base of MTV and locates it in an institutional context, as her analysis develops it increasingly centres on the nature of the music video text as if it were a separated art form. In some respects this is perfectly legitimate, as it is possible to study texts using structural and semiotic methods and so on, but it is important to remember that videos are embedded in a commercial context. Videos are produced in a very different context from the classical or even contemporary Hollywood film and cannot simply be analysed with concepts and categories derived from film and television analysis, without consideration of the specific applicability of such ideas to different media.

Second, the musical dimension of music video often takes a secondary position in many discussions of music video. Kaplan's work develops out of her previous background as an analyst and theorist of film. Distinctions in the visuals are central and musical differences tend to be discussed relative to these prior distinctions. In some writing the music in music video has been almost ignored. Thus Frith (1988b:221) criticizes the work of Browne and Fiske (1987) who he says:

> compare Madonna's song–and–dance routine in the 'Material Girl' video with Marilyn Monroe's 'Diamonds Are a Girl's Best Friend' in *Gentlemen Prefer Blondes*. 'The two songs', they assert, citing the lyrics in each case, 'are basically similar'. The differences are 'differences of tone'. Anyone who can hear a 1980s disco hit as 'basically similar' to a 1950s theatre song is obviously deaf. Alas, it has been the deaf who have dominated pop video theory.

Hence, our attention should be focused as much on music as on visuals and the spoken word in videos, suggesting that it is the relationship between these aspects that is important.

Third, Kaplan implies that the audience for the music video is of a particular type. However, this is based on an analysis of the text rather than an investigation of the audience itself (for more general discussion of this issue, see chapter 7). Kaplan argues that in the past rock music addressed different cultural groupings, but that MTV utilizes a mass address. She suggests that: 'MTV reproduces a kind of decenteredness, often called "postmodernist", that increasingly reflects young people's condition in the advanced stage of highly developed, technological capitalism evident in America' (1987:5). And later (p. 29), that:

> MTV simply takes over the history of rock and roll, flattening out all the distinct types into one continuous present. The teenage audience is now no longer seen as divided into distinct groups addressed by different kinds of rock music, but is constituted by the station as one decentered mass that absorbs all the types indiscriminately – without noting or knowing their historical origins.

However, it is not clear how this sort of approach can be reconciled with Kaplan's later comment (p. 159) that: 'Different groups of teenagers no doubt use MTV in different ways according to class, race and gender'.

Goodwin (1993) attempts to develop an analysis of video and MTV which takes into account these sorts of problem with the illuminating approach taken by Kaplan. Goodwin stresses the promotional and industry context of music video and MTV, emphasizing the way in which the different products of media or cultural industries interlock in relations of multitextuality (see also, Wernick 1991). This process:

> was exemplified, for instance, in the selling of the 1989 Warner Bros. film *Batman*, which involved tie-ins with the music industry (Prince's *Batman the Movie* LP, and the sound track from the film itself), publishing (including the Batman comic books, published by Warner Communications subsidiary D.C. Comics), television (through home video sales and rentals, and – eventually – cable and broadcast television rights), and merchandising (Batman bubble gum, breakfast cereal, and so on). (Goodwin 1993:27)

Ideas of the interlocking nature of the media industries and ideas of promotion and rights which were examined in chapter 2 are used by Goodwin to contextualize the development of music video. Video came about as a 'routine' way of promoting pop in the early 1980s at the same time as the development of the post punk 'new pop', which concentrated on issues of image and used new technologies in music making. Television itself was expanding and music videos were a cheap way to fill up airtime. Furthermore, 'music television very precisely addressed two trends in the 1980s: the aging of the rock audience and the growth (at least in the United States) of a youth culture that was *not* centred on music' (p. 39). Goodwin represents what he calls 'The music video cycle' in the way reproduced in figure 6.8. One important point to note about this cycle is the relatively insignificant role of the sale of music videos as commodities themselves, as their main use is in the promotion of other goods.

Goodwin shows how MTV has changed since it began in 1981, dividing its development into three stages: 1981–3, 1983–5 and 1986 onwards (with a fourth phase possibly developing from 1993). The first phase was studied by those like Kaplan, who focused on the visual and postmodern nature of MTV. At this point MTV did screen videos in a flow, and these videos themselves tended to break with narrative convention in the way identified by Kaplan (Goodwin 1993:134). However, Goodwin maintains that developments during the second phase led away from this format. Most importantly, MTV was increasingly divided up into programme slots, and the nature of the videos shown began to move increasingly towards the performance type with heavy metal music increasing in importance. In August 1985 the ownership of MTV changed hands from the founders Warner-Amex to Viacom International, and from 1986 on the trends which had appeared during the second period were consolidated. There are now more programme slots and different sorts of musical material appear, giving a typical MTV day in March 1991 as shown in figure 6.9.

This account contextualizes music video and MTV far more than other accounts have done. He also pays attention to the second problem with accounts like Kaplan's identified above: the relative neglect of music. He argues that it is important to recognize how musical and visual dimensions to video intertwine. Furthermore, he suggests that this is nothing new. Music has always made sense in relation to the visual associations that we in the audience give to it, hence certain forms of music suggest colours and images. Moreover, music has been connected with the visual through the media of film (early rock stars were promoted in film, especially Elvis Presley) and photographs. Goodwin's argument is that the 'visuals support the sound track' (1993:70). Thus, for Goodwin, music videos are not films and there is a clear danger of 'misreading the generic

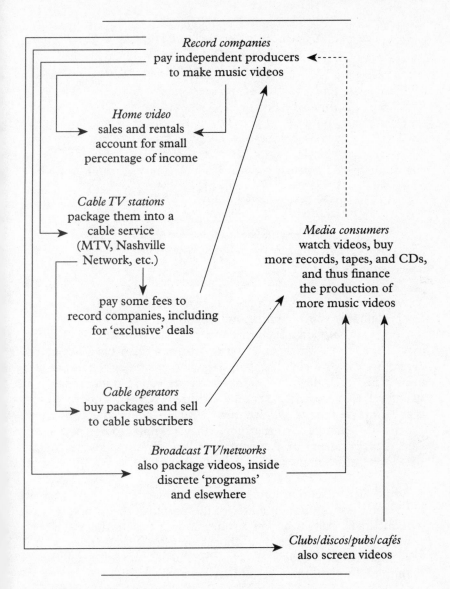

Figure 6.8 The music video cycle
Source: Goodwin (1993:43)

7:00 a.m.	*Awake on the Wild Side*
9:00 a.m.	Music videos (Daisy Fuentes)
12:00 m.	Music videos (Andrew Daddo)
3:00 p.m.	*Spring Bread '91*
4:00 p.m.	*Yo! MTV Raps*
4:30 p.m.	*Totally Pauly*
6:00 p.m.	*Dial MTV*
7:00 p.m.	*MTV's Half Hour Comedy Hour*
7:30 p.m.	*Hot Seat*
8:00 p.m.	*Prime with Martha Quinn*
10:00 p.m.	*House of Style*
11:30 p.m.	*Bootleg MTV*
12:00 p.m.	*120 Minutes*

Figure 6.9 A typical MTV day in March 1991
Source: Goodwin (1993:143)

conventions of the form by applying rules carried over from another (inappropriate) genre or medium' (p. 77).

Goodwin maintains that music in pop videos tends to close off meaning in ways which other writers on the form have neglected. He argues that 'we can find three kinds of closure or coherence that introduce a high degree of stability via the sound track: repetition, structural closure, and harmonic closure' (p. 79). Pop songs, he argues, are repetitive within themselves in alternating verse and chorus, for example. Furthermore, they resemble other pop songs (see the arguments of Adorno), and are repeated across 'media sites', where the same song can be heard on the radio, TV and so on.

While such repetition might be held to suggest that pop songs do not resolve issues in the manner of the narrative realist text, Goodwin maintains that structural resolution does this in 'the way a song ends with the repetition of a chorus or refrain that "ties up" the song, perhaps as it fades out' (p. 80). Such structural resolution is reinforced by 'harmonic resolution' which describes:

the organization of the music itself around conventions of tonality and musical arrangement that both ground the music in a system of tonal relations that may be seen as the aural equivalent of the realist systems of 'looks' in cinema and often enable it to end with a musical 'resolution' which may be seen as the aural equivalent of a realist narrative reaching its conclusion. (p. 83)

However, despite his strong arguments for the centrality of music in the meaning structure of the music video, Goodwin recognizes 'that music video is relatively autonomous from the music, to a limited degree, in a number of ways' (p. 85). He identifies and discusses four such ways:

'1   The visualization of the song may go beyond its meaning.
2   The clips seek to provide pleasure (sometimes, but by no means exclusively, of a narrative nature) in order to keep the viewer watching and to encourage repeated viewings.
3   The clips might promote other commodities (such as films).
4   The clips might narrativize/display images of stardom that exceed any given individual song.' (p. 85)

Goodwin, like Kaplan, points to the variety of different videos that are shown on MTV, and categorizes them as shown in figure 6.10. It is possible to see some overlap between these categories and Kaplan's. Thus, Goodwin's social criticism category is rather like the socially conscious category and the self-reflexive parody rather like the postmodern. However, Goodwin points to the way that video is used as a promotional device for other texts.

He suggests a number of different ways in which music and visuals interact in the music video, and also considers different visualization of videos by audiences. On the basis of a small-scale audience study he concludes (1993:55): first 'that the vast majority of students in this sample were able to note down visual images associated with the musical extract'; second, that there was 'a high degree of consensus on the kinds of iconography associated with each extract'; and, third, 'while a variety of mass-mediated imagery is invoked in these accounts, a significant amount of this imagery does *not* derive from music video (at least not in any clear, literal sense), and a good deal of it is clearly triggered by personal memory'. Goodwin also suggests that the kind of intertextuality in videos such as Madonna's *Material Girl* will not necessarily be recognized by the audience.

Goodwin's account is important, first, in developing a critique of the more unsubstantiated claims of those writers who have seen MTV and music video as postmodern in simple and clear senses; and second, in providing a clear and historicized account of the promotional and industrial context of video. His account alerts us to the interconnections of music and image in the way in which pop

Social criticism	Self-reflexive parody	Parody
SUN CITY (AAA)	DON'T LOSE MY NUMBER (Phil Collins)	BAD NEWS BEAT (Neil Young)
WAR (Springsteen)	JUST A GIGOLO (David Lee Roth)	LIFE IN ONE DAY (Howard Jones)
LIVES IN THE BALANCE (Jackson Browne)	THIS NOTE'S FOR YOU (Neil Young)	RIGHT ON TRACK (Breakfast Club)
TWO TRIBES (FGTH)	EAT IT ('Weird Al' Yankovic)	
RADIO CLASH (the Clash)	POP SINGER (John Mellencamp)	
JAMMIN' ME (Tom Petty)	ON THE GREENER SIDE (Michelle Shocked)	
SISTERS ARE DOIN' IT FOR THEMSELVES (Eurythmics)		
CULT OF PERSONALITY (Living Colour)		
ONE (Metallica)		

Pastiche	Promotion	Homage
RADIO GA GA (Queen)	A VIEW TO KILL (Duran Duran)	DON'T GET ME WRONG (Pretenders)
THE ULTIMATE SIN (Ozzy Osbourne)	ABSOLUTE BEGINNERS (David Bowie)	CHAIN REACTION (Diana Ross)
MONEY FOR NOTHING (Dire Straits)	STAND BY ME (Ben E. King)	DR MABUSE (Propaganda)
MATERIAL GIRL (Madonna)	DANGER ZONE (Kenny Loggins)[a]	$E = MC^2$ (BAD)
THRILLER (Michael Jackson)	LAND OF CONFUSION (Genesis)[b]	TELL HER ABOUT IT (Billy Joel)
WHERE THE STREETS HAVE NO NAME (U2)	BATDANCE (Prince)	R.O.C.K. IN THE USA (John Cougar Mellencamp)
BIG TIME (Peter Gabriel)[c]	HEARTBEAT (Don Johnson)	ROCKIT (Def Leppard)
MEDIATE (INXS)		

[a] DANGER ZONE is especially interesting because it both promotes the film *Top Gun* and references (as pastiche?) the opening scene of Francis Ford Coppola's *Apocalypse Now*.

[b] LAND OF CONFUSION is not a move trailer, as the other examples here are, but it does indirectly promote the British TV series *Spitting Image*, through its use of puppets. It also contains pastiche, in its joking reference to the montage sequence in Stanley Kubrick's *2001: A Space Odyssey*, in which the chimp's bone becomes a spaceship (here it is transformed into a telephone receiver held by the Phil Collins puppet).

[c] BIG TIME uses a pastichelike reference to the television series *Pee-Wee's Playhouse* (through its distorted, playful *mise-en-scène*), but the complicating factor here is that this can be read as an auteurist discourse, since the clip's director, Stephen Johnson, has also directed that television program. Read in that light, the clip should more accurately be classified as (self-?) promotion or homage.

AAA   Artists Against Apartheid
FGTH   Frankie goes to Hollywood
BAD   Big Audio Dynamite

Figure 6.10 Visual incorporation in music video
Source: Goodwin (1993:161)

creates meaning. He also develops an account of the place of the star system in such generation of musical meaning.

Stars and meaning

Goodwin develops his analysis of the importance of stars through an examination of Madonna's video for *Material Girl*. He suggests, against a number of other writers, that the narrative of this video is not actually very complex and that it moves 'through an initial lack, via action, to (romantic) resolution' (p. 99). Goodwin reads this video in a way which draws attention to the 'star-text'; a concept introduced through the work of Richard Dyer on stars (for example, Dyer 1979; Dyer 1987; Gledhill 1991). Goodwin interprets this video 'as if its central motif (the femme fatale who uses men to gain wealth and power) is co-terminus with Madonna herself precisely because this is one of the many images Madonna has portrayed in the promotion of her music' (1993:101).

Such an account connects to far wider themes concerning the ways in which stars function as trademarks which generate sales for the music business and the culture industries more widely (see chapter 2). However, it also raises issues concerning musical meaning. Thus, it can be hypothesized that in addition to focusing on the way in which the individual text can be shown to exist within a particular type (or genre), for example, analysis needs to consider how the meaning of a text may relate to the overall meaning that has been created by a star. Thus, a new record by Madonna may be seen in the context of the various meanings of Madonna, and not as, for example, another dance or disco hit. In this respect, it is possible to draw attention to these two ways of grouping products: by genre (e.g. the rock song, the ska track and so on) or through the activities of the star whose music can change significantly over a period of time (Goodwin 1993:103; Lury 1993:92).

Goodwin adopts the view that has developed in the study of stars, especially by John Ellis, that stars in the cinema expressed a form of incompleteness. He quotes Ellis as suggesting that 'The star image is paradoxical and incomplete so it functions as an invitation to cinema, like the narrative image. It proposes cinema as the completion of its lack, the synthesis of its separate fragments' (Goodwin 1993:117). This suggests that stars appeal, because the audience wants to understand or fill in the knowledge that is missing. It may be that the fan of a star feels that only he or she can possess such knowledge. Goodwin argues that this kind of 'lack' is recognized by stars such as George Michael, who observed that 'It's not the something extra that makes the star – it's the something that's missing' (p. 117). Goodwin traces the development of Michael's career to demonstrate the changing nature of his incomplete star text. Extracts from this informative discussion are contained in box 18.

It is possible to read Michael's legal action in 1993 over his contract with Sony (which was decided in Sony's favour in 1994) as another mutation in the development of his star text. This case sets a representation of Michael as an *artist* against the representation of the highly exploitative Japanese record company, who have only commercial aims. We might read the sober, but trendy, appearance and dress of Michael in court in relation to this narrative of stardom, which would potentially affect the meanings derived from his music (see figure 6.11).

Goodwin's argument, therefore, is that video texts need to be read in the context of the overall development of the star text, as well as in their own narrative or musical terms. Likewise, it can be suggested that the video or musical texts themselves contribute to the changing development of that star text, and can signal key moments of change in it very clearly. Hence, one way to map Madonna's changing star text is through the different images and meanings contained in her videos.

Other writers have suggested that contemporary stardom is actually rather different from that displayed in the classic Hollywood cinema. Thus Lury (1993:71) argues that:

> At the same time a new kind of star is emerging; these stars are sustained through the strategic and self-conscious manipulation of performative intentionality across media; their appeal derives from their capacity to make the actual virtual and the virtual actual, and their radiance flickers with an oscillation between two and three dimensions. Jack Nicholson, Madonna and Arnold Schwarzenegger are the most obvious example of this phenomenon. Within this mode of stardom, the 'value added' from an artist comes not from the management of the distance between their image and their creative abilities, but from its collapse.

This contributes to the process of 'branding' discussed in chapter 1 where the music industry (in common with other media industries) forms 'links of image and perception between a range of products'

Box 18   Extracts from FATHER FIGURE: a case study

POP STAR George Michael is someone who is capable of his own interesting and perceptive reflections upon stardom. During the 1989 MTV Video Music Awards program he observed: 'It's not the something extra that makes a star – it's the something that's missing.' Michael's star-text, which was initially constructed as one half of the duo Wham!, has exemplified the extent to which star imagery builds on vulnerability and ordinariness to establish points of identification for the audience.

. . . Michael became globally famous during his years with the British pop group Wham!, where, alongside childhood friend Andrew Ridgeley, he forged an identity that initially foregrounded fun and pleasure. The group's first release, 'Wham Rap!' was an ironic commentary on unemployment that became a hit in Britain only after its rerelease (in February 1983) following the success of 'Young Guns (Go for It)' in October 1982. It is worth pointing out that in their early days Wham!'s image as young innocents confronting a sometimes harsh parental world was mirrored in the real-life drama of major conflicts with their record company, Innervision Records, with whom they had signed a contract that was exploitative to a degree that has become somewhat legendary (although it was by no means unique) in the music industry. Wham! established themselves as fun-loving teen idols, with a string of hit singles over the next two years ('Bad Boys', 'Club Tropicana', 'Wake Me Up Before You Go-Go', 'I'm Your Man' etc.) . . . In a 1984

interview, Michael presented fame as an especially pleasurable kind of work: 'Suddenly you're in a position where you have as much money as you need, you feel secure, and you have no one to answer to. It's absolutely brilliant! What better job could you have than that?' (quoted in Tennant 1984; 195). Wham!'s video clips tended to stress happy-go-lucky themes and to present George and Andrew as star-objects, rather than as musicians or people . . .

The issue of Michael as a solo artist was emphasized early in Wham!'s career, when it became apparent that band-mate Ridgeley actually contributed very little to the music. Before Wham! split up, in June 1986, Michael had already released two solo singles – 'Careless Whisper' (which earned him considerable critical respect) and 'A Different Corner'. Both songs are brooding, introspective ballads, and they highlighted both Michael's songwriting talent and the beginnings of an emerging star-text that became the vehicle for the subsequent marketing of George Michael-as-auteur.

The solo trajectory begun by George Michael during his career with Wham! is visually present in the clips themselves. The group's early videos were set either in everyday British locations (mum and dad's living room, the High Street, etc.) or in exotic places. CARELESS WHISPER is a transitional video-text, in that the colorful, romantic settings where we see the narrator's ex-lover contrast with the bleak, less colorful *mise-en-scène* where George

Michael sings to us (backstage, on his own, surrounded by dangling ropes). Just as the singer is marked out from his more carefree past here, so is George Michael, pop star, isolated from the imagery of Wham! Indeed, the fact that CARELESS WHISPER was released as a solo project is revealing about the importance of the star-text in marketing music. Years later, Michael put it like this: 'We both had a definite attitude toward what a Wham! record should be about. Right up to 'Go-Go', they'd all been young and optimistic. It didn't seem right to abandon it for this one ballad' (quoted in Fricke 1986:85). The promotional clip highlights that calculation and underscores the importance of star imagery as a site of fictional construction. (Similarly, the video for Wham!'s final single, THE EDGE OF HEAVEN, includes extracts and multiple back-projection of excerpts from the previous videos – 'GOODBYE' runs across the bottom of the screen – and the line 'one day you'll wake up on your own' is thus unavoidably a comment on the fracturing star-text as well as a part of a romantic lyric.)

The bridge for the formal shift from Wham! to a solo career was a record George Michael made with Aretha Franklin ('I Knew You Were Waiting') in 1987. Simultaneously linking him with the authenticating power of classicism and soul (and indirectly with the word respect), this song foreshadowed his solo career, which was launched with the album Faith (Columbia Records) in the spring of 1987. I KNEW YOU WERE WAITING also broke with the homoerotic appeal of the Wham! duo, being a romantic song whose heterosexual interpretation is buttressed through its performance by a male-female duo – a convention that has often been used in video clips.

The first single from Faith was the controversial song 'I Want Your Sex', which Michael was forced to defend as an ode to monogamy – the video clip had a closing shot added to it in which Michael writes 'EXPLORE MONOGAMY' on his lover's back, in lipstick, following criticism that the song and video promoted permissive (and, by implication, dangerous) sexual behavior. 'Father Figure' was released in February 1988. In May, Faith became the first release by a white artist to top Billboard's Black Album chart. Michael also received an award as best soul/rhythm and blues act of the year at the American Music Awards (organized by the Recording Industry Association of America).

The context for the FATHER FIGURE video was thus one in which George Michael's image was undergoing considerable change, as he was established as a heterosexual solo artist (a key component of success in the United States) and as his music was increasingly associated with notions of authenticity, as opposed to the discourses of irony (the first three singles) and triviality (most of the subsequent releases) that dominated the music of Wham! The shift is apparent, for instance, if we compare two widely circulated long-form videos: Wham! in China: Foreign Skies (CBS/Fox Video, 1986, directed by Lindsay Anderson) and George Michael (distributed in video stores by CBS Music Video and made by London Weekend Television for The South Bank Show in 1990). Where the tone of the first documentary is partly that of a travelogue, with a commentary about Wham! as 'ambassadors' for British pop and perhaps even Western youth culture (material that is also deployed in the clip FREEDOM, which includes extracts from the film), the film offers an uncritical celebration of stardom that inevitably reverberates with the numerous clips in which Wham! appeared as young jet-setting pleasure seekers (CLUB TROPICANA, LAST CHRISTMAS). *George Michael*, on the other hand, utilizes the conventions of the art documentary in its mostly reverential delineation of his artistic development, which is elaborated in an interview with Melvyn Bragg, and offers the star's own self-conscious thoughts about stardom and his distance (as he sees it) from the world of Madonna and Prince . . .

Structurally, FATHER FIGURE is both complex and extremely simple in terms of narrative organization. The complexities arise from its confusion of time frames and because of uncertainty about the point of enunciation in some segments. For instance, in shots 1.7 and 1.9 we see George Michael pinning up a photograph of the model *before* he has met her. Since this is also the last shot, it seems reasonable to speculate that these images occur (in 'story time') later than they appear (in 'discourse time'). It also remains unclear whether in fact he has had an affair with the model, or whether some parts of the narrative might be taking place in his imagination, a parallel with the pop fan's real-life obsession. Since Michael is seen by the model when they are not alone (for instance, in shot 6.10) it becomes clear that the events really occurred, but that the time frame has been mixed up in ordering the narrative.

Rather than attempting to make sense of this narrative definitively in immanent terms, however, it is more appropriate to consider its relation to the sound track the song and the star-text. Visually, an important element running throughout FATHER FIGURE is the prevalence of slow-motion imagery, and the use of dissolves to link most of the shots gives the clip a languid mood, underlining its subtle eroticism and illustrating the music itself, which is slow and understated. Structurally, the video text offers a complete, self-contained televisual 'segment', one that illustrates Ellis's (1982a) approach to broadcast television narrative as well as my argument about the image and its relation to a three-minute song. The music itself returns to a moment of completion in its final chorus and coda, and the clip climaxes through two devices: first, sections 10 and 11 have more frequent cutting (during the choruses) and then, via a fade to black (shot 11.12), settle (like the music) on a single, final image (of the model). Second, the last sections are more repetitive than the rest of the clip, reviewing the plot and returning the George Michael character to where he began . . .

. . . FATHER FIGURE cashes in two symbols that have run from the earliest days of George Michael's career. The first is the black leather jacket – a familiar sign of rock rebellion that was originally worn with some irony (WHAM! RAP, BAD BOYS) and then became an integral part of Michael's iconography as a solo star. The BSA jacket, with its 'REVENGE' insignia, is the key visual *motif* of FAITH, and in a later clip (FREEDOM 90) it is this jacket that bursts into flames. Second, there is

George Michael's beard – often worn as low-level stubble, a trendy version of 'five o'clock shadow' first popularized by Don Johnson on *Miami Vice*. Again, this symbol made an earlier appearance in the days of Wham! (A DIFFERENT CORNER), but in the context of a bright, lively *mise-en-scène* that is quite different from the dark, almost monochrome tones of FATHER FIGURE. It is the new, brooding image of an unshaven Michael (often in dark glasses) that adorns the sleeve of *Faith* and is used repeatedly for advertising imagery and press photographs.

Taken together, the leather jacket and the stubble (along with the dark glasses and cigarettes) are not just character appropriate for a Hollywood version of a taxi driver; more important, they established 'classic rock' imagery for George Michael at a time when he was seeking mass acceptance in the United States. In fact, it would be more truthful to say that the characterization offered in FATHER FIGURE is secondary to these aspects of the star-text – it was probably chosen for that reason, not the other way around.

Source: Goodwin (1993:117–30)

(Lury 1993:87). Stars as brands (Michael Jackson, Madonna, Prince, Eric Clapton, Bruce Springsteen, Guns 'n' Roses) have become, on the basis of this sort of argument, a very important focus of musical meaning.

This chapter has identified a number of different aspects of musical meaning. It seems clear that the over-emphasis of one dimension can lead to a slanting of the analysis which neglects the potential effects of the others. However, the discussion of meaning leads into the ways in which meaning is understood or created by audiences. This is the topic of the next two chapters.

Summary

This chapter has considered a number of different areas of study and issues raised through the investigation of musical meaning. These have included:

- the critique of traditional musicology and contemporary arguments for the transformation of musicology to make it useful in the study of a variety of different forms of music;
- ways of studying musical meaning which derive in the main from the utilization of the approaches of structuralism and semiotics.

Figure 6.11 George Michael arriving at the High Court, 23 November, 1993
Reproduced by permission of The Press Association, photographer: Stefan Rousseau

Important concepts discussed here include code, structures and denotation and connotation;

- the interconnections between lyrics, words and music;
- music video, where Kaplan's (1987) work was used to represent a more text-centered approach. This was contrasted with the more contextualized perspective of Goodwin (1993);
- the potential importance of star texts in the generation of musical meaning.

PART III

AUDIENCE

7

Effects, Audiences and Subcultures

This chapter begins the consideration of the nature of the audience for pop music. It falls into three main parts. The analysis first reviews some of the different ways in which the relations between texts and audiences have been considered. This entails consideration of contemporary debates on the social effects of popular music and specific examples from pop music are fed into this more general discussion. This is followed by an examination of the contemporary consumption of pop music, which provides a context for the more detailed examination of how pop music is actually used in contemporary society. This theme will be addressed through an examination of the literature which considers how music is used within different subcultures. The following chapter develops this theme of the importance of considering the precise ways in which music is used in different social contexts.

The relations between texts and audiences

The earliest research on the mass media, in particular on film and radio, argued that there was a straightforward relationship between texts and audiences. The mass media were held to possess great powers to influence the behaviour of members of the audience. In a commonly used phrase, the media were held to act as a hypodermic syringe in injecting messages into the audience (J. Lewis 1991; Morley 1992; Moores 1993). The audience would accept such messages, often because they had no alternative sources of opinion, and would be 'brainwashed' by the media. Such a view was developed in the 1930s when fascist and totalitarian governments had come to power in various parts of Europe, partly, it was thought, through the use of propaganda. The earliest work of some of the writers of the Frankfurt School, including the work of Adorno considered in chapter 1, adopted a similar perspective. The mass media were a form of drug for the masses. Such a view of the media and television in particular, is often voiced in popular criticism. Thus, a recent record by the Disposable Heroes of Hiphopcrisy talked of 'Television, the Drug of the Nation'.

Such characterizations of the relations between texts and audiences often see contemporary society as divided into a very small elite and a large mass. The vast majority of the population were a part of the mass, which consisted of essentially similar people. The creation of such a mass was the result of the rise of industrialism or industrial capitalism, when people were moved from their 'traditional' communities into new industrial towns in the nineteenth century. They were seen to be living in similar places and working in large factories where they performed essentially similar tasks.

While in such theories the mass is made up of individuals, they do not possess true individuality or discrimination. They are 'massified' in that the ties between them have been, or are in the process of being, broken down. Hence, the old family or community ties from earlier days were held to be disappearing. It was argued that the development of such a mass society could have important ramifications. First, it was suggested by some writers that the mass could invade traditional or elite government, leading to its breakdown. This sort of view, which was often expressed by conservatives, held that government by the elite benefited everyone in society and that democracy would lead to social breakdown and turmoil. Likewise, it was thought that the masses were invading and contaminating 'good', 'proper', or previous 'folk' cultures. In such accounts, 'traditional' values were seen as threatened and under attack. Second, there was the fear that the masses would be manipulated by the power of the mass media, helping the elite to retain its rule and propagate its views. In both these accounts the media are seen to be very powerful in affecting how and what people think and how they behave.

Similar accounts of the power of the media have held that people respond to it in a very direct fashion: the media act as stimuli to particular forms of behaviour. In accord with such a view, there has been a great deal of research into the effects of the media. This has

recognize the complexity of the composition of the media audience, and the nature of some of the social relationships between its different members. However, there are criticisms which can be made of it. First, it tends to divide the audience rather strictly between those who are active and those who are passive. Second, it is not clear why there should be only two steps. There might in fact be a whole range of steps and the relationships between the members of the audience might be extremely complex.

An approach which attempted to shift attention away from the effects of the media was 'uses and gratifications'. As the name suggests, the focus here is on the way in which the audience uses the media to gratify certain needs or wants. This view is significant because it takes the everyday life of the audience rather more seriously than earlier approaches. For example, it would be possible, using such an approach, to argue that pop music can be used to satisfy a need for excitement or romance and so on. However, there is a danger of allowing the audience rather too much freedom in the uses to which they can put the media to the neglect of the point that the texts which they are using are structured in particular ways which may tend to restrict their uses. Hence, for example, categories like dance music which captive the primary use of a form.

More recent work on the audience has argued that it is important to recognize the complex two-way relationship between texts and audiences. Texts are structured in certain ways but are open to be understood or decoded by the audience in ways which are not necessarily determined by the text itself. Thus, in a very influential study of the early evening television magazine programme *Nationwide*, David Morley (1980), following the more theoretical work of Stuart Hall (1980), identified three categories of understanding of the programme among the audience. First, there was the *dominant* reading which followed the commonsense logic of *Nationwide* which had previously been identified by Brunsdon and Morley (1978). The structure of the programme is gone along with and audience members in this category do not question it. Second, there was the *negotiated* reading. These audience members would accept most of the message in the programme but would negotiate with it to some degree. The message would not be completely accepted, or there might be misgivings about some aspects of it. Third, there were those audience members who *opposed* the programme. They either saw it as a form of ideology, suggesting that it was putting forward a view of the world which suited the dominant class, or thought that it had no relevance to their lives.

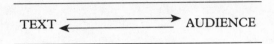

Figure 7.2　Two-way text–audience relationship

This study was influential for a number of reasons. First, it took audience response seriously and maintained that there could be rather different responses to the same programme. Second, these different responses to the programme were related to social background. They were not arbitrary or individualistic. Third, before doing this project, Morley had with Brunsdon carried out a detailed and sophisticated analysis of *Nationwide*. They argued that *Nationwide* tended to structure the viewer of the text in particular ways, so that it would not always be easy to perform an oppositional reading of the text. The relation between the text and the audience was therefore two-way, as shown in figure 7.2.

A number of criticisms can and have been made of this study of *Nationwide*, including the relative neglect of production: the most important for the current discussion is that the research was rather artificial in that groups of people were brought together to watch particular editions of *Nationwide* and then asked to discuss them afterwards. It can be argued that this is not the way in which we normally watch television. This was a point recognized by Morley and in subsequent research (for example, 1986) he has situated television as a domestic medium, and examined the way in which it is watched and viewed in the home. Since the early 1980s, there has developed an extensive literature which attempts to study the actual ways in which television is viewed by audiences. However, there has not been a corresponding expansion in the study of the audience for pop music, which would situate music use in the home, at concerts or dances to take just three possible contexts. One study which did examine this topic was carried out by Dorothy Hobson.

Hobson studied media use by housewives who were at home looking after young children. She found that the women listened to the pop station Radio 1 a great deal, using it as a background to their domestic work and as a way of structuring the routine of their days. The disc jockey provided 'the missing "company" of another person' (Hobson 1980:107), linking the women to others in the same position. In a sense, the male disc jockey would construct an 'imagined community' (Anderson 1983) between the women. The

Table 7.2 Albums: value of UK trade deliveries, by format

	1985	1986	1987	1988	1989	1990	1991	1992
All categories								
LPs	49.6	40.3	32.7	26.8	19.6	13.4	7.4	3.9
Cassettes	43.8	43.6	41.2	41.9	41.9	41.0	37.9	33.9
CDs	6.6	16.2	26.0	31.3	38.4	45.6	54.8	62.2
Total	100.0	100.0	100.0	100.0	100.0	100.0	100.0	100.0
Classical only								
LPs	32.0	21.0	12.0	10.8	6.6	5.5	2.0	0.6
Cassettes	36.0	27.0	27.0	27.0	31.1	33.5	28.0	19.6
CDs	32.0	52.0	61.0	62.2	62.3	61.0	70.0	79.8
Total	100.0	100.0	100.0	100.0	100.0	100.0	100.0	100.0

Source: *Cultural Trends* 19 (1993:46); from British Phonographic Industry Surveys

Table 7.3 UK trade deliveries of classical albums

Thousands of units and percentages

	1983	1984	1985	1986	1987	1988	1989	1990	1991	1992
Classical	5,784	7,864	8,693	9,374	11,869	12,012	13,973	16,688	15,500	12,350
Classical as a percentage of all trade deliveries (a)	6.4	7.8	7.8	7.2	8.2	7.5	8.6	11.1	10.9	9.2

(a) Albums only.

Source: *Cultural Trends* 19 (1993:47); from British Phonographic Industry Surveys

Box 19 World record sales figures 1992

GLOBAL sales of discs and tapes increased by over 9 per cent in 1992 according to statistics issued by the International Federation of the Phonographic Industry (IFPI). The retail market in the 59 countries surveyed by IFPI was worth $28.7 billion.

Almost all of the growth occurred in North America and Asia. The United States market for sound-carriers reached almost $8.9 billion due mainly to a 22 per cent increase in the numbers of Compact Discs sold there. US consumers accounted for over 400 million CD units out of the 1992 world total of 1.15 billion.

Music sales in South East Asia also expanded to reach over $2 billion in 1992. This was a 44 per cent increase over the figures reported in 1991. In this region, the main format for recorded music remains the cassette. Over 40 per cent of the world's tapes are sold here. After the US, India (240 million units) and China (150 million) are the largest national markets for music cassettes.

In contrast to Asia and the US, the record industries of Japan and Europe had a relatively poor year in 1992. Although the Japanese spent over $.3 billion on records and tapes, this was only 6 per cent more than in 1991. At 181 million discs, the CD market in Japan grew by under 6 per cent. In Europe, six of the eleven European Community members which report figures to IFPI showed a net loss in the value of sales in 1992. The position was worst in Greece where the record market fell by 26 per cent. The best performance came from Portugal where sales were up by 9 per cent although France and Germany also

reported slight increases.

The table below shows the year-on-year progress of the various formats in the world music market. While CD sales were up by 18 per cent this was significantly less than the 28 per cent increase shown by the format in 1990 and 1991. With the important exception of the US the Compact Disc revolution seems to have slowed considerably in the main industrialized countries and price factors have so far prevented CD from becoming a major soundcarrier in Asia, Africa and Latin America. The IFPI totals show a slight growth in cassette sales, although like the relatively low fall in vinyl LP sales this may be due to reporting variations in 1991 and 1992. The 1992 world listing includes Russia for the first time and the estimated cassette sales in that country were 100 millions units. Similarly, IFPI's 1992 returns show that 30 million LPs were sold in China, although none were reported for the previous year.

While the world total of singles sales remained almost static, the two-song or three-song format is now almost extinct outside Japan, the US and Western Europe. These countries accounted for 96 out of every 100 singles sold in world in 1992.

World sales by format 1992 (in millions of units)

Singles	331.6 (−0.4%)
LPs	126.1 (−19.5%)
Cassettes	1551.9 (+2.8%)
CDs	1152.9 (+18.0%)

Source: Laing (1993). From *Popular Music* published by Cambridge University Press

Table 7.4 Album purchases: by age, sex and social class, 1992 (a)

Column percentages

	16–24	25–34	35–44	45+	Male	Female
Classical	2	4	7	21	8	9
County/Folk	*	1	3	9	4	3
Dance/Soul/Reggae	17	10	8	4	10	10
Jazz	*	1	1	*	1	*
MOR (b)	2	3	5	26	8	11
Pop	38	45	39	22	31	40
Rock	35	28	28	9	30	19
Other	6	8	9	9	8	8
Total	100	100	100	100	100	100

	AB	C1	C2	DE	All
Classical	17	8	5	5	9
County/Folk	1	3	5	5	4
Dance/Soul/Reggae	10	9	13	8	10
Jazz	1	1	*	*	1
MOR (b)	8	10	11	9	10
Pop	28	35	35	41	35
Rock	24	25	25	25	24
Other	11	9	6	7	7
Total	100	100	100	100	100

(a) Based on recall of category of last album purchased.
(b) Industry-used abbreviation for 'Middle-of-the-road'.

Source: *Cultural Trends* 19 (1993:53); from Gallup Special Consumer Survey (SCS)/
British Phonographic Industry, 1993

2 Older people buy more classical albums. Classical music, in the main, is the province of the older and the better off.
3 The purchase of rock music declines with age, though the decline is gradual across the ages 25–44. Rock is not on these figures the music of youth, and more attention might be given to the middle-aged rock consumer by sociological research. It is important to note the success of magazines like Q and *Vox* which are orientated towards this market.

Table 7.5 Album purchases: profiles by age, sex and social class, 1992 (a)

Row percentages

	16–24	25–34	35–44	45+	Male	Female
Classical	6	11	16	67	46	54
County/Folk	*	9	20	71	52	48
Dance/Soul/Reggae	44	26	18	12	48	52
Jazz	..	..	..	..	..	..
MOR (b)	4	9	11	76	42	58
Pop	27	30	23	18	42	58
Rock	37	29	24	10	61	39
Other	20	24	23	33	51	49

	AB	C1	C2	DE
Classical	41	25	17	17
County/Folk	8	20	37	35
Dance/Soul/Reggae	21	24	34	21
Jazz	..	..	..	..
MOR (b)	18	26	31	25
Pop	16	26	27	31
Rock	20	26	27	27
Other	27	30	21	22

(a) Based on recall of category of last album purchased.
(b) Industry-used abbreviation for 'middle-of-the-road'.

Source: *Cultural Trends* 19 (1993:54); from Gallup Special Consumer Survey (SCS)/British Phonographic Industry, 1993

4 Country, folk and MOR music is most popular with older people; dance/soul/reggae with younger people.
5 Rock albums are more popular with men than women, the reverse being the case with pop albums. This seems to back up the arguments of Frith and McRobbie reviewed in chapter 4.
6 Jazz albums sell in very small quantities.

These figures on consumption are interesting but they can still only give a rather broad picture of music use. One of the ways in which such use has been studied in most detail is through the concept of subculture used in more ethnographic research.

Culture, subculture and music

Much research on subculture, which has focused on youth subcultures, draws on two different meanings of culture: first, that
which uses culture to refer to the works and practices of artistic and
intellectual activity. In this sense music or a painting is a form of
culture, where schoolwork for example is not. At times, this version
of culture involves a judgement of value. Thus certain forms of
music, such as Beethoven or Mozart, are held to be proper 'culture'
and works by such as Take That or Kylie Minogue to be trash. The
second sense of culture is rather different, referring to the idea of
culture as a 'way of life'. This more inclusive definition can be found
in expressions such as 'the American way of life' or 'British culture'.
Both of these definitions fed into the development of what has
increasingly become known as British Cultural Studies (Turner 1990)
and it is from within this context that many of the most important
studies of youth subcultures and music have been carried out. The
key definition of culture produced within this tradition (J. Clarke
et al. 1976:10) explains that:

> we understand the word culture to refer to that level at which social
> groups develop distinct patterns of life, and give *expressive form* to
> their social and material life experience. Culture is the way, the forms,
> in which groups 'handle' the raw material of their social and material
> existence.

Clarke et al. relate three aspects of social life in this definition: social
experience, social groups and patterns of life. In their account, social groups develop distinct patterns of life based on their own social
experiences in relation to other social groups and forms of experience. Culture is both a level or area of society and the forms in
which the raw material of social experience is handled.

The approach taken by Clarke et al. was greatly influenced by an
earlier paper by Cohen (1980), who examined the nature of youth
subcultures in the East End of London in the 1960s. He argued that
after the Second World War, from the 1950s onwards, the East End
working-class community was disrupted by three factors: first, mi-
gration out of the area; second, the redevelopment of housing involving the building of new tower blocks patterned on a middle-class
nuclear family model which destroyed the forms of communal space
and the patterns of female support which had been so important in
the area; and, third, a series of economic changes. This led to a

'polarization of the labour force' (p. 80) between more specialized, 'high tech' and well-paid jobs and more deadend, unskilled labour.

One outcome of this process of dislocation was the development of youth subcultures, which opposed the working class parent culture. In Cohen's argument, 'the internal conflicts of the parent culture came to be worked out in terms of generational conflict' (p. 82). Furthermore Cohen argued that youth subcultures 'express and resolve, albeit "magically", the contradictions which remain hidden or unresolved in the parent culture' (p. 82). Subcultures are ways of dealing with the difficulties which structural transformations in society have produced in the parent culture to which they belong. Following the pattern of the polarization of the workforce between an upward or downward option, Cohen argues that youth subcultures can express such routes in a variety of different ways. Hence:

> mods, parkas, skinheads, crombies are a succession of subcultures which all correspond to the same parent culture and which attempt to work out, through a system of transformations, the basic problematic or contradiction which is inserted in the subculture by the parent culture. (p. 83)

This sort of approach has been represented diagrammatically by Clarke et al. (1976) as shown in figure 7.3.

Cohen argued that there are two main components of the lifestyle of such youth subcultures, which he terms 'plastic' (dress and music) and 'infrastructural' (argot and ritual). Thus, music is an important part of the complex subcultural whole. However, Cohen paid relatively little attention to the detail of the music used by subcultures. Other writers who developed work within the 'Birmingham tradition' placed more emphasis on it. Some of the papers collected in *Resistance through Rituals* (Hall and Jefferson (eds) 1976) consider this dimension, but most detail can be found in the work of Paul Willis (1978) and Dick Hebdige (1979).

Willis (1978) examined various dimensions of the lives of two youth subcultural groups in the late 1960s: the motor-bike boys and hippies. While these examples are rather dated, it is the nature of the link that Willis makes between music and other aspects of the lifestyle of these groups that resonated through work on subcultures. Willis argues that the musical preferences of these groups were intimately connected to the nature of their lives. Thus, the motor-bike boys' preference for early rock 'n' roll in a single format and the hippies' liking for album-based progressive rock was no accident.

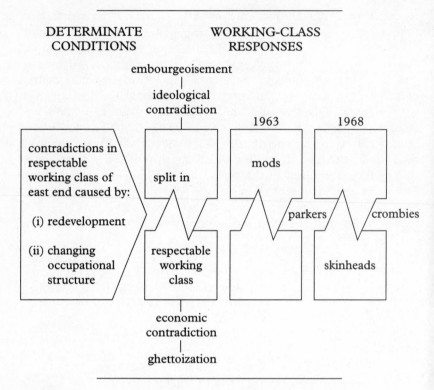

Figure 7.3 Class and subcultures: a version of Cohen's model
Source: Clarke et al. (1976:34) from S. Hall & T. Jefferson (eds) *Resistance through Rituals*, Routledge

Rock 'n' roll music matched the restlessness and mobility of the motor-bike boys' lives. Thus Willis suggests that:

> this music allows the return of the body in music, and encourages the development of a culture based on movement and confidence in movement. The classical European tradition has steadily forced the body and dancing out of music, and made it progressively harder to dance to. The absolute ascendancy of the beat in rock 'n' roll firmly establishes the ascendancy of the body over the mind – it reflects the motor-bike boys' culture very closely. The eclipse of tonality and melody in the music is also the eclipse of abstraction in the bike culture. (p. 77)

He further suggests that:

> the suppression of structured time in the music, its ability to stop, start and be faded, matches the motor-bike boys' restless concrete life

Date	Subculture	Class position	Style	Music	Shifts in post-war hegemony
1953–4	teds	unskilled	drapes		The construction of consensus Macmillanism
1955–6	teds	working class		rock 'n' roll	
1958–61	beats/CND	middle class	duffle coats, beards	jazz/folk	
1963	mods	semi-skilled	scooter	r 'n' b/Tamla	The construction of consensus Social democracy
1964	rockers	unskilled	motor-bike	rock 'n' roll	
1967–72	hippies	middle class/student	long hair, hallucinogenic drugs	progressive rock	Dissensus Protest and revolution
1967	rude boys	black underclass	hustling	ska	
1968–9	skinheads	unskilled	boots 'n' braces	ska	
1970	glams	working class?	bisexuality	glamrock	The Law and Order Society Authoritarianism and working-class resistance
1970	Rastas	black underclass	dreadlocks	reggae	
1976–8	punks	working class?	absurdity	punk rock	
1978–81	mod/ ted skinhead revivals				
1981	new romantics				
1982	?				

Figure 7.4   Chronology of subcultures
Source: Middleton and Muncie (1981:90)

style. As we have seen, it is no accident that the boys preferred singles, nor is it an accident that the rock 'n' roll form is the most suited to singles and its modern technology (fading, etc.). Both the music and its 'singles' form are supremely relevant to the style of the bike culture. (p. 77)

Willis mounts a similar sort of argument about the homologous relationships between different aspects of a youth subculture for the hippies (see especially, pp. 168–9). In Hebdige's words this expresses: 'the symbolic fit between the values and lifestyles of a group, its subjective experience and the musical forms it uses to express or reinforce its focal concerns' (1979:113). This means that subcultures are structured in that different aspects of the lifestyle of the subculture fit together to form a whole. So there is a homology between an 'alternative value system', 'hallucinogenic drugs' and progressive rock for the hippie subculture. Subcultures express a response to a set of conditions and the different aspects of the subculture are tied together into structured relatively coherent wholes. A schematic version of this approach can be seen in the chronology of subcultures produced in the Open University Course on Popular Culture reproduced in figure 7.4.

Hebdige read subcultural styles using the tools of the structural and semiotic approaches introduced in chapter 6. He focused on the different dimensions of the style of subcultural groups. Using the general definition of culture proposed by Clarke et al., Hebdige argued that the styles expressed by different subcultures are a response to social conditions and experiences. Furthermore, according to Hebdige, such styles often encode an opposition to the dominant or hegemonic forms of culture associated with dominant groups. Such challenges are often indirect and can involve the utilization and transformation of forms of culture which were previously the property of dominant groups. In engaging in such practices, subcultural members act as *bricoleurs* engaging in a process of *bricolage*, responding to the world around them by improvising in a structured fashion, creating meanings that are different from those of the dominant culture or dominant groups. As Hebdige says about the style represented in figure 7.5: 'In this way the Teddy boy's theft and transformation of the Edwardian style revived in the early 1950s by Saville Row for wealthy young men about town can be construed as an act of bricolage' (1979:104).

Hebdige argues that subcultures often resist the dominant social order, though indirectly and in symbolic ways. However, he also argues that forms of subcultural expression are often incorporated into the dominant social order through two main routes. First, there is the commodity form which involves 'the conversion of subcultural signs (dress, music, etc.) into mass-produced objects'. Second, is 'the "labelling" and re-definition of deviant behaviour by dominant groups – the police, the media, the judiciary' (Hebdige 1979:94) in a process of ideological incorporation.

This sort of account of the ways in which subcultural groups produce new and resistant meanings which are then bought off or incorporated by the capitalist system is now relatively familiar. It entails the notion that there is some kind of sphere where 'authentic' meanings are produced which are then corrupted. However, as has been pointed out in other parts of this book, this thesis has always been rather difficult to sustain, especially now. Nevertheless, it is also important to note that this sort of characterization of the processes of change in social life is often produced by young music fans themselves.

On the basis of research carried out in 1972, Frith (1983:205–12) drew a distinction between 'sixth-form culture' based around progressive rock which stressed the individual nature of taste, a 'lower-fifth-form culture' made up of people who 'bought singles and

Figure 7.5 Teddy boy, 29 May 1954
Reproduced by permission of Hulton Deutsch Collection Ltd.

watched *Top of the Pops*, went regularly to youth clubs and discos
but rarely to concerts, emphasized beat and sound in their tastes
rather than meaning, and identified with specific youth styles'
(p. 206). He also identified a group of prospective sixth formers
who had a 'missionary zeal for progressive rock and hatred of

commercial pop' (p. 207). This group were very assertive in their views about music and taste. As Frith explains:

> One of the paradoxes in my survey was that the group which most stress individual music choice also most stressed the importance of shared musical taste for friendship – music served as the badge of individuality on which friendship choices could be based. One of the ironies was that because music was taken as a symbol of a cluster of values, the most individualistic groups were the ones most thrown by their musical heroes changing direction. This was particularly a problem for the hairies because they differentiated themselves from the masses as a self-conscious elite by displaying exclusive musical tastes. Their tastes weren't just a matter of identification, they also reflected a different – more serious, more intense – relationship to music. The hairies thought of themselves not as just another teenage style, but as people who had transcended the trivialities of teenage style. Their music *meant* something, and when one of their acts 'sold out', became part of mass taste, there was great bitterness. (p. 208)

Frith tied age and class together, through noting that the sixth formers were more middle class than the more mixed younger groups. He also discussed some important gender differences which will be addressed in more detail below. Frith found a clear distinction between rock and pop audience tastes and that the rock audience was very critical of commercialism. It might be thought that such a division is now rather dated, since Frith's study was undertaken over twenty years ago. However, it can be argued that the structure of the division he found continues to exist even if the contents of rock have changed. For example, it may be the audience for 'indie' is rather like the one that there used to be for progressive rock, though some evidence suggests that there is also an allegiance to pop music within such subcultures. However, this is not the pop music associated with the Top 40 charts (Kruse 1993). There certainly seems to be evidence for an 'oppositional' stance in the studies of local music-making by Cohen (1991) and Finnegan (1989) discussed in chapter 3.

One of the most important problems with the literature discussed in this section so far is the fact that its attention fell almost completely on boys or men. This myopia was first challenged by Angela McRobbie in an article co-authored with Jenny Garber, in which they asked four main questions:

> (1)   Are girls really absent from the main post-war subcultures? Or are they present but invisible? (2)   Where present and visible, were

their roles the same, but more marginal, than boys; or were they different? (3)   Whether marginal or different, is the position of girls specific to the subcultural option; or do their roles reflect the more general social-subordination of women in the central areas of mainstream culture – home, work, school, leisure? (4)   If subcultural options are not readily available to girls, what are the different but complementary ways in which girls organize their cultural life? And are these, in their own terms, subcultural in form? (McRobbie and Garber 1976:211)

In response to question (1) they argued that, at least partly because of the male bias of previous investigations, this was a very difficult question to answer. The men who had studied subcultures had not looked at girls' possible participation in them, and so girls' invisibility tended to be a self-fulfilling prophecy. In pursuing questions (2) and (3) they looked in more detail at the parts that women have played in three subcultures. First, the rocker, greaser or motorbike subculture like that described by Willis. They saw women as being in a very subordinate position in this subculture. Women were passengers on the motor-bikes – they did not drive them. Second, they considered the mod girls of the early 1960s, whom they see as prominent within the mod subculture. Third, they examined hippie culture, identifying two particular roles for women: the earth mother and the Pre-Raphaelite fragile lady. Furthermore, they suggested that this period saw the development of two particular styles for women in music: first, the introspection associated with singer/songwriters such as Joni Mitchell; and second, the boozy blues singer, as exemplified by Janis Joplin. These roles have continued to be important for women in rock music, where it might be argued that Kristin Hirsh is an example of the former and Courtney Love of the second.

McRobbie and Garber argued that the places for women in the subcultures so far described were related to their other roles in life. However, they also suggested that girls tended to organize their cultural life differently from boys, forming a more home-based, romantic or 'teenybop' culture. This point and others made by McRobbie were developed in her subsequent critique of the male-dominated nature of research on subcultures. McRobbie (1980) argued that there are two main approaches that can be taken to previous male-dominated writing on subcultures. First, such accounts can be dismissed, or accepted as applicable only to boys, and attention placed on the different nature of girls' culture. This extended the point made in the earlier article written with Jenny Garber

(1976). Second, previous accounts, such as those by Willis and Hebdige, can be read 'against the grain' to see what they can offer for the analysis of masculinity, both in the nature of the subcultures and the writing on them.

In developing her points about the different nature of girls' culture, McRobbie argues that the street is a potentially dangerous place for girls and that: 'younger girls tend to stay indoors or to congregate in youth clubs; those with literally nowhere else to go but the street frequently become pregnant within a year and disappear back into the home to be absorbed by childcare and domestic labour' (p. 47). She further contends that the use of drink and drugs can induce the same sort of perils: 'it is clear from my recent research, for example, that girls are reluctant to drink precisely because of the sexual dangers of drunkenness' (p. 47).

McRobbie suggested that the working-class girls she studied tended to form a teenybop culture based around romance. These girls spent more time in the home, at least partly because of the dangerous nature of public places, like the street. Frith (1983) added three other aspects to this when he argued: first, that girls are more subject to parental control and discipline than boys are; second, that girls are often expected to carry out work in the home, in a way that boys are not, a point that was illustrated graphically by McRobbie (1978) where she pointed out that girls were expected to perform large amounts of work in the home for very little financial recompense; and, third, girls spend more time at home getting ready to go out than boys do.

To summarize, this form of girl's subculture identified in the 1970s consisted of the following features:

1   The centrality of the home and often of the bedroom. Girls tended to get together with other girls and listen to records by their favourite artists in each other's bedrooms.
2   Girls formed a teenybop culture, where there was a romantic attachment to one star or group. There is a history of different stars and groups which have filled such a role.
3   When girls did go out it was most likely to be a youthclub. Though, as Cohen and Robins (1978) pointed out, in the extract in box 20, such youthclubs, like the one they studied in north London, could be a site of conflict.
4   Dance was important to girls in ways that it was not for boys. McRobbie (1984, 1993) has continued to stress the importance of dance to girls.

5 For the girls in McRobbie's study, the relationship with a best friend was very important and they valued this more than their relationships with boys.
6 The idea of romance was very important. Many of the girls, despite at times showing a 'realistic' appreciation of some of aspects of marriage, placed great stress on the idea of romance and the romantic attachment to one boy. This can be related to the continued existence of a sexual double standard, where girls could easily become known as 'slags' if they went out with several boys.
7 McRobbie argued that the girls she studied stressed some dominant ideas of femininity in an exaggerated fashion. This may form part of a culture which opposed the perceived school ethic of responsibility, hard work and seriousness. The girls spent much time talking about boys and wanted to bend the school rules about dress and make-up in as fashionable a direction as possible. McRobbie argued that this culture, while it may oppose official culture in some ways, reinforces the culture of romance and the idea of femininity which is a part of this. This parallels the argument advanced by Willis (1977) concerning the way in which the exaggeration of masculinity among working-class boys, in opposition to school norms, suited them for manual labour.

The way in which this teenybop culture of femininity connects with music in more detail is discussed in the article on rock and sexuality by Frith and McRobbie (1990), which was reviewed in chapter 4. Various writers have identified some problems with this idea of the teenybop culture of romance.

First, McRobbie may have underestimated the participation and seriousness of the commitment of some girls to subcultural groups. Smith (1978) argued that the 'delinquent' girls she studied were heavily involved in fighting that took place between subcultural groups. However, she also noted that girls were less committed to the groups in terms of length of time of membership. Second, Cowie and Lees (1981) found that girls had a more realistic appraisal of the potential problems in marriage than McRobbie found in her group. Cowie and Lees found far more emphasis on having a good time before marriage. Third, Cowie and Lees (1981) suggested that McRobbie's work tended to isolate a discrete female youth subculture, overintegrating and separating it off from the relations between men and women which existed in society more widely. Relatedly, they argued that too much emphasis is placed on the resistance entailed in the culture of femininity. Fourth, McRobbie's work concentrated mainly on white working class girls, and more evidence is needed about black and middle class girls for comparison. Furthermore, it might be that some of this work is now rather dated. This point can be considered through an examination of McRobbie's more recent work.

In her earlier work, McRobbie had drawn attention to the role of magazines like *Jackie* in the culture of romance. In reconsidering this argument, McRobbie (1991) demonstrated the difference between *Jackie* and contemporary magazines like *Just Seventeen*. Romance has drastically declined in importance and pop and fashion are central, leading to a greater emphasis on image and the pop star. McRobbie argues that 'It is pop rather than romance which now operates as a kind of conceptual umbrella giving a sense of identity to these productions' (p. 168). In such girls' magazines:

> there is an overwhelming interest in personal information. The magazines increasingly play the role of publicist for the various bands who fall into the teenybopper camp. In return their pages are filled with glossy pictures and they can claim to have a direct line to the stars. This makes for cheap and easy copy. Three pages can be covered in a flash with the help of a transatlantic telephone call, a tape-recorder and a selection of publicity shots often provided by the record company. (p. 169)

In McRobbie's view, pop music is more important to girls now than it was in the 1970s. However, girls are not only involved with pop music of the teenybop type, and McRobbie has also drawn attention to their participation in rave culture. She argues that such culture can be connected to drastic changes in femininity over recent years in Britain, suggesting that 'girls both black and white have been "unhinged" from their traditional gender position while the gender and class destiny of their male counterparts has remained more stable' (McRobbie 1993:408). In an article on rave culture, McRobbie reiterates some the points already made about the changing nature of girls' magazines, but develops her arguments about dance. She points to the continuity of rave culture with earlier cultures in that 'dance is where girls were always found in subcultures. It was their only entitlement.' However, 'in rave it becomes the motivating force for the entire subculture' (1993:419). The centrality of dance allows a far more important place for girls within such contemporary subcultures. However, in continuity with earlier work, McRobbie still sees the danger of these occasions for girls, even if at this later date it is as a parent rather than as a sociological observer.

At this point it is necessary to consider some of the main points made against the kind of writing on youth subcultures that has been discussed in this section so far. A very useful overall critique has been produced by Gary Clarke (1990) who makes a number of particular criticisms of work from the Birmingham Centre for Contemporary Cultural Studies. These are:

1 Much of this writing is imprecise on the nature of the 'structural location' of subcultures and the nature of the problem-solving involved in the subculture.
2 There is relatively little explanation of where the different subcultural styles actually come from.
3 There is a rigidity in the analysis, as the subcultures which are identified tend to be 'essentialist and non-contradictory', meaning that there is little attention paid to variations of style and commitment within different subcultures.
4 There is a lack of attention to the way in which individuals move in and out of subcultures. Thus, Clarke (1990:82–3) argues that 'Cohen, for example, classifies crombies and parkas as distinct subcultures, but surely the only "problem" which distinguished them from skins and mods respectively was the need to keep warm'.
5 There a tendency for these analyses to start from subcultures and work backwards to class situations and contradictions. This leads to a kind of 'freezing' of distinct subcultures.
6 There is a dichotomy between subcultures and the rest of the young people.

Clarke identifies three important consequences which stem from these criticisms. First, there is the lack of consideration of 'subcultural flux and dynamic nature of styles' (p. 84). Second, there is the separation of subcultures from the rest of society which is incorporated into a 'consensus' or dominant social relations. Third, there is the point that a 'vague concept of style' is elevated 'to the status of an objective category' (p. 84).

Hence, Clarke argues that there is a need to study what all categories of youth are doing, rather than just subcultures, as he says: 'It is true that most youths do not enter into subcultures in the elite form described in the literature, but large numbers do draw on particular elements of subcultural style and create their own meanings and uses of them' (p. 92).

Furthermore, he suggests that there are important differences in the early 1980s from the situation described in the 1960s and 1970s by the classic writers from Birmingham. Thus, there was the combination of styles involved in movements like punk and Two Tone, and the argument that 'new wave' broke the 'distinction between "teenyboppers" and youth' based around the distinction between LPs and singles. Thus, Clarke's general conclusion is that: 'what is required is an analysis of the activities of all youths to locate continuities and discontinuities in culture and social relations and to discover the meaning these activities have for the youths themselves' (p. 95). Some recent literature has attempted to take up this challenge and it is reviewed in chapter 8 below.

So far this section has focused on class and gender in relation to youth subcultures and music use. There is also a developing body of literature which considers the racial dimension to subcultures and music. Some general aspects of this have been considered in chapter 5, and at this point I consider one of the more specific studies of this topic which appeared within the 'Birmingham tradition' of studies of subcultures.

Simon Jones's book on *Black Culture, White Youth* (1988) falls into two relatively discrete parts. In the first he presented an overview of the development of reggae and its connection to forms of culture in Britain and Jamaica. However, it is the second half of the book which contains an ethnography of black and white youth in Birmingham which is of more interest for present purposes. Jones discusses the formation of identity in a multiracial area of the city of Birmingham in the English Midlands. Thus many white boys had adopted forms of culture which would in more conventional analyses be seen as black. 'Black' language was used to express opposition to authority on the part of white children (p. 149).

Reggae was adopted by the young white people growing up in this environment, and Jones shows how different themes from Jamaican music were adapted by young white men and women. Thus, he maintains that:

Black music generally and Jamaican music in particular have functioned as transmitters of oppositional values and liberating pleasures to different generations of whites for nearly three decades. They have consistently supplied white youth with the raw material for their own distinctive forms of cultural expression. Through the political discourses

of Rastafari, reggae has provided young whites with a collective language and symbolism of rebellion that has proved resonant to their
own predicaments and to their experiences of distinct, but related,
forms of oppression. (1988:231)

However, Jones recognizes contradictions which existed around these
modes of appropriation. Thus, 'Powerful feelings of attraction to
black culture could easily coexist with perceptions of that culture as
threatening and with resentment and fear of black people' (p. 216).

Jones suggests that new forms of 'racial' identity are being formed
in parts of Birmingham and other inner-city metropolitan areas. He
ends his book with a quotation from one of the people he studied
which captures this. He says:

> [in Jojo's] eloquent conclusion is captured both the reality of the new
> 'England' that is already emerging, as well as the hope that such an
> England might itself not be 'recognizable as the same nation it has
> been', or perhaps, one day, 'as a nation at all':
>
> 'It's like, I love this place . . . there's no place like home . . . Balsall
> Heath is the centre of the melting-pot, man, 'cos all I ever see when
> I go out is half-Arab, half-Pakistani, half-Jamaican, half-Scottish, half-
> Irish, I know 'cos I am [half-Scottish-Irish] . . . Who am I? . . . Tell
> me? Who do I belong to? They criticize me, the good old England.
> Alright then, where do I belong? . . . you know, I was brought up with
> blacks, Pakistanis, Africans, Asians, everything, you name it . . . Who
> do I belong to? I'm just a broad person. The earth is mine. You know,
> "we was not born in England, we was not born in Jamaica" . . . we
> was born *here* man! It's our right! That's the way I see it . . . That's
> the way I deal with it.' (1988:239–140)

Jones's general discussion resonates with the postmodernist arguments, outlined in chapter 4, which suggest that there has been a
'decentering' of our identities in contemporary culture. For example, it has been suggested by a number of writers that we no longer
have the same attachments to place as earlier generations because
we live in a society where in some respects it is easier to see what
is going on the other side of the world through television coverage
than it is to observe events at the other end of the street. Some
themes concerning postmodernism and the study of youth culture
have been addressed by Redhead.

Redhead (1990) criticizes the idea of a neat fit between different
elements of youth subcultures and music, which are entailed in the
concept of homology used by Willis (1978) and Hebdige (1979).

He also suggests that it is problematic to see music as the straightforward expression of a subcultural community. For example, it is often difficult to specify the community of which music is an expression. This echoes the critique of the realist theory of representation in lyrics developed by Frith which was examined in chapter 6. Furthermore, the subcultures and communities from which music is often held to issue or which put it to use, do not simply exist, but have to be examined within language and communication. They are in important senses constructed within writing about them, or in other terms, discursively constructed.

Redhead considers whether there was ever the clear fit between music and subcultural use in the way identified by the Birmingham writers, or whether there has been a change in the articulation of music with subcultures in the period since punk rock in the late 1970s. In some accounts postmodernism in pop has developed through the 1980s, leading to the breakup of the forms of association identified by earlier writers. However, Redhead argues that in many respects pop music has *always* possessed some of those features which are characteristic of postmodernism. He maintains that pop music has broken barriers between high and popular culture at different points. In common with theories of postmodernism, he argues that the best way to understand contemporary pop music is not through some of the conventional 'oppositions' which have often been used to study it, like those between 'rock and pop', 'authentic and synthetic', 'true and false' and 'high and low', but through the distinction, and relationship, between the local and the global. Thus 'world musics' are affecting local music making in a number of complex and diverse ways.

Redhead's work raises a number of issues about the complex contemporary interaction between forms of cultural production and consumption of contemporary pop music. However, he does not provide, or attempt to provide, a blueprint for how these relationships should actually be studied.

More recent work has considered different dimensions of contemporary music and youth. Rietveld (1993) examines a number of different dimensions of rave culture in the north of England in the late 1980s. The account given of this form of culture is not dissimilar from that of the 'Birmingham' writers. For example, Rietveld argues with respect to rave culture that:

> Not only the lack of finance, but also the intensive dancing and the use of the drug Ecstasy determined the style. It makes a person

words themselves. Thus, music can be used, and be made, to express feelings, as well as to structure everyday life. An example given of the latter is the use of the personal stereo: 'the ultimate artefact in providing a personal soundscape that can be carried around, quite literally, inside the head, while travelling, walking, waiting or negotiating public spaces' (Willis 1990:64–5).

Dance is the fourth dimension to creative consumption. The argument is made that 'Whereas dancing used to be seen as something of a feminine activity by some working-class young men, it has become more acceptable for males to express themselves through body movement. Some of the ties between dance forms and codes of masculinity/femininity have been loosened' (Willis 1990:68). Finally, it is suggested that there is often a strong identification with the 'lyrical themes, imagery and symbolism of popular music' (Willis 1990:68).

These forms of creative consumption can often develop into production. Four different aspects of the development of consumption into production are considered by Willis (1990):

1 sound systems
2 black music and oral poetry
3 DIY recording and mixing
4 music-making and performance

First, there is the sound system which, as was noted in chapter five has been particularly prominent in black musical traditions. This form has also become prominent in rave culture (McRobbie 1993:421). The sound system was an institution 'where the activities of consumption merge into and become intertwined with more conventional forms of production' (Willis 1990:72). Furthermore:

> Besides being one of the principal focal points of musical activity within the black community, the sound system also involves a number of primary private production processes, which embrace electronics, sound technology and carpentry. These informal processes are motivated by specifically musical enthusiasms and operate to their own cultural agenda. They often involve the use of independently gained technical knowledge and skills, picked up from electronics magazines. (Willis 1990:72)

Second, connected to the sound system is the form of production engaged in by the DJ, who in black tradition may draw upon forms of oral poetry. Again, the DJ is important within rave culture. Third, there is the increased importance of DIY recording. Especially with the increased availability of cheaper forms of recording equipment (see chapter 3), there have been greater opportunities for the involvement of young people in music making. 'In this process the hardware and software of *consumption* have become the instruments and raw materials of a kind of cultural production' (Willis 1990:77). Finally, there is the way in which young people develop their interests in music to become involved in the production of music themselves, especially through performance.

This discussion raises a number of issues concerning the nature and relation of production and consumption and how they can be analytically separated. These issues have relevance beyond the cultural activities of young people. The final section of this chapter explores these issues in detail and outlines some possible directions for future analysis. It emphasizes the complexity of contemporary musical production and consumption and the importance of social context.

Production, consumption and music-making

Dave Laing (1990:186) has argued that:

> It is a commonplace that production and consumption are interdependent. Without production of material or cultural goods, there can be no consumption. Without a demand for, and consumption of, the use-values embodied in these goods, there is no impetus for continuing production. In certain areas of popular culture, the relation between production and consumption has another aspect. There, the producers of today are frequently the consumers of yesterday. Through the experience of consuming music as a listener, many individuals are drawn into producing music of their own.

Recent work has attempted to examine the relationships between production and consumption in more detail. For example, Warde (1992) has argued that discussions of production and consumption are often rather confused, especially between the levels of systems of production and consumption and those of individual production and consumption. Warde argues that it may be possible to show that there are linkages between mass production of goods in a factory system and the mass consumption of such goods. For example,

been done it may not be possible to say that some aspects of a form of music are progressive, while others are less so. For example, consider again the Madonna phenomenon. Madonna may be an empowering figure for some young women, but she may also be used as a pin-up for men, replacing pornographic images. Some writers may emphasize the former, others the latter. Yet other analysts might suggest that it is precisely such ambiguity that makes Madonna so important and politically relevant.

In general, my view is that even what seem to be the most commodified products of the culture industry need to be examined in their social contexts of production and consumption before any judgements of value can even begin to be made. I am suspicious of accounts which 'write off' whole forms of music because they do not seem to conform to traditional standards of high art or because they have mass appeal. Who is to say that children's enjoyment of Kylie Minogue or Take That *necessarily* has pernicious effects, before detailed sociological study has been carried out?

If this sounds like a call for appreciation of the relativity of worth and the suspension of critical judgement in the interest of sustained empirical enquiry informed by theoretical innovation then so much the better. However, one of the clear obstacles to this is the lack of funding available for precisely the sort of empirical work into contemporary pop production, textual form and audience that is so necessary to advance the state of knowledge reviewed in this book.

It is clear that the study of cultural forms in general, and pop music in particular, has come a long way in the last twenty years, but unless there is investment in detailed empirical work informed by theoretical advances in cultural studies, media studies and the sociology of culture, the field will not advance in the way necessary to understand the rapidly changing nature of some of the key contemporary aspects of social life. This may sound like a rather depressing note on which to end, but then there is always new and old music to compensate for gloomy thoughts.

Further Reading

A number of the most important books and articles on pop music are discussed in the individual chapters of this book. The Bibliography that follows provides full references for these and other cited texts. In this section, I briefly comment on the key books in this field, primarily as an initial guide for students. Publication details can be found in the Bibliography.

The best place to start in the sociological study of popular music is with Frith and Goodwin's excellent edited collection *On Record* (1990). This is a very impressive and useful book, which stands comparison with the best of sociological readers. Lull's (1992) rather shorter edited collection, *Popular Music and Communication*, is also useful, though more patchy in quality. The pre-eminent sociologist of pop is Simon Frith and any of his work is worth study. His most well-known book is *Sound Effects* (1983) which was itself a revision of his earlier *Sociology of Rock* (Constable, 1978). *Sound Effects* is still worth reading, though it is obviously now rather dated in some respects. *Music for Pleasure* is a good collection of Frith's essays and journalism. Frith is one of the editors (along with Bennett, Grossberg, Shepherd and Turner) of *Rock and Popular Music: Politics, Policies, Institutions* (1993) which is another useful collection.

Middleton's *Studying Popular Music* (1990) is a thought-provoking, musicologically based discussion of a number of issues arising in the study of popular music. It can be hard-going in places but the considerations of Adorno, folk culture and subculture are particularly rewarding. Relatively little attention has been given in the current book to the more philosophically based studies of the role of music